Anasazi Archite

EDITED BY

BAKER H. MORROW AND V. B. PRICE

WITH A FOREWORD BY

ROBERT C. HEYDER

Anasazi Architecture and American Design

UNIVERSITY OF NEW MEXICO PRESS

Albuquerque

© 1997 by the University of New Mexico Press
All rights reserved. Second paperbound printing, 1998

Library of Congress Cataloging in Publication Data applied for.

Anasazi Architecture and American Design grew out of the Mesa Verde
symposium on the Anasazi built environment, an interdisciplinary
exchange of ideas involving historians, architects, archaeologists,
urban planners and critics, and landscape architects held at Mesa Verde
National Park 17–19 May 1991.

Library of Congress Cataloging-in-Publication Data

Anasazi architecture and American design / edited by Baker H. Morrow and
V. B. Price ; with a foreword by Robert C. Heyder. — 1st ed.
p.   cm.
Results of a conference held at the Mesa Verde National Park in
May 1991.
Includes index.
ISBN 0-8263-1778-2 (cloth). — ISBN 0-8263-1779-0 (pbk.)
1. Pueblo architecture—Congresses.
2. Pueblo philosophy—Congresses.
3. Pueblo Indians—Antiquities—Congresses.
4. Southwest, New—Antiquities—Congresses.
I. Morrow, Baker H., 1946-.
II. Price, V. B. (Vincent Barrett)
E99.P9A48   1997
720'.979—dc20   96-25381
                                                              CIP

To JoAnn, Susie, Hazel, Roz, Julie, and Tom. —*BHM*

For Rini, Jody and Amy, Keir and Kady, and Ryan and Talia, Chris and Cheryl, Marc and Jerri, Toria and Danae, Mary, Jim, Jackie, and D.O.D. —*VBP*

The Anasazi are a reminder: Human life is fundamentally diverse and finally impenetrable. That we cannot do better than a crude reconstruction of their life . . . a thousand years ago is probably to our advantage, for it steers us away from presumption and judgment.

—Barry Lopez

Contents

Acknowledgments

This book is based on presentations and essays derived from the Mesa Verde Symposium on Anasazi Architecture and American Design.

We are grateful to the National Park Service, and in particular to Robert C. Heyder, former superintendent of Mesa Verde National Park, as well as to Becky Brock and Art Hutchinson of the park administration, for their assistance and support.

We would like to thank Beth Hadas, Dana Asbury, Liz Varnedoe, Sue Niewiarovski, Peter Moulson, Annie Brown, and Joe Wesbrook of UNM Press. In addition, our thanks go to Rosine McConnell and Robert Torres at Morrow and Company, Landscape Architects, and to Sue Lowell.

Leonora Dowdy and Pat Curkendall of the Hilton staff served us gallons of coffee and orange juice at the Casa Chaco Coffee Shop in Albuquerque as this project took on shape and substance over the years. Thank you, friends.

And we appreciate as irreplaceable the patience, kindness, and love of JoAnn and Rini.

Baker H. Morrow, ASLA • V.B. Price

Foreword

Robert C. Heyder, former superintendent,
Mesa Verde National Park

The cultural heritage of the American Southwest as expressed by the architecture of the Anasazi epoch is monumental. The genius of these people may well be best remembered through future centuries by their remarkable buildings. To understand their architecture one must also have a well-grounded understanding of the legacy that has been left to us of their great construction works.

To comprehend the people who designed and built these marvelous structures, one has to observe the ruins that remain scattered throughout the Southwest. It is during the time one spends in observation that one begins to come to the realization that we can never know all the reasons the Anasazi built as they did a thousand years ago. One must contemplate how and why they built where they did. That understanding will not come like a bolt of lightning, but by serious thought over time. The scholar will have to study Cliff Palace, Spruce Tree House, Long House, and other cliff dwellings of Mesa Verde National Park, then compare these magnificent prehistoric dwellings in counterpoint to the equally magnificent free-standing structures of Pueblo Bonito, Chetro Ketl, Pueblo del Arroyo, Pueblo Alto, and their attendant structures at Chaco Canyon National Historical Park. This study in counterpoint provides many avenues for future studies in the architecture and related archaeology of the Southwest.

The science of archaeology has generated a profound study of the Anasazi epoch, taking this civilization from the Basketmaker phases I, II, and III through the Pueblo phases I, II, and III and on to the present. The evolution of Anasazi architectural style is still an ongoing phenomenon in the Pueblo cultures of the American Southwest and in the design of many modern buildings. It would be interesting to see where this continual use of the Anasazi genius will lead in the next millennium.

This collection of critical essays is the beginning of a process of bringing together different disciplines to study the vanished past as seen through the eyes of present-day scholars. These monuments of our southwestern heritage are about as close as one can get to a total harmony of architecture with the surrounding landscape.

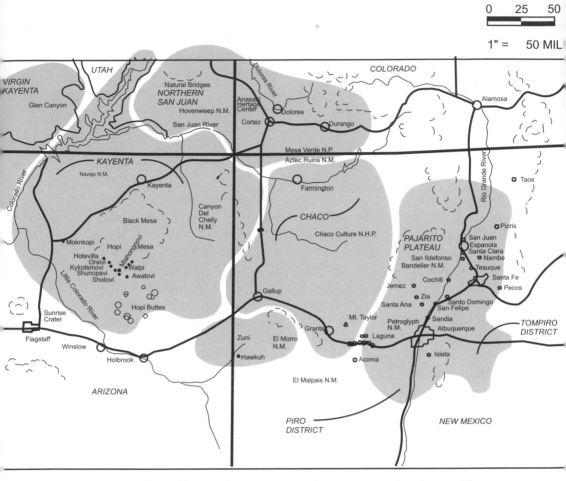

The Puebloan Tradition Anasazi Settlement Areas and Modern Pueblos

Preface

In May 1991, some twenty-two thinkers and scholars—among them archaeologists, art and cultural historians, architects and landscape architects, artists, poets, urban planners and critics, Euroamericans and Native Americans—came together for a unique multidisciplinary symposium at Mesa Verde National Park called "Anasazi Architecture and American Design." The symposium focused both on the place that Anasazi built environments have in the history of American architecture and urban planning and on the lessons that might be learned from ancient builders about making humane and ecologically safe new cities in the future. This book is a direct result of the Mesa Verde symposium.

Organizers of the symposium, including ourselves, realized that a diverse group of high-powered scholars, artist professionals, and planners would need a freewheeling atmosphere in which specialization would not become an obstacle to communication. The stimulating, open-minded exchange of insights gave the participants, and the more than 150 people from across the country who attended the two-day symposium, a rare opportunity to converse and incorporate fresh perspectives and useful new metaphors from other disciplines into their own view of the Anasazi built environment.

We believe the Mesa Verde symposium was the first of its kind to treat Anasazi sites directly in terms of their architecture, landscape planning, and "urban" form. It was also the first public discussion of the subject to begin with the assumption that the environmental sensitivity and problem-solving strategies of Anasazi designers and builders have an unexplored utility for contemporary urban planners and architects.

Transforming the tolerant and stimulating atmosphere of the symposium into a book for general readers and others of various disciplines requires a translation of diverse terminologies and a brief explanation of multiple starting points and perspectives of symposium participants.

When southwestern archaeologists talk about the Anasazi, for instance, they are referring to a culture that endured a vast span of time over many regions. When architects and others use the term, they are generally referring to the people who built the "great house" structures of Chaco Canyon and the cliff dwellings at Mesa Verde.

The term *Anasazi* is a Navajo word that means, depending on the translation, "enemy ancestors" or "ancestors of others." The Hopi equivalent of the term is *hi'sat'si'nom*, which means "our" ancestors or forebears. The term *Anasazi* was taken up by early archaeologists and explorers in the nineteenth century who traveled and worked with Navajo guides and laborers. As the term implies, Navajos are not culturally related to the people who constructed the ancient structures that so attract us.

Archaeologists use the term *Anasazi* to describe prehistoric—or pre-conquest—Puebloan peoples living anywhere from approximately 800 B.C. to when the Spanish arrived in A.D. 1540. Pueblo Indians of today, all of whom claim ancestry with places such as Chaco Canyon, inhabit the Rio Grande Valley region of New Mexico from Taos to south of Albuquerque at Isleta, and from west of Albuquerque to Acoma to Zuni in west-central New Mexico and northwest to the Hopi villages of Arizona. "Remnant" Pueblo peoples (Tiwa and Piro) also live in and around Ysleta near El Paso, Texas.

The prehistoric Pueblo or Anasazi area covers a much wider region than the contemporary homeland of the Pueblo world. The Anasazi lived in a geographic region that reaches from northeastern and central Arizona and northwestern and central New Mexico into southern Utah and southern Colorado. This area is sometimes referred to as the Four Corners region. The archaeological precincts most popularly associated with the Anasazi are around Kayenta, Arizona; Mesa Verde, Colorado; Chaco Canyon, New Mexico; and Hovenweep, Utah. But there are perhaps tens of thousands of Anasazi sites—most very small and some very large— throughout the four-state area. Anasazi people lived in "pueblos," or towns, and in smaller community units in such diverse places as the Gila Wilderness in southwestern New Mexico, in Santa Fe in northern New Mexico, in fortress sites in New Mexico's Jemez Mountains, and in huge cities in the Galisteo Basin between Albuquerque and Santa Fe.

The most common dating system for the Anasazi was coined by archaeologists at a conference held at the ruins of Pecos Pueblo and its abandoned mission church east of Santa Fe in 1927. This system is known as the Pecos Classification, and it divides southwestern archaeology into a number of major cultural periods. This schemata, used by most southwestern archaeologists, was first developed in 1927 and was embellished continually until the 1950s. A. V. Kidder, who convened the first Pecos conference and is widely considered the founding architect of this temporal framework, had become concerned with both its rigidity and its uncritical use, as he noted in the foreword to the final edition of his classic text, *Southwestern Archeology.*

The fundamental problem with the Pecos Classification is that it purports to describe cultural change but schizophrenically alternates its focus between fine-grained details of changes in architecture and changes in artifacts like pottery. In several of this volume's essays, authors have stood back a bit and described broader patterns of change in quite different terms, thus giving the reader access to fresh insights into the evolving organizing principles of Anasazi society at different time periods. David Stuart casts these in terms of power/efficiency and ecological adaptation, while John Stein, Judith Suiter, Dabney Ford, and Michael Marshall explore the dimensions of time, space, and religion. Their results will be debated for years to come.

Though by no means the only dating system used by archaeologists, the Pecos Classification is still the most common. Chaco Canyon and Mesa Verde, the sites most frequently referred to by nonarchaeologists in this book, fall under the Pueblo II and Pueblo III categories of the Pecos Classification, going from roughly A.D. 950 to the mid 1200s. The great sites in Chaco Canyon—known sometimes as "Classic Bonito," were abandoned midway in Pueblo prehistory, sometime around A.D. 1150. The four hundred or so remaining years before the arrival of the Spanish saw many large Anasazi sites develop south of Chaco and Mesa Verde, sites that are not generally referred to in this text. Despite this expansion of the Anasazi world, Chaco and Mesa Verde have become synonymous in the layman's mind with Anasazi culture because they have been popularized as national landmarks.

The multidisciplinary mix of participants at the Mesa Verde symposium was challenged and enlivened by the tensions that grew among three distinct perspectives—the scientific, the pragmatic, and the metaphoric.

The southwestern archaeologists in this book belong to a nearly hundred-year-long tradition of workers in the field who have labored to make sense of the immensely complicated archaeological terrain of prehistoric Pueblo remains. Although many of these archaeologists have a romantic, and even a poetic bent, they are first and foremost research scientists who collect data, test hypotheses, and continually revise their reconstructions of the Anasazi world based on the evidence of hard-won data collected in the field. Some believe it is appropriate to interpret Anasazi remains by referring to contemporary Pueblo cultural patterns; others do not. Although the schism runs deep, no one seems to dispute that the Anasazi are not an isolated cultural phenomenon but still have a living place in southwestern cultural history. Like the archaeologists, the historians at the conference come from a tradition that puts data at the service of evaluation. The question always asked is "What picture or reality arises naturally and clearly from the data?"

By contrast, architects and urban planners are not primarily interested in the technological exactitudes of archaeological and historical research: they are interested in the results. And they take a more pragmatic view of the Anasazi cultural remains. Their perspective emerges directly from their art form and from the design problems they are trained to solve—as architects for individual and corporate clients and as planners for governmental and public clients. They tend to be more interested in how Anasazi design strategies and environmental sensitivities actually worked and whether these strategies have any practical application for contemporary design in the arid Southwest.

Many architects also are interested in the aesthetic power of Anasazi artifacts and ruins. They join writers, critics, poets, and artists in exploring the metaphorical implications of Anasazi design and its relationship to contemporary American culture. The essence of their perspective comes from the search for appropriate metaphor, describing one thing in terms of another so that both terms energize each other. Like scientists and architects and planners, cultural writers insist that their metaphors have a real-world accuracy, that they do not falsify the past in their effort to explain it. Their underlying goal is to give the past new life in the present, to counteract the false notion that the past is somehow dead and disconnected from the living world, and to reveal the connections, the hidden pulse, between what was and what is now.

What all these thoughtful people believe about the nature of Anasazi architecture and how they think it applies to the present is the subject of this multidisciplinary anthology.

Baker H. Morrow and V. B. Price

Anasazi Architecture and American Design

Prologue

Baker H. Morrow

Modern Americans who know the stone cities of the ancient Anasazi—the ancestors of today's Pueblo Indians—cherish the architectural remains as symbols of the antiquity and enduring beauty of human life on this continent. But the proper place of Anasazi architecture within the broader framework of American design has never been determined. Is it a prehistoric curiosity with no relevance to our time? Is it simply a picturesque setting in which we can imagine characters from southwestern legend, such as Billy the Kid and Francisco Vásquez de Coronado, playing out their lives against a backdrop of red mesas and cobalt blue skies? Anasazi architecture has unquestionably influenced modern buildings, but can twentieth-century attempts to re-create it do anything more than suggest ancient building masses and masonry techniques?

The answers to these questions have proven to be as remarkable and surprising as the Anasazi themselves. Architects, archaeologists, historians, city planners, architecture critics, landscape architects, and art historians who have reviewed the evidence have begun to sketch a new picture of the original nature of Anasazi architecture.

By the eleventh century A.D., a simple love of masonry buildings and a tremendous facility in creating them had allowed the Anasazi to develop a highly stylized regional tradition having many local variants. The Anasazi built underground constructions as well as aboveground multistoried structures as essential parts of great complexes scattered across the modern Four Corners area. An Anasazi town or city often consisted of a ceremonial center around which several outlying hamlets were arranged, with field houses even more distant clustered near agricultural lands. The open spaces of patios, plazas, terraces, and courtyards were carefully planned to serve as living spaces and to complement the nearby building masses.

The Anasazi frequently oriented their towns and key buildings to the cardinal directions. Moreover, startling evidence suggests that the Anasazi of Chaco Canyon may have organized many of their buildings and building complexes in patterns that are harmonious with the cycles of the sun and the moon, thus bringing architecture firmly into the service of ritual. Anasazi landscape elements such as platform mounds and road networks also may have served religious purposes.

The Anasazi, showing an uncommon restlessness, constantly built and rebuilt their stone cities, only to abandon the cities after a century or two in favor of new townsites many miles away. As was the case with Rome, the center of gravity of the Anasazi world ultimately shifted east from Chaco and the Mesa Verde country to the valley of the Rio Grande. Many Puebloans will tell the curious visitor that the heart of the modern Pueblo world is Santo Domingo, a bustling small city on a spectacular site having fine views of the line of the great river and the Jemez Range to the north and west. Perhaps we might think of Santo Domingo as the modern Byzantium of the Ancient Anasazi world. Thus, in a sense Anasazi architecture is with us yet as Pueblo architecture, an evolved but nevertheless continuous form. The modern Pueblos represent an unbroken tradition that is now well over a thousand years old. A close look also suggests that the celebrated "Santa Fe" style might more accurately be called "Anasazi traditionalism" because it continues to evoke the spirit of the region more deeply than any other building approach.

The following essays may allow us to determine what is the rightful place of Anasazi architecture in the history of American architecture and, if it has something to offer the late twentieth century beyond its appealing style, how we may best make use of it.

Part One   *Archaeology, Architecture,*
                            and the Anasazi

1 The Rhetoric of Formalism

Interpreting Anasazi Architecture

J. J. Brody

We begin this anthology with art historian and museologist J. J. Brody's keynote address to the Mesa Verde symposium "Anasazi Architecture and American Design," May 1991. Brody's is a cautionary message about the dangers of misinterpretation that arise when trying to apply the lessons to be learned from ancient civilizations. Since the nineteenth century, artists, architects, and social thinkers have used images from the past to help catalyze their vision of a better future. This appropriation of imagery has often resulted in a confusion between the images or artifacts and the rhetoric used to describe them. Cultures of the past are subject to distortion when seen through the lens of social idealism.

I discuss Anasazi architecture in this essay, but only within a broad context that is my true theme. My point of departure is the symposium itself, and two tangential facts about it that I thought were interesting. The first, its association with four other events that were celebrated at Mesa Verde in the spring of 1991: International Museum Day, the seventy-fifth anniversary of the United States National Park Service, the eighty-fifth anniversary of the establishment of Mesa Verde National Park, and the Nordenskiold Centennial Exhibition, which was inaugurated at the park following the symposium. The second, the extraordinarily diverse and multidisciplinary character of the symposium's participants.

These two facts provide my thematic base. I conceive the conjunction of events that spring at Mesa Verde to have been more than coincidental, for they provided an appropriate historical context within which to regard the uncommon mix of disciplines and professions that were represented at the symposium. Several issues are suggested by that context. One deals with aspects of two different histories: that of modern museums and that of modern architecture. Another deals with the relationships between conventional museums and the things they preserve, as well as between less conventional ones (such as Mesa Verde National Park) and the architectural and natural things they preserve. Then there are broad social issues raised, including those dealing with the uses people make of architecture and art, the meanings they give to those activities, the rhetoric with which they surround them, and the consequent need to distinguish between art and rhetoric if we are ever to learn anything about the past histories of any art or architecture for which no written documentation exists.

I shall first establish some of the historical associations that I perceive among those celebratory events and suggest how those associations might give added meaning to the cross-disciplinary symposium. I shall then discuss how those events and associations might either clarify or obscure our understanding of Anasazi architecture. Throughout, I shall briefly touch upon some of the problems that are created when our appropriation of the past intersects on the one hand with our desire to discover expressive meanings in man-made objects, and on the other with our wish to build a better future. All my discussions of rhetoric, art, and Anasazi architecture will address that intersection.

Local Celebrations and the Crossover of Disciplines

Among participants in the symposium either as auditors or presenters were archaeologists and ethnologists, historians and art historians, architects and architectural historians, poets and painters, bureaucrats and landscape architects. Some of these trades are obviously compatible, some appear to be quite the reverse, and many have no very obvious connection one to another. Some participants wore two or more hats. So diverse an assortment has the potential for making any long meeting intellectually uncomfortable, especially for those who come to it with high confidence in the stability of the academic and workplace categories that structure the boundaries of their working lives. My guess is that most who participated in the symposium accepted the legitimacy of all interests and were likewise open, at least provisionally, to the notions that academic disciplines as we know them were born yesterday or the next thing to it and that workplace categories become obsolete the instant they are thought of as rigid. I think most were willing to walk on academic quicksand if need be, were likely to be bored by the limits of workplace categories, and accepted that all man-made boundaries and classifications are artificial and provisional.

If I am correct, there are nice linkages here with the scholars who first did academic research at Mesa Verde, with the idealists who created the prototypes for Mesa Verde National Park and of modern museums, and with the innovators responsible for the invention of modern architecture. Both Gustaf Nordenskiold and J. Walter Fewkes, the pioneer scholar archaeologists at Mesa Verde, were trained as natural historians rather than ethnologists or archaeologists; Artur Hazelius, who conceived of and created the modern outdoor museum, was a linguist and orthographer; Frank Lloyd Wright was a draftsman, Mies van der Rohe a brick mason, and neither they nor any other founding master of modern architecture was trained within the structure of an academic architectural discipline. It is almost as though academic and workplace categories were a burden upon and incompatible with the kinds of creativity exercised by these people. They epitomize disciplinary crossovers.

Gustaf Nordenskiold was a Swedish Finn who for two months in 1891, at age twenty-two, did his archaeological work at Mesa Verde. He published the results in 1893 and died two years later (Nordenskiold 1893; Steen 1979). Though his excavations began almost as an afterthought to a casually planned tour of the Southwest, they were technically sophisticated for their time and place, and his beautifully illustrated publication is still a valuable scientific report a century later (Lister 1979). Most of the collection he made at Mesa Verde was ultimately given to the Finnish National Museum in Helsinki, a museum acquisition that involves much more than the mere disposition of a collection of objects. To approach that acquisition we have to ask two questions: first, what prompted Nordenskiold to investigate the Mesa Verde ruins? and second, why were obsolete and broken objects excavated from so alien a place of any interest at all, either to him or to a national museum in Scandinavia?

The clue to answering both questions lies in Nordenskiold's close participation throughout his short life in a Swedish intellectual movement that closely paralleled similar intellectual movements throughout the Western world in focusing on the study of what they called folklore and folk culture (Steen 1979:17–20). His interest in Mesa Verde and the interest of a Scandinavian museum in the artifacts of an ancient American Indian society can both be understood only in the context of that international intellectual movement. Modern natural history, anthropology, and history museums (and many of our art museums) were created by or profoundly modified by it. One branch of that movement evolved into modern ethnology, another into modern archaeology; social Darwinism was mightily influenced by it, as were such unlikely intellectual bedfellows as the communism of Marx and Engels and the theosophy of Madame Blavatsky. It was a movement that not only ushered in the modern urban-industrial world that we all know, but was triggered by it.

Chekhov and Kipling, Gauguin and Kandinsky, Louis Sullivan and Le Corbusier were all acting and reacting each in quite different ways to the same sets of social problems, having to do with overcrowded, technologically complicated, urban-industrial societies that were quickly becoming internationalized. All turned to, co-opted, and appropriated remnants of some preindustrial past to develop and support their vision of a better future. We are still caught up in that movement, which is the link that unifies the four events separately celebrated at Mesa Verde in 1991 with this symposium. It explains why we spend so much of our national product (as do people in all other parts of the world in equivalent circumstances) on efforts to preserve and interpret the ancient architecture of Mesa Verde and others of our publicly owned parks and monuments. It explains why millions of people from all over the world come to these places, all over the world, year after year. It is why this symposium was held, and why the questions it addressed from so many different perspectives all boil down to a single issue: the modern-day appropriation of the material remains of an ancient society as a tangible expression of the desire to give meaning to the present and to control the future.

That desire inspired Nordenskiold to carry the discipline of folk studies through ethnology into archaeology. His older contemporary J. Walter Fewkes, who came to Mesa Verde later but was ultimately of greater importance to the history of its archaeology, also took folklore studies through ethnology into archaeology. Fewkes published extensively in the *Journal of American Folklore* and was much more systematic in his ethnology and in his merging of the three disciplines. He also commanded infinitely greater resources and spent considerably longer than two months of a long and full life as a field archaeologist and two years of it as an anthropologist (Hough 1931; Swanton and Roberts 1931).

But museums take center stage here. In the same year that Nordenskiold was at Mesa Verde, his countryman Artur Hazelius opened the Skansen Museum in Stockholm. The Skansen was the world's first modern, permanent outdoor museum. The Skansen evolved from Hazelius's efforts, begun in 1873, to preserve and publicly exhibit and interpret collections that represented the distinctive regional traditions of Scandinavian folkways (Alexander 1983:239–275). Urbanization, modernization, cosmopolitanism, and all of the other universally leveling, homogenizing impacts of the Industrial Revolution were rapidly erasing all traces of traditional rural life in Scandinavia, and Hazelius was trying to salvage what he could. But his interest was more than antiquarian. His concern for preserving the physical remnants of this newly obsolescent past was driven by a conviction, almost an obsession, that the social values expressed through those remnants were in some mystic sense Scandinavia itself. They were the soul of his nation and must not be lost (Alexander 1983:242-244).

The Skansen is in every way a national museum. It is also, as are all museums, a philosophical and political statement. It is the prototype for Colonial Williamsburg, Ellis Island, Alcatraz, the Little Big Horn Battlefield, Mesa Verde, Gettysburg, and all the rest of our outdoor museums and national parks and monuments. Throughout the world, all such institutions are expressions of political and social values and are tangible evidence that self-conscious control of the past is an exercise in attempting to control the future.

In those years—in Sweden, Russia, Austria, Germany, England, France, the United States, all over the industrially impacted world—were many related movements to study, preserve, memorialize, and interpret the products of preindustrial societies. Usually the subject societies were those most closely related geographically, physically, historically, or economically to the nation-state involved. Related to these movements were every conceivable variation of handcraft art industry, every utopian social movement, every socially directed innovation in architecture, including the technological ones. These were all philosophically grounded upon some variant of the notion that positive metaphysical, mystical, ethical, and moral values could be expressed through material objects, especially if they were handmade, handcrafted, and beautifully proportioned.

Aesthetics was always involved in these movements, as were associations with a variety of artistic and scientific phenomena, but considerable variation from place to place and time to time was visible in the philosophical particulars that impelled them and in their products. They could be religious or secular, nationalist or internationalist, scientific or metaphysical, industrial or anti-industrial, aesthetic or antiaesthetic, reactionary or revolutionary. Wagner and Mahler, Ruskin and Whistler, Tolstoy and Nietzsche, Sullivan and Gaudi, Darwin and Agassiz were all involved in one way or another with the study or interpretation of a real or imagined national or international, natural or man-made, preindustrial past.

The Rhetoric of Formalism 9

And, as well as modern museums, modern art and architecture and all of the modern social sciences are built upon some variant of the notion that obsolete or endangered objects contain values that are important to the present and the future and should be preserved.

If we believe that social values have material expression, if we read ideals into objects, it then becomes our duty and our right to appropriate those objects and preserve them for ourselves and posterity. That is what modern museums, including outdoor museums, are all about: the preservation of obsolete, useless, broken, dead, endangered, exotic objects that have acquired or been given important new social values. But there is great variety and little agreement as to just what those values might be. That variety and lack of agreement partly explains the categorical variety of our museums, the sometimes radically different values that they give to very similar objects that are in their care, and the difficult moral and ethical issues that are raised if ever legitimacy is given to questions about the accuracy, quality, or ethical propriety of any new meanings that may be given to old objects.

What are we to think when the same, or similar, or obviously related phenomena inspire diverse and sometimes mutually exclusive interpretations by so many apparently legitimate interests, institutions, and intellectual giants and heroes? Have these gods gone crazy, or have they simply been blinded by their own rhetoric?

Form, Meaning, and Context in Anasazi Architecture

The analysis of material objects, especially those that we categorize as art or architecture, is always subject to distortion resulting from the rhetoric of social idealism. Analysis is always couched in the rhetoric of whatever fundamental social values and beliefs are held by an investigator, and it may be impossible for that person either to recognize the consequent distortions or to accept that an analysis is necessarily subjective. Our definitions of art and architecture are so dependent upon the expressive and emotional values we ascribe to objects that art analysis often has less to do with facts of artistic form and history than with the social history and social values of the analyst. Not only art analysis is as much inspired by the rhetoric of social issues and ideology as by the objects that are analyzed; the same is true of object analysis based upon other modes of thought or types of classification. Anthropologists, historians, and sociologists are also constrained by their own ideologies and social histories, even those who are trained to be self-consciously aware of that fact.

Here again, I will lump together categories just as I did earlier by classifying national parks as a type of museum. We define the two categories "art" and "architecture" by recognizing a single attribute, which we call expressive content, in all objects of each class. For that reason, I am comfortable in subsuming architecture as a subtype of art for the purpose of this discussion. As every art historian must learn, the rhetoric that surrounds art should never be confused with the art under consideration. No matter who creates the rhetoric or why, or how one feels about its validity, it always acts as a form of static that interferes with objective, critical examination of an art object or of its history. What is true about art analysis is equally true about all other forms of analysis: the baggage of sociopolitical beliefs and values as well as religious and philosophical sentiments that an investigator brings to objects distorts perception and must be ignored if objects are to be examined objectively. But rhetoric is tricky, and in a convoluted way it can disguise its own nature.

As a case in point, look at Mies van der Rohe's 1951 apartment houses at 860 Lakeshore Drive in Chicago. These are pure geometry defined by steel and glass, and they seem to exemplify the structural and ethical rhetoric of the International style of architecture, which Mies helped invent a generation earlier. Mies was antiaesthetic, pragmatic, utilitarian, idealistic, and committed to creating useful artistic objects that he felt were expressive of eternal physical and spiritual values. He believed that "technology was the most significant force animating this or any other age" (Zukowsky 1986). In 1923 he wrote, "Form by itself does not exist— form as an aim is formalism; and that we reject!" (Honey 1986:40); in 1938 he said, "The long path from material through function to creative work has only a single goal: to create order out of the desperate confusion of our time" (Honey 1986:37). Structural purity, refined craftsmanship, sensitive use of materials (especially those associated with industrialization), and the absence of applied ornament were central features of his work.

Chicago fire safety ordinances require that steel be encased in concrete. Therefore, the exposed steel which appears to be structural that defines the geometry of his brilliant buildings on Lakeshore Drive is in fact ornamental, nonstructural appliqué. The purity is illusion, and the apartment houses are a marvelous self-contradiction—a pure artistic form that is at one and the same time a physical, critical commentary upon his verbal rhetoric and a powerful, self-conscious visual expression of his rhetorical ideals. In Mies's case we can look separately at the physical qualities of his objects and at his words and by comparison can fairly conclude that he deliberately stepped outside his own self-imposed aesthetic boundaries to make a rhetorical point.

The physical qualities of Anasazi architecture and the rhetoric that surrounds it must also be looked at separately and compared, each as a potentially enlightening yet obfuscating contradiction of the other. But in the Anasazi case, there is a gross disjunction between the objects and their verbal rhetorical surroundings. Rhetoric now is imposed upon the objects many hundreds of years after the facts of their creation and obsolescence, and usually by people of an alien society. Analysis of this art in the context of its verbal rhetoric, no matter how it is done or who does it, cannot tell us anything about the relationships between expressive form and the social and aesthetic ideals of its Anasazi creators. Analysis can only inform about relationships between its forms and the social and aesthetic ideals of very much later, far removed, and often entirely alien people. Is it possible to approach an Anasazi view of Anasazi art, and if it is, how can we do so?

It seems to me that there is only one way. Artistic forms are embedded within layers of history and surrounded by layers of rhetoric, and we must peel away and evaluate all of those layers until the bare, abstract structure of the work is exposed. Abstract qualities are the only parts of the art complex that remain substantially intact through time, across space, and despite overlays of perhaps unrelated cultural and social values and ideologies, which are all that any rhetoric can ever express. The point of tension between rhetoric and analytical vision is the place where we can identify those abstract qualities that must be defined if discussions of art traditions are to lead anywhere.

Anasazi architecture served practical tasks of daily life; it was as utilitarian as can be. But we can believe that much of it was also made as works of art, for it is also expressive and visually and emotionally stimulating to us. The fascination that Pueblo II and Pueblo III masonry architecture of the Four Corners has held for the nineteenth and twentieth centuries is focused precisely where the abstract visual qualities of the architecture are associated with positive rhetorical values of those centuries. We see the forms of Anasazi architecture as being simple and basic, in the sense of being fundamentally geometric—sphere, cone, cylinder— and as having the social virtues and values that we associate with those qualities. We have only to look at Cezanne after about 1880 and at the

12 *J. J. Brody*

International School of architecture after World War I to see how Anasazi architecture complements the avant-garde Euroamerican aesthetic attitudes of the late nineteenth and early twentieth centuries and fits the rhetoric that surrounds those forms.

We can perceive "great house" and "cliff house" buildings and communities as deliberate artistic expressions because of their use of sun and shade, of sharply defined or carefully rounded forms, of planes and textures that clearly and consistently articulate expressive geometry and large-and small-scale spatial relationships. Because we can see them so clearly, we read these structures as art, intellect made tangible in objects of social action, and then we build our rhetoric around that reading. But now consider the large number of Anasazi structures in New Mexico and Arizona—south, east, and west of the Four Corners region and generally not quite as old as those of the San Juan drainage—that have aged less gracefully because they were built of mud or poor-quality stone. Many that have now melted into the landscape were as large as or larger than, as complex, deliberate, and rational as any of the most impressive Chaco or Mesa Verde or Kayenta buildings, and they surely once articulated light, shade, space, and geometry with all the skill and drama of the now more famous structures of the San Juan region.

If we could read the artistic expressions of this other Anasazi architecture as clearly as we can those of the Four Corners, if it had been preserved as well, as dramatically, as romantically, would we talk so easily of Chacoan villages as though they were urban centers or suggest that abandonment of the Four Corners by the Anasazi represented a loss of artistic quality and social complexity? I think not. I then ask if we are reading the history of Anasazi architecture and deciphering its implications correctly, or are we misreading it because our eyes are blind to certain classes of ruined buildings and to other Anasazi artistic values and expressions?

I propose that the aesthetic, social, metaphorical, and metaphysical qualities that we perceive in Anasazi architecture must be examined within the framework of all of Anasazi art history, and only within that framework. I think we would find then that its abstract, structural qualities more closely parallel those of other Anasazi domestic arts than of any Euroamerican art and that those parallels held during all Anasazi times and in all Anasazi regions. Examination of painted pottery, decorated basketry, textiles, and architecture would show that the formality of Anasazi domestic arts, including architecture, contrasted sharply with the informality, less deliberate, and even random structuring of Anasazi rock art and other nondomestic arts. Further, those nondomestic arts ordinarily occur outside of Anasazi domestic or built spaces, or on their margins, in the liminal places where culture met nature. We might be puzzled then by the occasional mixing of these co-traditions that we sometimes see in rock art, in architectural spaces, and on pottery, and we might be guided by our puzzlement to ask questions that are generated by Anasazi traditions and artistic rhetoric rather than by our modern or alien ones (Brody 1991).

Only then will we find clues to the artistic values of the Anasazi and to their artistic rhetoric. Abstract formalism is the fundamental quality that Anasazi pottery shares with Anasazi architecture: can we postulate that formal geometry expressed culture, domesticity, and areas of female concern, while informal abstract or representational expressionism was about nature, the wilderness, and areas of male concern? In this construct, since Anasazi architecture belongs in a class with the other domestic arts, we can read its formalism as a metaphorical expression. It *may* have had practical values but it *always* had rhetorical and metaphorical ones, and its basic aesthetic features changed hardly at all from place to place within the Anasazi world or with the passage of time. Any fit there may be between the forms of Anasazi architecture and those of more modern and alien architectures must then be read as purely coincidental formalism in Mies's sense, which I also would reject.

Neither the forms of Anasazi architecture nor its metaphors had anything at all to do with the ethical ideals and rhetoric of any modern movement. The use of stone masonry was always an accident of circumstance and largely irrelevant to Anasazi rhetorical intentions, and the great stone ruins that so capture our imagination are, for all of their present magnificence, a kind of visual static that misleads our reading of Anasazi artistic systems and of its history. We may appropriate any of their forms and metaphors for our own use, but when we do so, it is in terms of our ideals, our visions, and our rhetoric.

References

Alexander, Edward P. 1983. *Museum Masters.* American Association of State and Local History, Nashville.
Brody, J. J. 1991. *Anasazi and Pueblo Painting.* School of American Research Book, University of New Mexico Press, Albuquerque.
Honey, Sandra. 1986. "Mies van der Rohe: Architect and Teacher in Germany."

In *Mies van der Rohe: Architect as Educator,* ed. R. Achilles, K. Harrington, and C. Myhrum, pp. 37–48. Illinois Institute of Technology, Chicago.

Hough, Walter. 1931. "Jesse Walter Fewkes." *American Anthropologist* 33:92–97.

Lister, Robert H. 1979. "Interpretive Forward." In *The Cliff Dwellers of the Mesa Verde, Southwestern Colorado,* Gustaf Nordenskiold, pp. 31–36. Reprint of 1893 edition. Rio Grande Press, Glorieta, N. M.

Nordenskiold, Gustaf. 1893. *The Cliff Dwellers of the Mesa Verde, Southwestern Colorado.* Reprint, Rio Grande Press, Glorieta, N. M., 1979.

Steen, Charlie. 1979. "Introduction." In *The Cliff Dwellers of the Mesa Verde, Southwestern Colorado,* Gustaf Nordenskiold, pp. 17–29. Reprint of 1893 edition. Rio Grande Press, Glorieta, N. M.

Swanton, J. R., and F. H. H. Roberts, Jr. 1931. "Jesse Walter Fewkes." *Smithsonian Institution Annual Report for 1930,* pp. 609–619. Washington, D.C.

Zukowsky, John, et al. 1986. *Mies Reconsidered: His Career, Legacy, and Disciples.* Art Institute of Chicago.

2 The Changing Image of the Anasazi World in the American Imagination

Richard Ellis

Although by no means a conspicuous part of American popular culture, the Anasazi world has played a steady, if marginal, role in how our nation has defined itself historically. Colorado historian Richard Ellis traces how Euroamericans encountered the Anasazi and incorporated their ruins into the mythology of the American West.

Early in the American period in the Southwest, a number of factors were at work that focused the American mind on the Anasazi world, and some of those were at least partly contradictory. One factor, I think, was that the United States was a new nation without much of a history when compared to Europe, and thus Americans sought a special legacy, an ancient record of which they could be proud. As a result, the American mind seized upon the Anasazi, this unique civilization that had thrived in the Southwest—an area that was, itself, clearly exotic. The ruins of this strange civilization were of obvious antiquity and thus provided an ancient past that was distinctly American.

Yet, while Anglo Americans exhibited a sense of inferiority because of the brevity of their national history, in the early nineteenth century they also were confident that the United States was politically the most advanced nation in the world. They believed that the United States served as a political beacon, encouraging the people of other nations to emulate the American experience. These two forces—a sense of inferiority and a sense of superiority—helped to make the Anasazi heritage of the Southwest important in the American mind.

Commerce was a third factor that emerged with the discovery of the ruins on Mesa Verde in the late nineteenth century. Westerners in the nineteenth century were largely developers; they were eager to see their communities grow and sought to identify special features that would attract people to their area. The discovery of the "Aztec Ruins" (as they were often called) in Mesa Verde provided the opportunity to develop tourism, which could provide economic growth. Thus as early as 1880—before the town of Durango, Colorado, was effectively formed and when all that existed in the Animas Valley was the little community of Animas City—residents began to advertise visits into Mesa Verde to see the ruins. This effort to develop businesses to exploit this new resource brought knowledge of the existence of Anasazi sites to a large audience through advertising while also giving other Americans direct contact with Anasazi remains.

The Anglo American world received its first impressions of the ancient Southwest beginning in 1846 with the outbreak of the Mexican War and with subsequent official American exploratory expeditions in the area. Americans engaged in the fur trade and in the Santa Fe trade had previously seen or heard of Anasazi ruins, but the first reports of such sites reached the East through official government explorers. Usually those explorers were sent out by the United States Army Corps of Topographical Engineers, which was the institution that conducted the great surveys of the West. The tradition already had developed to send artists with the engineers and also occasionally with military expeditions. Artists provided Americans with the first visual record of what existed in the Southwest. The written and artistic records were available through government publications of the reports of these expeditions.

Some of the earliest visual descriptions of ruins in the Southwest were provided by John Mix Stanley, who visited New Mexico with the Corps of Topographical Engineers in 1846. His drawings of the ruins of Pecos Pueblo appeared in the 1848 publication of Lieutenant William H. Emory's report, which went through three printings. The combined work of Emory and Stanley has been credited with marking the beginning of anthropological studies and of the visual reconnaissance of the Southwest, although Emory, perhaps influenced by best-selling books by William A. Prescott and by John Lloyd Stephens, spread the erroneous interpretation that these ruins were tied to Montezuma and the Aztecs.

Whereas Stanley and Abert had introduced Americans to the exotic and romantic ruins in New Mexico, the work of artist Richard Kern and the report of Lieutenant James H. Simpson provided broader knowledge of antiquities in the Southwest. Richard and Edward Kern, who had survived the disastrous fourth Frémont expedition, joined Simpson of the

Corps of Topographical Engineers on a reconnaissance of Navajo country in August 1849. At Jemez Pueblo in New Mexico, Richard Kern was permitted to enter and to sketch the interior of a kiva. There he also met Hosta, the governor of the pueblo, who reported that the kiva was connected to Montezuma.

Leaving Jemez with Hosta as a guide, Simpson traveled westward and descended Chaco Wash. Kern stopped to sketch Pueblo Pintado, the easternmost of the large Chacoan sites, which some called the Pueblo of Montezuma. Hosta described the sites in Chaco as Aztec ruins, a label that Simpson (who had read the work of Prescott and Alexander von Humboldt) readily accepted. Kern, however, was more inclined to link these Anasazi sites to historic Pueblo Indians. Knowledge of Montezuma and other aspects of Mexican Indian traditions apparently had entered Pueblo mythology, perhaps transmitted by the Mexican Indians who had accompanied Spanish expeditions and had become part of the Spanish occupation of New Mexico. As another alternative, Hosta and other Pueblo Indians may have told Simpson what he wanted to hear. Moreover, Hosta was a significant figure in imparting the Montezuma legend because he guided others, including the great photographer William Henry Jackson, through the area and continued to describe the sites as Aztec ruins.

As the expedition traveled down Chaco Wash, Kern prepared a visual record of major sites. Seven major and several smaller ruins were studied and documented, and Kern sketched the interior as well as the exterior of buildings and also attempted artistic reconstruction of what the sites may originally have looked like. Kern's concentration on creating accurate renditions of the ruins may have led him to connect the Anasazi to modern Pueblo people because he previously had sketched Pueblo villages and the ruins of Pueblo villages with Spanish missions. The publication of Simpson's report with Kern's drawings provided the first description of Chacoan sites, in addition to ruins in Canyon de Chelly in what is now Arizona.

The belief in Aztec origins for Anasazi sites was widespread by the 1850s. For example, when George Douglas Brewerton traveled across New Mexico and published an account in *Harper's Weekly* in April 1854, he described abandoned Pecos Pueblo as an Aztec temple, and his article was accompanied by illustrations taken from Emory's report. So it was, too, that Private Josiah Rice, who saw Pecos on his way to Canyon de Chelly in 1851, described the ruins of the "Aztec church" at Pecos.

The 1870s ushered in the age of the great surveys, exploring expeditions funded by the federal government and led by such individuals as Clarence King, Richard Wheeler, Ferdinand Hayden, and John Wesley Powell. Timothy O'Sullivan, a veteran Civil War photographer, worked for both King and Wheeler. During his service with the Wheeler survey he produced the first real photographic record of Anasazi ruins, and the photographic record had a far greater impact on the American mind than did the paintings of previous expeditions. O'Sullivan's photographs of White House in Canyon de Chelly are justly famous.

The 1870s were also notable because of the work of William Henry Jackson, a photographer with the Hayden surveys. In that decade Jackson and William Holmes worked down the Mancos Valley along the southeastern edge of Mesa Verde. Jackson had heard of the Mesa Verde ruins and hired John Moss, leader of a mining enterprise at the mouth of La Plata Canyon, as his guide. Moss took Jackson's party—which included Ernest Ingersoll, a writer for the *New York Tribune*—directly to the ruins in Mancos Canyon. Jackson noted that the discovery attracted "considerable attention," causing Hayden to send him back to the area in 1875.

In 1875, Jackson used 20 inch by 24 inch glass negatives to photograph Anasazi sites in Colorado, Arizona, and Utah as he traveled to the Hopi villages and back. Publication of his reports for the Hayden survey was significant for focusing attention on the connection between the Anasazi and historic Pueblo people. Jackson reached an even wider audience when he prepared a scale model of Anasazi sites for the Centennial Exposition in Philadelphia in 1876 and also lectured on the subject.

Even the mass media took note of changing interpretations. The 22 May 1877 issue of *Harper's Weekly* included a lithograph entitled "The Watch for Montezuma" by Paul Frenzeny and Jules Tavernier but carried an explanation that recent research had shown that the Hopis, or Puebloan people, of New Mexico and Arizona were a distinct group and were not the descendants of the Aztecs as previously believed. The more provincial *Rocky Mountain News,* however, still referred to Anasazi sites as ancient Aztec villages in 1876, and in 1880 businessmen in Animas City, now part of Durango, advertised trips to the Aztec ruins.

If the study of archaeology and anthropology in the Southwest began with the work of Simpson and Kern, as some believe, it received a boost from the work of Jackson and Holmes and grew dramatically after the creation in 1879 of the Bureau of Ethnology, which in 1894 became the Bureau of American Ethnology. The bureau sponsored serious ethnologi-

Fig. 2.1. *The Watch for Montezuma.* Lithograph by Paul Frenzeny
and Jules Tavernier, *Harper's Weekly,* May 22, 1875

cal and archaeological research by such individuals as Frank Cushing, Victor Mindeleff, James and Matilda Coxe Stevenson, photographer John Hillers, and others. Such work firmly established the relationship between the Anasazi and the people of the modern Pueblos.

Meanwhile, other scholars and popular writers worked independently. Among them was Adolph Bandelier. Bandelier was a major figure in the study of southwestern anthropology and archaeology in the nineteenth century and also played a major role in destroying the Aztec theory and in stressing instead the connection between the Anasazi and the modern Pueblo world. Bandelier is important, too, because he wrote a novel, *The Delight Makers,* thought by many to be one of the great novels of the Southwest. Archaeologist Edgar Hewett described *The Delight Makers* as the best novel written about American Indians. Despite Hewett's praise, the book is difficult to read because of a stiff writing style, excessive romanticism, and nineteenth- century literary conventions. Nonetheless, it gave to a broader audience a fictional account of what life was like in precontact days in Frijoles Canyon near Santa Fe and thus gave a wider knowledge of the Anasazi world. Bandelier's friend Charles Lummis debunked the Aztec myth and supported the scientific work of Bandelier and others in his many popular books on the Southwest.

The individuals who probably did more than anybody else to disseminate information about the Anasazi were the Wetherills of Mancos, Colorado. The Wetherill brothers served as guides for a number of people who visited Mesa Verde to observe the ruins. They put together exhibitions of artifacts that were displayed in Durango, Pueblo, and Denver. One artifact collection was bought by the Historical Society of Colorado and then was shown to the public in the state capitol in Denver. The Wetherills also went to the World's Columbian Exposition in Chicago in 1893 and exhibited Anasazi artifacts to a new and much broader audience. Richard Wetherill received the backing of the Hyde family, which allowed him to explore in the Grande Gulch area of southern Utah from 1893 to 1897, and he was prominent in the early fieldwork in Chaco Canyon. The Wetherills also worked with Gustaf Nordenskiold, the Swedish archaeologist who also was a superb photographer and whose photos of Mesa Verde sites were displayed not only in the United States but also in Europe.

The early twentieth century was noted for the continued development of scientific archaeology, distinguished by the work of A. V. Kidder and others. At the same time, the mass media also became interested in the Anasazi. Both still and motion pictures were made of Anasazi sites, and

Fig. 2.2. A scene from *Vanishing American,* Paramount Pictures (1925)

even the prominent Pathe film company worked in Mesa Verde in about 1920. The 1920s also were marked by the work of Zane Grey, whose novel *The Vanishing American* was converted into a Hollywood film of the same name in 1925. Accuracy was not important to the filmmaker, who provided a rather absurd portrayal of the Anasazi residents of a cliff dwelling who were attacked and defeated by invading enemies. However, the visual image was significant, and *The Vanishing American* provided the first coverage of the Anasazi in a commercial film.

Through the late twentieth century, film has continued to be important. Professional documentaries of the Anasazi have reached classrooms and also have gained a national audience through public television. Even the British became involved and produced a high-quality program on the

Wetherills and their work, indicating the international interest in the Anasazi.

During the same period archaeological fieldwork continued. University field schools and salvage archaeology developed. The National Park Service also authorized the Wetherill Mesa Project in Mesa Verde National Park (1958–1965) and the Chaco Canyon Project (1973–1985), which made major contributions to knowledge and pioneered new scientific techniques for the study of the Anasazi world.

By the 1980s, the Anasazi had become the subject of best-selling popular fiction. In 1987 Louis L'Amour, author of some ninety books, published *Haunted Mesa,* in which a modern southwesterner passes through a time warp into the third world of the Anasazi-Pueblos where some descendants of the Anasazi continued to live. Mystery writer Tony Hillerman also used archaeologists and Anasazi remains in his novel *Thief of Time* (1988).

By the 1990s, the American public was familiar with the Anasazi and exhibited fascination with this unique prehistoric culture and also with historic Pueblo people. Such interest can be identified by increasing visitation to Anasazi sites, many of which have been preserved by the National Park Service. By 1990, some 800,000 people a year visited Mesa Verde alone. Public interest in the Anasazi will undoubtedly continue at a high level, because of the exotic nature of the Anasazi world and the promotion of tourism in the southwest, and will continue to be stimulated by new discoveries and by scholarly debates.

Part Two   *The Patterns of Settlement*

3 Anasazi Communities in Context

Stephen Lekson

*The prehistoric Southwest was not solely Anasazi territory. Nor were
structures in Chaco Canyon the largest or most spectacular in the ancient
North American world. Southwestern archaeologist Stephen Lekson reminds
us that other peoples such as the Hohokam and Mogollon made their own
contributions to the settlement patterns of the ancient Southwest. They have
much to teach us, as well, about adapting built environments to harsh and
precarious desert landscapes.*

Chaco Canyon contains the most famous Anasazi building in the Southwest: Pueblo Bonito. Pueblo Bonito (Fig. 3.1g)is evocative and, for various
reasons, impressive. The hype of choice on Pueblo Bonito is its large size:
it is immense, massive, huge, monumental, BIG. Pueblo Bonito was big,
but not really all *that* big by southwestern standards. Unfortunately for
the Chaco chamber of commerce, Bonito is not the biggest ruin, nor the
biggest Pueblo ruin, nor the biggest stone masonry Pueblo ruin, nor the
biggest excavated stone masonry Pueblo ruin, nor the biggest anything—
except, perhaps, the biggest building in Chaco Canyon (and Chetro Ketl
might actually be larger). But size is one reason that Pueblo Bonito has
become an architectural archetype. Why?

Many Pueblo ruins are undeniably bigger. Pueblo Bonito would get
lost in some of the really big northern Rio Grande ruins, like Sapawe or
Kuapa. And some living pueblos are bigger. Bonito would fit comfortably
into the plaza of the modern pueblo of Taos (Fig. 3.2u), for example.

Yet we dwell on Bonito's size. There are aspects of size and implications
of size that are of real importance, but I fear that our fixed interest in
Pueblo Bonito's size says more about the twentieth-century United States
than it does about eleventh-century Chaco Canyon. We are impressed
by size. Bigger is better, and size legitimizes. And Bonito is the biggest
ruin that we all know about. The last statement is critical: we have built
a whole mythology around Bonito's size, but it is false. Most of us simply
do not know about the other sites. That fact can have a disastrous effect

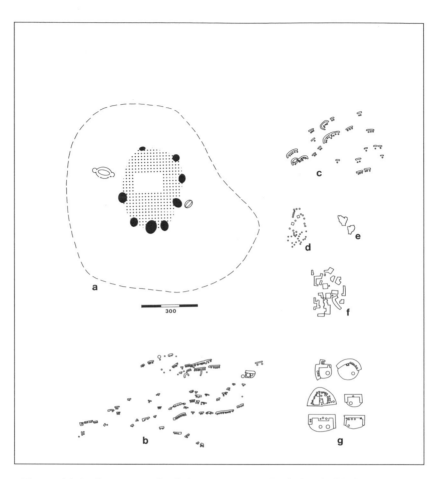

Fig. 3.1. (a) Snaketown, south of Phoenix, Arizona (Hohokam); (b)Skunk Springs
(Anasazi ca. A.D. 1150); (c) Example of a unit pueblo (Anasazi ca. A.D. 750); (d)
Typical pit house village, Mimbres area; (e) Masonry village, Mimbres area,
ca. A.D. 1000; (f) Masonry village, Mimbres area, ca. A.D. 1000;
(g) Great houses, Chaco Canyon area (Anasazi)

on architectural evaluations of the Anasazi or any other southwestern
people. When people generalize about the Anasazi based solely on Mesa
Verde or Chaco Canyon, it is like talking about Western literature based
on five novels, drawn at random, from an airport newsstand—far off the
mark.

This paper offers a flying tour of prehistoric southwestern communi-

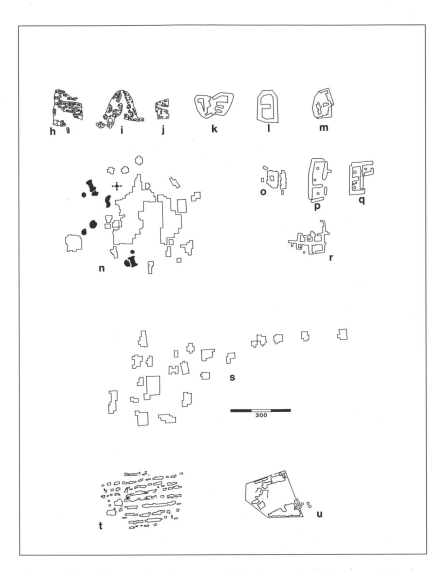

Fig. 3.2. (h)Sand Canyon site, Montezuma Valley (Anasazi); (i) Goodman Point site, Montezuma Valley (Anasazi), ca. A.D. 1200; (j) Yellowjacket; (k) Example of Zuni development; (l) Example of Zuni development; (m) Example of Zuni development; (n) Casas Grandes, Chihuahua, Mexico, ca. A.D. 1400; (o) Example of buildings in Rio Grande/Mogollon uplands area ca. A.D. 1500; (p) Example of buildings in Rio Grande/Mogollon uplands area ca. A.D. 1500; (q) Example of buildings in Rio Grande/Mogollon uplands area ca. A.D. 1500; (r) Example of buildings in Rio Grande/Mogollon uplands area ca. A.D. 1500; (s) Los Muertos, Phoenix, Arizona (Hohokam); (t) Santo Domingo; (u) Prehistoric Taos Pueblo

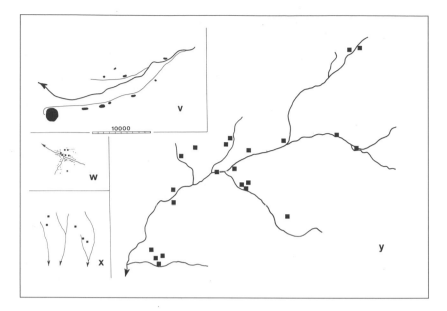

Fig. 3.3. (v) Casa Grande, example of a canal community in Hohokam area, south of Phoenix; (w) Chaco Canyon community; (x) Hovenweep; (y) Prehistoric Zuni

ties, more to show the scale of the problem than to survey the field. I would like to broaden the context of Anasazi architecture and Anasazi communities to the *real* Southwest, well beyond the immediate Four Corners. The Four Corners area—the area around Mesa Verde—is traditionally defined as the Anasazi homeland, the ancestral origin of the Pueblos. We are beginning to realize that to understand what happened in the Southwest, we have to look not just at the Four Corners, but much further afield, far south into the deserts of southern Arizona and even into the northern reaches of old Mexico, and into areas that have traditionally been considered separate "cultures" unrelated to the Anasazi-Pueblo world—those would be the Hohokam area of southern Arizona and the Mogollon or Mimbres area of southwestern New Mexico. Those areas can help us think about Anasazi building as part of a real world, the world of the ancient Southwest, and not as isolated frames in a picture book.

In the Montezuma Valley, just to the east of Mesa Verde, several large villages were built about a century after Chaco. These include sites like Sand Canyon (Fig. 3.2i) and Goodman Point (Fig. 3.2h). They are comparable and maybe a bit larger, at least in plan, than the Chaco sites. And at exactly the same time that Goodman Point and Sand Canyon were being built, even larger buildings were going up in the Zuni area to the south (e.g., Figs. 3.2k, 3.2l, 3.2m). In fact, while Mesa Verde was at its peak, an entirely comparable building boom was going on around Zuni.

The Zuni development may have been on an even larger scale than Mesa Verde, but no cliff dwellings and no national park call attention to it, so nobody knows about it. Only a handful of archaeologists have picked up on the fact that the Mesa Verde climax—renowned in story and calendar—is more than matched by Zuni.

Thirteenth-and early fourteenth-century sites at Mesa Verde and Zuni set a scale for Pueblo building that continued into early historic times. Compare the large Mesa Verde and Zuni sites to fourteenth-and fifteenth-century buildings in the Rio Grande and Mogollon uplands (Figs. 3.2o, 3.2p, 3.2q, 3.2r). The scale set by individual Mesa Verde and Zuni buildings, which continued on to later Rio Grande and Mogollon pueblos, is an important point of reference to which I will return later.

Confusing the issue of building scale is the seldom appreciated fact that many Anasazi and other prehistoric southwestern communities were more than a single site or an individual building. We are often inclined to mistake a single archaeological building (or a single site) for a complete settlement, a self-contained community. During the latest Pueblo periods, a large building *might* really be a complete, self-contained settlement (e.g., Figs. 3.2h—r). But more often than not, single buildings are simply one element of a much larger settlement, much as a house is simply one element of a town (e.g., Fig. 3.2s, Los Muertos).

Arthur Rohn introduced the idea of Anasazi communities—clusters of sites that make up a larger settlement—quite some time ago. But the notion that individual buildings equal individual settlements is still quite pervasive: if not so much in archaeology, then in related fields that use, consider, or take inspiration from archaeological sites.

What constituted a settlement, a community in the ancient Southwest? Over the entire Southwest, people initially lived in pit houses and pit house villages. They continued to live in pit house villages for a *long* time. In fact, if you measure by seniority and persistence, the pit house—not the pueblo—is the archetypal southwestern building.

Pit house villages were the rule, and some of these were quite large. A typical—let us say modal—large pit house village of southern New Mexico (the Mogollon or Mimbres area) is shown in Fig. 3.1d. All the smaller blobs are pit houses, and the bigger blobs are great kivas. Pit house villages in southern New Mexico were replaced by single-story, masonry buildings clustered into villages, such as those shown in Figs. 3.1e and 3.1f, at about A.D. 1000. These villages represent some of the earliest massed, contiguous, masonry-room villages in the Southwest. Outside of Chaco Canyon—Alice's own wonderland of architectural anomalies and unique cases—the first real Pueblo-looking structures in the Southwest were not in the Four Corners area but along the Mimbres River in southwestern New Mexico.

In the Anasazi or Four Corners area, pit houses persisted rather longer than that. They were not replaced, but rather were supplemented with small, aboveground room blocks—the beginnings of the "unit pueblos"—by about A.D. 750 or 800. Unit pueblos did not exist in splendid isolation but instead were parts of much larger communities. Fig. 3.1c shows an exceptionally large example of an Anasazi community of this type—larger spatially, but perhaps not in population, than the southern New Mexico villages.

In the deserts of southern Arizona, pit house villages were extraordinarily long-lived. A single location would be occupied for centuries, unlike the much shorter-term Anasazi pattern. Since pit houses themselves lasted only fifteen or so years before the timbers rotted and a new dwelling was needed, a long-term occupation of a single place might ultimately create a very large site, such as Snaketown (Fig. 3.1a; note that individual pit houses are not shown on this map). Snaketown and sites like it seem huge when compared to the largest contemporary Anasazi sites. Some of this disparity is the result of long-term use, but in fact sites like Snaketown were probably much larger than most contemporary Anasazi sites.

Snaketown and many other communities in what is today southern Arizona also included a bewildering variety of public architecture: ball courts, platform mounds, plazas, roads. Hohokam pit houses were shallow, and their superstructures were highly perishable. As a result, a large pit house village, like Snaketown, leaves a very big but very flat site. Because the remains of pit houses are flat, things that stick up, like platform mounds and ball courts and roads, are almost impossible to ignore—they are the only things above grade.

Hohokam archaeologists have been comfortable with earthen architecture—mounds, ball courts, and the rest—from the earliest days of Hohokam archaeology. In the Four Corners area, with the many dazzling stone buildings to distract, it has taken nearly a century for us to realize that earthen architecture—mounds, berms, roads, and the like—was also a major element of Anasazi communities. We are only now starting to see it.

Snaketown, which is full of mounds and ball courts, reached its peak about A.D. 1100 or 1150. One of the largest Anasazi sites of that time was Skunk Springs (Fig. 3.1b). Skunk Springs is a classic Anasazi community, with scores of "unit houses" clustered along streets into a village or settlement. Like many of the larger Anasazi communities, Skunk Springs also included several elements of much more massively built public architecture: great houses (like one of the smaller Chaco buildings in Fig. 3.1g) and great kivas (in the upper right corner of Skunk Springs, Fig. 3.1b). In the eleventh and twelfth centuries, this pattern typifies the Anasazi settlement, with many small unit houses or small aggregates of unit houses either around or more often to one side of a cluster of larger-scale, presumably "public" or "communal" architecture. The public or communal building forms the architectural, if not the geometric, center of the community.

The great houses of Chaco Canyon were also part of a much larger settlement (Fig. 3.3w—note the scale change). Chaco was by far the largest single community, in the sense of a multibuilding settlement, in the Anasazi world. But other, later settlements elsewhere in the Southwest were even larger. The largest sites in the deserts of southern Arizona and northern Chihuahua from about A.D. 1350 to 1450 reached phenomenal sizes (for the Southwest). Casas Grandes (Fig. 3.2n) was perhaps the largest Pueblo-style building ever; it consisted of two massed, terraced, adobe room blocks with a spacious central plaza. Around the exterior were a number of fascinating specialized structures: ball courts, platform mounds, and so forth. These Mesoamerican-looking structures have been used to argue that Casas Grandes is, in fact, a Mesoamerican site. But the bulk of the architecture—and most important, the domestic architecture—is almost a stereotype of the Pueblo style. Walking into the central plaza at Casas Grandes would be much like walking into a version of the modern pueblo of Taos (Fig. 3.2u), only much bigger. Casas Grandes was a pueblo on a truly awesome scale.

But even Casas Grandes was not the largest settlement of its time in the Southwest. Consider Los Muertos (Fig. 3.2s), one of many sites located under modern-day Phoenix. This cluster of large adobe buildings stretched for well over a kilometer. (It is likely that most, if not all, of these buildings were contemporaneously occupied.) Los Muertos was a big community, but it was only one of about a dozen similar sites in the

Phoenix area, settlements like Las Colinas, Mesa Grande, Pueblo Grande, and Casa Buena.

Sites like Los Muertos could exist only because of the elaborate system of impressive canals that brought agricultural and drinking water from the major streams—the Salt and Gila Rivers—to the broad expanses of the upper terraces. The terraces supported both the large settlements and the fields that fed them. But canal systems demand a degree of community integration far beyond that needed for smaller Anasazi settlements. Canals might stretch for miles, with a series of villages strung along—or, more appropriately, tethered to—the canal. Fig. 3.3v shows one such system associated with the famous site of Casa Grande. Casa Grande is a large site in southern Arizona, much like Los Muertos, and should not be confused with Casas Grandes in Chihuahua. Since water distribution required cooperation and coordination among all the settlements along the canal, archaeologists have termed this pattern a "canal community."

"Canal community" is correct on more than just a descriptive level. The associated community for sites like Los Muertos was thus much larger than the site itself—and hugely bigger than any community in the Anasazi world. Fig. 3.3w shows Chaco Canyon, which was the largest single Anasazi community prior to historic times; compare its extent with that of the Casa Grande canal community in Fig. 3.3v.

In late prehistoric and early historic times, after A.D.1500, Pueblo community size may have reached the scales implied by Los Muertos and Casa Grande. Zuni, in particular, has always been large, in both its population and its areal extent. Fig. 3.3y shows the late prehistoric settlements that combined to form today's Zuni—in effect, the Zuni community. The spatial extent reaches the scales of the later communities of the Phoenix area.

In summary, I want to make two points. First, Anasazi communities were, prior to A.D.1300 or 1400, almost always larger than the site. The individual ruin, be it a mesa-top unit pueblo or cliff palace, is *not* a community. The appropriate context for understanding Anasazi architecture or town planning—which are essentially the same thing—is much larger than we could ever grasp from coffee-table books, photo essays, and calendars that focus, literally, on the individual building. Second, a note of caution is necessary on how we appropriate Anasazi architecture. Most nonarchaeologists who look at prehistoric southwestern building believe that Pueblo Bonito and Chaco were the architectural apex. That simply is not true. Using Anasazi monuments (the postcard and calendar view) is fine and proper for purely formal inspiration; but using the coffee-table book presentation of Anasazi building as a point of entry for trying to understand Anasazi intentions is pernicious. The sample is hideously skewed.

Santa Fe's Museum of Indian Arts and Culture, where I worked, has a world-famous collection of pots. Do the pots represent Indian life? Only obliquely; in fact, they represent the collecting tastes of rich white people in Santa Fe during the 1930s and 1940s. Anasazi monuments (and I mean this to include the parks and monuments that preserve the "best" prehistoric architecture) are likewise a biased sample from which to understand Anasazi architectural intentions. At places like Mesa Verde and Chaco, we see what appealed to Euroamerican tastes, the selection of Euroamerican people whose job it was to pick and choose monuments. Some parks are simply an accident of preservation, like Mesa Verde, and some simply reflect the pragmatics of archaeological logistics. Bandelier comes to mind; it is a national park because it was a day's ride out from Santa Fe.

4 Power and Efficiency in Eastern Anasazi Architecture

A Case of Multiple Evolutionary Trajectories

David E. Stuart

Southwestern archaeologist David Stuart relates architectural massing and design sophistication in the Anasazi world to fluctuating socioeconomic conditions. For Stuart, built environments reflect either the values of the powerful or the needs of those who must be efficient to survive. Stuart argues that there was not a single, fluid line of architectural development in Anasazi history but rather a flexible pattern of formal and informal buildings that matched the political and economic conditions of the times.

This essay draws together preliminary observations about changes in Anasazi architecture from roughly A.D. 350 to A.D. 1450. Many of these trends in architecture have been noted and commented on for more than half a century—others have not. More important, these trends appear to be interrelated in ways that have not previously been considered. Architecture is more than a space for living, more than elements of design, more than the manifestation of a society's inner values: it is also direct, hard evidence of the state of a social system, including its health, its economy, and its life cycle. The trends in Anasazi architecture addressed in this essay are systematic changes in room size from A.D. 350 to A.D. 1450; a separation of architectural trajectories between small-room farmsteads and "big house" architecture associated with the Chaco Phenomenon; a repeated regression to pit house architecture (long after such forms would have been expected) at critical times of reorganization in Anasazi society; an unstable separation of sacred versus secular architecture ("kivas" vs. "pit houses"); and radical, cyclical changes in the standing mass of architecture at different times in the life cycle of Eastern Anasazi society. Many archaeologists have commented on the dramatic fluctuation in the number of rooms, room size, and wall thickness, but no one has adequately explored the possibility that the total "standing mass" of architecture at a given time is direct evidence of the power and energy available to a society.

My explanation for these interrelated phenomena is simple. In times of great structural and economic change, there is no energy left over to invest in a "powerful" mass of standing architecture. Survivability becomes all-important, so efficiency becomes the dominating factor. Pit houses are a more efficient form of architecture, for thermal buffering and mass, than is aboveground masonry architecture.

Power and Efficiency

Some years ago, while explaining to myself how some hunter-gatherer societies eventually become agriculturists while others remain hunters and gatherers, I hit upon the idea that two great evolutionary trajectories pertain to human societies: "power" versus "efficiency" (Stuart and Gauthier 1981).

The hunter-gatherer society is typically highly efficient. The population is fairly stable over long periods of time, often in rough equilibrium with the environment and its carrying capacity (Stuart 1980). Little energy is invested in material goods or architectural features. Indeed, energy taken in from the environment in the course of daily economy and energy expended that same day tend to be roughly equal. Such societies are basically mobile, and most "standing mass" consists of the living bodies of the individuals who constitute the population. Such societies tend to be highly resistant to change; one generation is rather like the next. In short, most hunter-gatherers have societies that, at least anecdotally, approximate a physicist's definition of thermodynamic efficiency (Stuart 1982).

In contrast, agricultural societies (which *all* arose from transformed hunter-gatherer societies) tend to grow and "flouresce." In periods of flourescence, or "power," change is rapid and the rate of energy consumption is dramatic when compared to that of hunters and gatherers; population growth is explosive and fluctuates episodically. Indeed, as Stephen J. Gould would put it, "the life-cycles of more complex societies are 'punctuated equilibria' " (Eldridge and Gould 1972). Such societies are susceptible to rapid change. One generation is not necessarily like the next.

Often huge amounts of energy are wasted in the process of transforming some of it into the fixed materials that support the society. Much of the remaining energy is invested in "things": material goods, technology, architecture, and infrastructure. Eventually, in a large agricultural society, only a minor proportion of its energy is directly fixed as "standing mass" in the human bodies that constitute the population.

Of course, many hunter-gatherer societies never became agriculturists at all, while some agricultural societies are known to have eventually de-evolved back into a semisedentary hunter-gatherer state (Stuart 1986). Clearly, these great trajectories in evolution are not discrete and exclusive; rather, they can be viewed as the two ends of an adaptive spectrum between which all human societies are suspended through time, some fluctuating modestly (in the case of efficient societies) and others dramatically (in the case of powerful societies). In short, all evolutionary events can be viewed as a balancing act between the need for power, which is necessary for short-term competition, and efficiency, which enhances the durability or "immortality" of a society (Stuart 1982).

One irony merits serious contemplation: the powerful societies that have created the most architecture have not endured. Ancient Egypt, Rome, Byzantium, Chaco Canyon—they come, they go. Only the truly efficient hunter-gatherer society endures over many millennia. Even when "destroyed" by more powerful, developed societies, many nomads have re-established themselves in the shadows of former civilizations. The dynamics of "power" and "efficiency" can be observed right here in the Southwest as Anasazi society rhythmically fluctuated, suspended between these two polar parameters of evolutionary adaptation. As Anasazi society went through its "punctuated equilibrium," one sees fundamental changes in archaeology and architecture, which can be measured and analyzed.

Trends in Architectural Change: A.D. 350 to A.D. 1450

Changes in Room Size

Virtually every archaeologist who has worked in the Eastern Anasazi world has noted dramatic changes in room size between different archaeological phases, or time periods. Yet the tendency in doing meticulous archaeological fieldwork in one geographical locale is to become so enmeshed in the details of such local changes that the larger regional pattern is lost. Those regional patterns relate to fundamental organizational transformations in Anasazi society over time.

Between A.D. 200 and 500, prior to Basketmaker III times (about A.D. 500), northern Anasazi sites are characterized by large cobble-ringed pit houses, small storage cysts, and *no* pottery. Such sites, a number of which are found south of Mesa Verde between Durango and the San Juan country, are the direct outgrowth of even earlier pit houses that arose out of the Desert Archaic tradition. The earliest of these are small and architecturally inconsistent. Eventually, they grew in size, consistency, and numbers, until early Basketmaker III times—characterized by well-formed pit houses (Cordell 1984).

Small pit houses were replaced by larger ones by Basketmaker II—only to go through a radical transformation when pottery was introduced into the Eastern Anasazi heartland, transforming Basketmaker II into Basketmaker III. During the course of Basketmaker III times, there was a powerful surge in village construction. With it came increased differentiation between the largest and smallest pit houses, which peaked in the A.D. 700s-800s (Pueblo I times).

By the early A.D. 800s, aboveground masonry architecture began to replace the last of the pit house villages. Because of the dates, many archaeologists associate this architecture with Pueblo I, but I view it as part of the early Pueblo II period. Comparatively large Anasazi pit houses and associated aboveground storerooms inhabited at the end of Pueblo I times were quickly replaced by small-roomed, aboveground masonry room blocks in the early Pueblo II period.

More important, the pit house architecture in the Anasazi country that overlapped for the greatest length of time with the "new" aboveground masonry architecture is found largely in isolated upland sites with surprisingly large, deep pit houses (those of the Rosa phase in the Gallina country between Dulce and Lindrith come quickly to mind). Invariably, it was the unusually large pit houses which survived beyond their time to overlap temporarily with aboveground masonry architecture. This is a pattern we shall see again.

Meanwhile, in the homeland of the Chaco Anasazi, from the Red Mesa Valley near Gallup eastward to Mount Taylor and northward along the east slope of the Chuska Mountains, housing starts were at an all-time high. A frenzy of building activity characterized very early Pueblo II so-

Fig. 4.1. Pueblo Bonito at Chaco Canyon illustrates the architectural mass, diversity, and technical complexity typical of a "power phase" in Anasazi architecture. Photograph by Baker H. Morrow.

ciety. Most of the sites created between the early A.D. 800s and the mid 900s were small "farmsteads" of six, eight, ten to twenty rooms. Small rooms, often two rows deep, were built in L's or C's. Adjacent to many, centered in a small plaza, were comparatively large "kivas" or "proto-kivas." I argue that these were pit houses in the process of becoming sacred and stylized into religious chambers, or kivas.

By A.D. 950, Pueblo II society in the San Juan Basin was in full swing. Indeed, in the years between approximately 950 and 1100, 43 percent of all of the Anasazi sites discovered by archaeologists in the 125 years between 1856 and 1981 were built (Stuart and Gauthier 1981)! In short, during the approximately 150-year-long period of episodic building booms (A.D. 950–1100) in Chacoan society, a staggering proportion of the total "standing mass" of architecture ever created by the Eastern Anasazi was "fixed," through construction. This is evidence of a "power phase" (see Fig. 4.1).

Increased Diversity between "Large" and "Small" Architectural Features

During that same building boom, dramatic changes were taking place in both site and room size. Chaco Anasazi society began to build what are now called Chacoan "outliers." At the same time, tens of hundreds of farmsteads continued to be built in an architectural model typical of modest Pueblo II house blocks. The small sites are often classified as Hosta Butte phase, and slightly earlier ones, Red Mesa. The large outliers are typically classified as Bonito phase, or if they are very late in Chaco times, late Bonito or even Chaco/McElmo phase (roughly A.D. 1080–1120).

The important trend, however, is that size differences between both large and small rooms and large and small sites increased dramatically. The late 900s to early 1100s are marked by repeated, powerful episodic surges in architectural activity *and* dramatically increased coefficients of variation between "bigs" and "littles." Indeed, field archaeologists have correctly noted that many Eastern Anasazi rooms at smaller "habitation" sites were often only a meter and a half on a side, too small to actually serve as habitations. Therefore, many scholars assume living and working areas to have included rooftops and plaza areas as well.

In contrast, the "big house" architecture of the Bonito phase consisted of immense sandstone strongholds with thick masonry walls, kivas set into square rooms, and rooms that are enormous even by contemporary standards. Sites like Pueblo Pintado, which contains sixty-odd immense ground-floor rooms and six stepped-in kivas, are impressive in size, height, and mass in any time period. They are in stark contrast to the architectural mass of smaller farmsteads built at the same time.

By the early 1100s, however, Chaco Anasazi society was beginning to suffer burnout. Its great "power phase" could not be sustained. Those sites that hung on and remained inhabited, indeed even expanded, tended to be the "big house" architecture, not the small farmsteads. By the early 1100s, Anasazi farmers were abandoning the lower, drier areas of the San Juan Basin in droves and returning to the surrounding uplands. By the mid 1100s, many hundreds of families had built new sites in the uplands. These were not aboveground architecture—they were highly efficient *pit houses* of modest scale (Stuart and Farwell 1983). These pit houses were followed in the late 1100s by the resurgence of aboveground masonry architecture consisting of small to moderate-sized pueblos—ten, twelve, sixteen, twenty rooms—with medium-sized, rather uniform rooms.

By 1200, another building boom and peak of diversity in Upland architecture became evident just to the north of the earlier Chacoan development. Mesa Verde is tangible evidence of this surge in construction, which created both "cliff palaces" and "mesa-top" pueblos. Like similar ruins at Bandelier, the Chuska Mountains, the Gallina highlands, and Gila Cliff Dwellings National Monument, the Southwest's uplands—rather than the low, drier basins—became a new heartland for reformulated Anasazi society in the 1200s. Some archaeologists refer to these sites as Pueblo II/Pueblo III, but they are distinct enough from the earlier Chacoan heyday to be considered a separate phenomenon. I refer to this as the Upland period.

By 1300, yet another set of pit houses—smaller, shallower, and rectangular— were being constructed in the lower river valleys, particularly along the Chama River and the Rio Grande. These pit houses marked the decline of Upland society at Mesa Verde and Bandelier. A final transformation in Anasazi society brought the population downhill, following streams that flowed from the cooler, wetter east slopes of mountainous areas. This move to the rivers has been called Rio Grande Classic society. I call it the Riverine period. It began, like its predecessors, with modest, efficient pit houses constructed in the early 1300s (Stuart and Farwell 1983).

Through time, the rhythmic changes were from small to large rooms, the largest rooms and pit houses tending to be "survivors" that often overlapped the next archaeological phase having small rooms or small pit houses and found in a slightly different ecological setting. As the economic and energetic power built up in any phase, there was a rapid divergence in size and function between large and small architectural elements. Such temporal episodes of maximum diversity reflect the deep tensions inherent in growth and signal yet another oncoming reorganization in society.

Think of it like 1959 in the United States with the divergence between Cadillacs and Volkswagens. One could research population records, Wall Street stock values, and housing starts to document that 1959 was a "powerful," or good, year in America—a year when the powerful (Cadillacs) had begun to diverge from the efficient (Volkswagens) and when society was on the verge of transformation. All of us would argue that the succeeding decade was a period of radical transformation in American society. That decade constituted a protracted debate on power—an unwinnable war, a president assassinated, values changed, a rejection of materialism, a resurgence of idealism, an increasing secularization of the nation, a remarkable liberalization in race and ethnic relations. These characteristics of political economy in the 1960s have not endured.

If that decade was a period of surprising secularization in American society, then the early 1990s can be demonstrated as a period of religious resurgence, even fanatic forms of it. This resurgence has far more to do with surrounding economic, social, and political fragility than it does with *sui generis* changes in the values of people who live in our society. As the rich get richer and the poor get poorer, most of us get a little more rigid. It is just that simple, or complex, depending upon your point of view.

In times of prosperity, "liberalism" and great change are more plausible than in times of want. Times of prosperity breed social "liberalism," not because we are saints, but because we can more easily afford to be generous to "others," thereby satisfying our own egos. "Diversity" also requires higher power inputs to sustain than does homogeneity. Is anyone surprised that the recession of 1990–1991 carried with it a national debate over "cultural diversity" in America? Or that race relations have hardened as the buying power of many families has declined?

There is a great cost to society merely to sustain diversity, whether of religion, of political viewpoint, or in architecture. After all, social "class" itself is about technological, political, social, and economic power and its differentiation. Different "classes" in society have different amounts of power. Societies cannot afford to sustain the costs of a high coefficient of diversity indefinitely, so they do not.

The Anasazi world was no different. In late Chacoan times, its remarkable diversity resulted in architecture so complex and so divergent that some archaeologists continue to argue that there were "big house" people and "small house" people who interacted but were not truly part of the same society.

There are even more useful parallels with "modern" American architecture. Grand American homes of a Gold Coast, a Main Line, a Westchester County are almost always created very late in a cycle of great power and prosperity. The end of the Gay Nineties, the end of the Roaring Twenties, and the end of the 1980s—these are among the periods most likely to create large, elegant architecture, even as those with less economic power are displaced from the pinnacles of economic enterprise and build unpleasantly small townhouses and duplexes or move to trailers. More to the point, nowadays one finds America's "great" houses along Philadelphia's Main Line, indeed in almost every city's grand old close-in suburbs, to have been broken up into small apartments or converted to new uses, such as funeral parlors. That is what happens to the large, elegant survivors of prior "grand ages."

Again, it was no different in the Chaco-Anasazi world. By the mid 1200s, Chacoan great houses had been reinhabited by Mesa Verdean peoples, and the large, elegant rooms had been cut up into twos and threes, using coarser Mesa Verde masonry. As a consequence, most archaeologists have tended to conclude that those Chacoan outliers continued to be inhabited more or less continuously from the 1000s to the mid 1200s. I suggest not. To my way of thinking, most were either very nearly or altogether abandoned by the mid to late 1100s, only to be divided up into smaller apartments and reoccupied for a time by "poorer folks" in the mid 1200s.

Repeated Regression to Pit House Forms of Architecture

As already noted, pit houses precede major shifts in settlement patterns and reorganization of Anasazi society at roughly 1150, 1220, and 1310—times when they would not have otherwise been expected if one adhered to a neat, unilinear, architectural progression. Those Anasazi farmers who lived modestly in the "small house" architecture of the San Juan Basin moved into the uplands to build pit houses again as Chacoan society became fragile and fragmented in the mid 1100s. Slightly later, in the early to mid 1200s, small to medium-sized, aboveground masonry pueblos were being built even as the largest, and last, of the Upland pit houses were renovated and refurbished one final time before abandonment *as* habitations. Again, one sees an overlap with the larger "survivor" forms of architecture as growing elements of upland society reorganized into numerous, smaller succeeding community structures nearby. By the late 1200s, the modest masonry pueblos of the early 1200s had been replaced by large mesa-top sites (like Grasshopper in Arizona or LA 12,700 near Los Alamos). These, too, were short-lived. Those in the uplands were typically abandoned in the late 1200s. Due to droughts and upland crop failures, Anasazi society throughout the Four Corners region once again reorganized and moved on, resettling in the lower river valleys by about 1325. They *first* announced this movement (ca. 1300) by creating still more new pit houses in lowland elevations along the primary rivers and streams.

The facts are clear. Late pit houses are an episodic feature of the uplands throughout the Southwest. In areas where piñon meets ponderosa, the first important cluster of pit house dates was 1153 and includes "different" archaeological phases geographically spread from southern Colorado to Sierra Blanca near Mescalero, New Mexico—350 linear miles from north to south (Stuart and Farwell 1983).

As noted earlier, pit houses are efficient. Clearly, in the mid 1100s, Anasazi society was starved for energy as it adapted to rapidly changing conditions. Just as Anglo-American plainsmen coming to the Southwest in the 1880s first built sod dugouts, thereby earning the name of "sodbusters," while getting several crops in and harvested before they built their farm houses, so, too, did Anasazi farmers a millennium before. Systematic regression to pit house architecture is not a sign that Anasazi society had "failed"; rather, it is a sign that many were forced into an "efficiency phase" to conserve energy that was needed to reorganize and adapt to new ecological conditions as settlement patterns shifted to the uplands (see Fig. 4.2).

Unstable Separation of Sacred Versus Secular

A huge literature has been created on kivas in the Southwest and on the details of kiva architecture. Many archaeologists have spent good portions of their careers tracing the details of kiva construction and from these details trying to discern migration routes, religious patterns, and, indeed, the histories not only of individual language groups but even of separate lineages and clans. To my way of thinking, both the notable architectural ambiguity between "kivas" and "pit houses" and the shifting usage of these architectural forms is far more fascinating.

I believe that pit houses became sacred and some became "kivas" because they represented the way things had once been done. They were tangible connections to an increasingly remote past during Chaco's fast-paced era of growth. Indeed, one can look at small Pueblo II pueblos of the late A.D. 800s and early 900s in the Anasazi country and easily argue that a generation of grandparents still lived in the "kiva" in the courtyard of the plaza, while the younger folks lived out back in the aboveground masonry room blocks that we call Red Mesa phase. This is quite like

Fig. 4.2. A small pithouse settlement of A.D. 800s illustrates the uniformity, simplicity, and modesty typical of an "efficiency phase" in Anasazi architecture. Courtesy of the National Park Service Chaco Culture National Historic Park Museum Collection, Site No. 29SJ628 in Chaco Canyon.

grandparents on many contemporary Navajo "outfits," who live out back in an eight-sided hogan while the kids live in trailers or small H. U. D. houses just fifty feet away. In Anasazi times, once the grandparents were gone, their pit houses became more sacred, and many were eventually altered to include more of the formalized architectural features associated with "kivas."

46 *David E. Stuart*

By the A.D. 1000s, Chaco Anasazi society had begun to construct an enormous number of kivas, actually built inside square rooms—integrating the sacred and the secular into the same room block. Fifty to seventy years later, the kivas moved out into plazas again, re-establishing a more traditional separation. That should not really come as a shock. We have modern parallels as storefront churches are first created, then abandoned as new, formalized, "real" churches are later established for the same congregation, usually in different geographic settings. As a generalization, no specific form of architecture in the Anasazi world was more consistently renovated, refined, reused—or, when purposefully abandoned, done so with more finality—than the kiva.

Changes in Standing Mass of Architecture

Dramatic changes took place in the raw mass of architecture built at different time periods and in different stages of the life cycle of Eastern Anasazi society. I offer the tentative estimate that 80 to 90 percent of all currently visible Eastern Anasazi architecture was built in five peaks— late A.D. 700s to early A.D. 800s, roughly 950–1100, 1220–1270, mid 1300s, and mid 1400s—comprising less than three hundred years out of the approximately fifteen hundred years of Eastern Anasazi prehistory. These peaks were the comparatively brief "power phases" of Eastern Anasazi society (corresponding roughly to Basketmaker III/Pueblo I, late Pueblo II, Pueblo III, and early and late Pueblo IV in the Pecos Classification).

The most spectacular of these, beginning about A.D. 950 ("the Chaco Phenomenon"), generated both rates and scales of construction that were awesome in comparison to any prior or subsequent period. As already noted (Stuart and Gauthier 1981), 43 percent of all of the archaeological sites, and an even higher percentage of the most massive architecture ever found in the Anasazi world, was built between roughly A.D. 950 and 1100 in a series of erratic construction episodes.

There were also at least three lesser peaks in aboveground building activity. The first was between approximately 1220 and 1270 in the uplands. It was followed by another from 1325 to 1375 along the rivers of the Southwest. A second surge in Riverine period building came in the early to mid 1400s. Each of these peaks preceded major reorganizations of society. They were comparatively short periods in which Eastern Anasazi society managed to focus its energy and generate record "housing starts" and surprising architectural mass, only to be subsequently interrupted by conditions beyond ordinary control.

Each of these power peaks had a distinctive character reflecting the particular tensions and problems that arose as the previous adaptational peak failed. For example, the architecture of Mesa Verde is not representative of a "secure" adaptation—it is the architecture of nervous people. The far walls of the canyons are too distant to offer much threat from enemies armed with spear throwers or twenty-five-pound bows. Indeed, access to these great cliff palaces from either above or below is very easily controlled.

Mesa Verde's cliff dwellings are also efficient. Facing south, southeast, or southwest, as nearly all cliff palaces do, this architecture minimizes the need for exterior fuel sources, for most are large solar collectors. These are elegant, defensive locations that minimize the need for outside resources. These are far more like small, feudal cities or citadels than they are like the open towns of the expansive Chacoan world. The citadels of Mesa Verde, Bandelier, and Gila Cliff Dwellings are not about dominating 30,000 or 40,000 square miles. They are efficient but relatively short-term adaptations to isolation, social unease, defense, and strategic domination of the surrounding canyons and mesa tops—not the open, expansive architecture and connecting roadways of folks whose social world is well under control and whose competitors are not feared (Stuart 1989).

Many archaeologists have lumped the late Chacoan great houses and the impressive Upland citadels together, calling them both Pueblo III. But Chacoan towns and the Upland cliff palaces were not *both* part and parcel of a single Pueblo III "great house" phenomenon—they are separated in time by nearly a century (roughly A.D. 1075–1120 vs. 1220–1270), in space by 500 to 1,000 feet in elevation, and in ecology by piñon/juniper (Chaco) vs. piñon/ponderosa (Upland) vegetation communities. They are also separated by great transformational episodes that make them no more socially and economically related than the 1880s and the 1980s. One of those intervening transformational events, as already noted, is the upland pit house/small pueblo construction, social isolation, and scarcity of pottery trade wares of the mid 1100s.

By Upland times (1150–1300), the great trading networks of the Chaco basin were gone. Pottery styles and technology had changed. These were replaced by a trading network that connected upland areas to other upland areas through the exchange of valued items like St. John's Polychrome bowls. Mesa Verde was most closely connected by trade to the

Bandelier area and to the uplands of Arizona, not primarily to scattered populations living in decaying room blocks down in the Chaco country. In contrast, the Riverine period architectural peaks (mid 1300s and mid 1400s) created a network that connected settlements strung out along most of the Southwest's permanent rivers.

Conclusions

In concluding, I want to focus again on the primary patterns of architectural change in Anasazi society. Two consequences of these patterns merit further discussion: first, the separation of the socially and economically powerful from the efficient, and second, the fact that powerful societies tend to be short-lived. Even when powerful and efficient social elements are not separated into distinct societies, the most powerful *phases* of fundamentally efficient societies are comparatively short-lived.

Because of this, Chaco Canyon is particularly compelling as a metaphor for the story of our own times in modern America. Chacoan society, like ours, sought to transform the world around it politically, economically, socially, and ideologically. There's no doubt that, for a time, it succeeded. The population of Chaco undoubtedly believed in the myth of Chacoan power every bit as passionately as we believe in the infallibility of modern American power.

Like modern American society, Chacoan society faced typical problems. Time alone brought economic, organizational, population, and ecological changes that could not have been anticipated. Subsequent Eastern Anasazi society, however, learned from the Chaco experience and never again attempted to change and control so large a geographical area. The absence of later road systems on a Chacoan scale is eloquent testimony to that realization.

A second fascinating lesson of late Chacoan times comes from the period of roughly 1050 to the early 1100s. This was the time of maximal creation of standing mass in architecture—the absolute maximum amount of energy ever fixed in buildings by the Anasazi within a short time span. It was also the time of maximal investment in infrastructure: roads, district trading villages, outliers, and religious centers (Vivian 1990). Thus, it was also the time of greatest divergence between "great house" architecture and "small house" architecture. Archaeologists who primarily excavate at the large Chacoan sites have one picture of Chaco-

Anasazi society—but those who survey and excavate the small farmsteads have quite another.

As the tensions of unforeseen consequences brought the first wave of protracted economic stress to the San Juan Basin in the 1050s to 1070s, sites like Pueblo Pintado were built and road networks were expanded. Much of this building activity did not arise as a natural consequence of service to clusters of long-established surrounding farmsteads, for sites like Pueblo Pintado were plunked down in the middle of nowhere. Michael Marshall eloquently points out (elsewhere in this volume) that many, if not most, of the formal Chacoan roadways were built to serve "religious" purposes. Whether the organizing principle of a society is religion (Anasazi) or money (Wall Street) matters little. In a power phase, that society's primary organizing principle is elaborately mobilized to focus energy.

Quite frankly, all this is surprisingly similar to the Works Progress Administration and Civilian Conservation Corps projects of the 1930s. Some archaeologists have argued that because of differences in units of measurement at adjacent rooms, some late Chaco sites were built by work crews who were ethnically different and so used different basic units of measure. One can easily argue that excess labor was being absorbed in massive "public works" projects throughout the San Juan Basin in the late eleventh century. I enjoy the plausible irony that many ruins of Chacoan society, built to reverse a deepening economic depression, were enshrined by public works projects 850 years later that were designed to reverse the Great Depression of the 1930s. I suggest that as a response to regional stress just prior to A.D. 1000, Chaco society went into an orgy of activity, thus putting the "icing" on its own elaborate cake. Most archaeologists look back on it through the depths of time and the imperfections of archaeological analysis and pronounce this episode the very height of Chacoan society. I argue that it was far more like an elegant, but essentially hollow, shell.

This "public works" strategy, however, did not adequately relieve stress on all elements of Chacoan society as it neared A.D. 1100, for during crisis the fate of those tied to the modest, more efficient "small house" architecture took on a separate history from those of the large and elegant "big houses." Small farmers drifted away from Chacoan society by the hundreds, if not the thousands, in the early to mid 1100s, abandoning the elites in large Chacoan towns.

As the agricultural underpinnings were pulled out from under Chaco

Anasazi society, the top simply collapsed downward. Those who occupied the lowest economic tiers abandoned the Chaco country first and rebuilt in the uplands—it was they who created modest pit houses. Others, likely better off, moved en masse, leaving evidence of "site intrusions" along the northern perimeter of the Plains of San Agustín and elsewhere. One way or another, many endured, but some of the most complex elements of Chacoan society were forever lost.

The lesson for us in modern times is that when societies go into a powerful phase, things begin to differentiate internally. A "class" system, however benign, emerges. We can see this in modern American architecture. It differentiates, as architecture did in late Chacoan times, between those who have more power and energy available to them and those who have less. More profoundly, each class faces different risks in that same society when true crisis arrives. Once a crisis has transformed (even fragmented) the original whole, much esoteric knowledge is lost for all time; however, the more fundamental "everyday" knowledge of those who always had to practice efficiency to survive as a class within a complex society is most likely to endure.

The Anasazi indeed may offer us the ultimate lesson in social values. Their architectural trajectories suggest that it is not the meek who inherit the earth. Rather, it is the *efficient,* through greater rates of survival, who inherit all.

Anasazi architecture was not one grand, progressive, uninterrupted trajectory of development that culminated in an illuminatingly vibrant style based on genius. It, like all other evolutionary adaptations in the real world, is best understood as a series of punctuated equilibria where periods of great resurgence and power are interrupted by periods of painful transformation that require the modesty of efficiency. Our "modern" view of these adaptations is one-sided, largely because efficiency does not impress; it only endures.

References

Cordell, Linda S. 1984. *Prehistory of the Southwest.* Academic Press, New York.
Eldridge, N., and Stephen J. Gould. 1972. "Punctuated Equilibria: An Alternative to Phyletic Gradualism." In *Models in Paleobiology,* ed. T. J. M. Schopp, pp. 82–115. Freeman, Cooper, & Co., San Francisco.
Smith, Watson. 1952. "When Is a Kiva." In *Excavations in Big Hawk Valley, Wupatki National Monument, Arizona.* Bulletin No. 24, Museum of Northern Arizona, Flagstaff.

Stuart, David E. 1980. "Kinship and Social Organization in Tierra del Fuego: Evolutionary Consequences." In *The Versatility of Kinship,* ed. L. S. Cordell and Beckerman, pp. 269–284. Academic Press, New York.

———. 1982. "Power and Efficiency: Demographic Behavior and Energetic Trajectories in Cultural Evolution." In *The San Juan Tomorrow,* ed. Plog and Wait, pp. 127–162. U.S. National Park Service, Santa Fe.

———. 1986. "The Rise of Agriculture: An Essay on Science, the Rule of Unintended Consequences, and Hunter-Gatherer Behavior." In *Award Winning Essays,* pp. 11–16. New Mexico Humanities Council Third Annual Humanities Award Program, Albuquerque.

———. 1989. *The Magic of Bandelier National Monument.* Ancient City Press, Santa Fe.

Stuart, David E., and Robin Farwell. 1983. "Out of Phase: Late Pithouse Occupations in the Highlands of New Mexico." In *High Altitude Adaptations in the Southwest,* ed. J. Winter, pp. 115–158. CRM Report No. 2, U.S. Department of Agriculture Forest Service, Albuquerque.

Stuart, David E., and R. P. Gauthier. 1981. *Prehistoric New Mexico.* New Mexico Historic Preservation Division, Santa Fe. Reprint, University of New Mexico Press, Albuquerque, 1989.

Vivian, R. Gwinn. 1990. *The Chacoan Prehistory of the San Juan Basin.* Academic Press, Inc., San Diego.

5   A Planner's Primer

Lessons from Chaco

Stephen D. Dent and Barbara Coleman

*Departing from purely archaeological or historical points of view in this
fresh analysis, architect Stephen Dent and urban planner Barbara Coleman
examine the ruins of Chaco Canyon from the perspective of modern urban
planning and design. They conclude that many principles of sound city planning seem to have been followed by the Chaco Anasazi. Dent and Coleman
ask intriguing questions: Was an overall site plan for the canyon created and
then patiently executed, perhaps over a period of centuries? Was there a need
for a local consensus in site planning, or did some person or class of persons
make authoritarian development decisions? When viewed from a pragmatic
planning point of view, the architecture and open space of Chaco Canyon
provide successful models for modern designers in the arid Southwest.*

Urban Form

If we look at the overall physical plan of Chaco, we see a highly
articulated composition even without the infill pattern of fields and
small structures that has largely disappeared. Using the noted city planner Kevin Lynch's urban form determinants of paths, edges, nodes, districts, and landmarks, we can test the legibility of Chaco (Lynch 1960:47–
90). Is it easily comprehended? Could one understand one's place in the
community both socially and spatially? Are the important values of the
society expressed in the physical forms? On all counts, we say yes. Impor-
tantly, all of Lynch's determinants are clearly perceptible both at the
larger scale of the extended community and at each separate structure
within.

The regionwide road network leading to Chaco Canyon had a major
impact on the overall composition of the site and reinforced its prominence and special status. Travelers on those roads knew they were going
to, or coming from, only one place. Within the canyon, a network of
larger and smaller paths connected structures, intermittent streams, and
fields. Even today, carved steps and narrow paths up the cliffs are remind-

ers of this network that tied together all aspects of daily life. Without beasts of burden or wheeled vehicles, the pace of life slows and face-to-face contact is reinforced by the connecting pathways.

The edges of the overall settlement were clearly marked by natural features (cliffs and streams) and by large structures placed at roughly the four cardinal points: Pueblo Alto to the north, Una Vida to the southeast, Tsin Kletzin to the south, and Peñasco Blanco to the northwest. Within structures, the limits are particularly well defined, in many cases by enclosing walls. Edges define limits of control, areas of influence, and social groupings—and Chaco reflects all of these attributes.

Nodes are concentrations of activity. When they become quite large they are thought of as centers, as at Pueblo Bonito. A vital community has numerous nodes of activity, which contribute to social interaction and physical coherence. Kivas and plazas were certainly nodes of activity, as were common places for everyday events such as collecting water, bathing, or irrigating. Major centers in Chaco would appear to be Pueblo Bonito and Chetro Ketl, with their large plazas and numerous kivas (see Fig. 5.1). These centers, along with nearby Casa Rinconada and Pueblo del Arroyo, create the most intense center of buildings and activity—the center of the centers, or "Downtown Chaco" as Stephen Lekson (1986) has called it.

Districts at Chaco are, at their simplest, the man-made and all that is beyond. Even the natural environment is at a scale that can be articulated as definable districts: bosque, valley floor, cliffs, and mesa tops. The man-made would have been perceived as the fields and the settlements. And there would have been no confusing the different individual settlements, due to the unique character of the major structures coupled with the specifics of the adjacent natural setting, small residential clusters, and pattern of fields.

The number of identifiable landmarks in Chaco is clear to this day. At the east end is Fajada Butte, which must have had special significance owing to its physical prominence. Specific cliff walls, the stream, feeder canyons, and distant peaks gave constant reference points. Each of the major structures would also have marked one's place in the whole from almost all vantage points in the canyon.

Significantly, all of the critical determinants in creating a legible and meaningful urban form are in evidence at Chaco—and at both the smaller scale of immediate experience and the larger scale of the whole. This means that both visitors and residents were never lost or confused

Fig. 5.1. Pueblo Bonito Plaza. Photograph by Baker H. Morrow.

about their place in this "metropolis." We can assume that this clarity also extended to one's social place. The quality of legibility at Chaco is typically missing in modern cities. When legibility is present, however, the "sense of place" so often talked about by designers will almost always be perceived. Chaco, even in its skeletal remnants, has that special character that intrigues and holds us.

Environmental Response

Major settlements in delicate ecosystems, however, have a difficult time surviving for long periods owing to their susceptibility to environmental change. A rational strategy for extended survival would be twofold: first, plan and design to "fit" with the natural forces of the site; and second, extend systems of infrastructure and social order beyond the immediate ecological zone. Both approaches are evident at Chaco.

The structures at Chaco generally show a high degree of environmental sensitivity in their response to climatic forces both at the building scale and in site planning. Generally, forms step down and open up to the south or southeast. Such configurations provide the plazas and most openings in the buildings with shelter from the prevailing northwesterly winter winds, shade from the hot afternoon summer sun, and warmth from the winter sun. Ralph Knowles (1974:40–41) has shown that the radiant energy distribution in winter over the entire mass of Pueblo Bonito is remarkably even—a highly sophisticated environmental response. Whether the building was to shelter goods or people, the design works to give all parts of the structure nearly equal solar exposure during winter days.

Ample evidence also indicates that solar design response transcended the provision of summer shade or winter heat. Knowles (1974:38–39) observed several special solar relationships in the plan and form of Pueblo Bonito besides those noted above. Of special interest are the solar alignments of Bonito, which apparently mark the summer and winter solstices. As Pueblo Bonito grew and evolved, these solar marking aspects of the form were altered, and other, perhaps more sophisticated relationships replaced them. Recent research reveals a widespread net of solar, lunar, and cardinal markings and relationships both within the individual structures and connecting the major buildings in the canyon. This research materially alters the way in which we see the overall plan of Chaco. Rather than a collection of individually interesting structures that were built to respond to their immediate environment, they are seen as part of a large-scale "cosmic" composition of great richness and intellectual depth.

Frankly, it would surprise us if the Chacoans did *not* comprehend and mark solar geometry and its relation to natural cycles. Anyone who has slept beneath those clear skies or walked in the valley can attest to the impact and power of the sun, moon, and stars in one's perception of place.

If Chaco, and Pueblo Bonito in particular, was a center for trade, administration, and ceremonial functions, the public outdoor space is appropriately scaled and designed for meetings, trade, and religious events. Evidence of ramadas or shade structures on the plaza edges further reinforces the idea that these were not just leftover spaces but had social func-

Fig. 5.2. Pueblo Bonito blends with cliff. Photograph by Baker H. Morrow.

tions. The terraced form would permit numerous possibilities for inter-action and observation at the various levels.

The environmental "fit" of almost all early architecture is reinforced by the use of immediately available building materials. The easy access to tabular sandstone in Chaco Canyon influenced both construction methods and building placement. The manner in which the remaining stone structures seem to meld with the landscape reminds us of how little influence natural features or systems have with most city planning today—and we are not the better for it (see Fig. 5.2).

A strongly expressed separation between the settlement and its surround seems to be the norm in early settlements in arid regions. In true desert habitats, the enclosed, compact settlement provides security from both invaders and the climate. A compact form of high-mass walls, an insulated roof (minimal though that insulation was), small openings, and narrow shaded paths and open spaces is a consistent vernacular design response in arid regions.

The pattern of placement of structures within the canyon reveals a high level of sensitivity to environmental factors. Each of the three earliest settlements in the canyon is located close to Chaco Wash and the confluence of major tributary drainages, as noted by Lekson (1986:264). As the settlement increased in size and complexity, the unpredictable water supply was further strained by a growing population and by additional farmland. The construction of check dams in the cliffs to catch and control runoff was required. Perhaps the very value of these water systems, once they were in place, influenced the location of each successive building phase in the canyon.

The other approach to environmental survival is to extend social systems and infrastructure beyond the immediate area. This is another major determinant in reviewing the planning of Chaco. The road system emanating from the canyon unequivocally marks Chaco as the center of a network of related Anasazi settlements. It made the transport of timber for construction easier, and it shaped the settlement pattern. The need, functionally or symbolically, for markers to monitor movement in and out of the canyon is expressed clearly at Chaco. Pueblo Alto, located on the north mesa, is usually considered a gateway to the main canyon settlement from the major road north. The location of Tsin Kletzin due south of Pueblo Alto on the south mesa and of Peñasco Blanco and Una Vida mark other entry points as well.

Planning Processes and Lessons

We all like to believe that our observations about the world around us are valid, even universal, and that what we have learned in our work can be applied to the larger world beyond. From our experience as city planners and urban designers we have observed basic principles or processes that must be followed to implement a coherent physical plan. It was gratifying, then, to see that (to our eyes at least) many of these essential processes were evidently employed at Chaco.

We will address these processes and lessons primarily from our viewpoint as physical planners. The complexity of our world today requires comprehensive city planning that utilizes expertise in determining the physical and spatial disposition of the city's elements and in numerous related and underlying issues. Typically, urban designers and physical planners are but a part of a professional planning staff and are charged with translating extensive background analysis, policies, and goals into physical plans.

Let us note right away that earlier peoples clearly dealt with a comprehensive array of issues when planning. However, those issues were not overwhelming or isolated from their experience; they were instead comprehensible to a population that was not as specialized and intellectually removed from the land they inhabited as we are today. The following six general planning principles or processes appear to have played an active part in creating the Chacoan built environment.

First, there must be a vision or image of the desired result that can be understood by all. This image or vision must be compelling. Otherwise, why would one put considerable effort and resources into play to achieve an unsatisfying result? The image is usually visual (though it may be more ephemeral), and it must galvanize action toward achieving the end goal. At Chaco, there is strong evidence of building to a long-range plan: the enclosed plaza at Pueblo Bonito and the final plan at Chetro Ketl would appear to be clear examples. What is less clear to us is how that vision/image was communicated. Was it a drawing in the sand? A mud model? A word picture? Whatever method or methods were used to convey the idea, the extended period of more than two hundred years of intense building certainly took commitment and perseverance.

Second, the leaders or decision makers of a community must "buy into" the plan. A successful plan has many enthusiastic supporters. In a democratic society, a broad-based coalition of government, business, and other leaders must feel included in the planning process as major contributors. If so, the chances of long-term commitments are much greater than when plans are imposed. In hierarchical societies, an imposed plan may be successful—as long as there is continuity in leadership.

The formal structure of decision making at Chaco would, we suspect, have been of a group nature (though we have no basis other than what we know of contemporary Pueblo society to make that conclusion). The length of the building campaigns would suggest that the group commitment was strong and broad-based.

Third, all relevant factors must be fairly evaluated and included in shaping the plan. This does not mean that all elements are given equal weight. Before modern land economics came into play, the symbolically important elements of the built environment, such as sacred sites, were always prominent, usually at the very heart of the community. Such a pattern seems to be the case at Chaco. Additionally, in the harshness of the high desert environment, a settlement could not survive for more than a brief period without successful responses or adaptation to all of its environmental pressures. Survival is itself the test of inclusive and responsive design.

Fourth, the plan must be flexible and adaptable so that it can adjust to changing conditions over time. For example, additions to Pueblo Bonito exhibit changes in direction and concept that transform a completed building into a much larger structure. Innumerable decisions must have modified the original intentions; yet the whole has a sense of completeness and clarity that is powerful to this day.

Fifth, implementation policies must be included as part of the plan. It is difficult to imagine the Chacoans developing plans for the expansion of fields, roads, and structures without the intention or ability to carry them out. Yet that is often the case today. Plans, particularly visionary or utopian plans, are often intended to generate interest or test theoretical waters for new ideas. However, good plans that include the steps that lead to actual implementation are particularly valuable to decision makers and leaders.

Sixth, results will take *years* to become visible; thus, all of the above factors, including patience, are important if long-range goals are to be achieved. Indeed, short-term city planning does not exist. The shortest-term modern plans are capital budget plans for the next year in pursuit of five-year goals. One must have patience to be a planner, as results are often measured in decades. The incredibly complex man-made organism that is the city cannot alter or regenerate itself quickly.

Architects, by contrast, may expect results in days (for designs), months (for small buildings to be completed), or a few years (for the completion of the largest buildings). The architect tends to see the built environment as a series of finite design problems, while the planner sees an ever-changing set of relationships that, with great effort and perseverance, can be nudged into a more pleasing environment.

Chaco's built forms exhibit the sense of design and order that come from both the singular vision of the architect and the perseverance over time of the planner. Consequently, we see these remains as evocative of a better way to plan and build—a way that has, perhaps, been lost in our fragmented, complex cities.

References

Knowles, Ralph L. 1974. *Energy and Form.* MIT Press, Cambridge, Mass.

Lekson, Stephen H. 1986. *Great Pueblo Architecture of Chaco Canyon.* University of New Mexico Press, Albuquerque.

Lynch, Kevin. 1960. *The Image of the City.* MIT Press and Harvard University Press, Cambridge, Mass.

6 The Chacoan Roads

A Cosmological Interpretation

Michael P. Marshall

Architectural forms and even costly engineering projects are not
always designed to meet purely functional goals. Contrary to the dictum
of modernism, an illuminating interpretation of Chacoan roads can be made
on a cosmological rather than a functional basis. Archaeologist Michael
Marshall compares the vast Chacoan road system with the sacred roads of
contemporary Zuni and Acoma Pueblos. Like major sites in Mexico and
Mesoamerica, Chaco appears to have been in part designed to reflect mytho-
logical and astronomical principles, a concept completely foreign to modern
architects and planners, but one that clearly imbues the built environment
with deep religious meaning and emotional significance.

Recent investigations in the Chacoan province have revealed evidence of a cosmographic organization that has implications for the entire Anasazi world. A cosmological model or evaluation involving aspects of Chacoan architecture, roads, shrines, and other sites can be defined in terms of the basic mythic themes of the traditional Puebloan worldview. These include such themes as origin and emergence from the underworld, the ancestral search for the Middle Place, the importance of directional symbolism, the use of a complex astronomical-ceremonial calendar and elaborate New Year ritual, the recognition of the underworld land of the dead, and other pan-Puebloan beliefs. In this worldview, peaks and pinnacles, springs and lakes, caves and other topographic features have cosmic significance, and the organization of pueblos, kivas, and roads is sometimes linked to topographic features and to solar and lunar orientations.

We are only beginning to comprehend the cosmological implications of Chaco Canyon and other Anasazi sites. I will attempt in this paper to outline some of the observations regarding the cosmology of Puebloan-Anasazi roads that have been recently made by students in this field.

Sacred Geography

Essential to Puebloan cosmology and religious belief is the concept of sacred geography. Most of the great mythic events recounted in the origin legends are associated with topographic features. Many of these places are considered to be sacred shrines. The Pueblo people have often said, by way of explanation, that "our Bible is the land," meaning that the story of creation and ancestral mythology can be read from the geographic features of the earth.

Mountains, pinnacles, caves, lakes, springs, and other topographic features in the Puebloan worldview are considered to be elements of a divine cosmography or holy land. These sacred sites are revered as the location of miraculous events and the home of supernaturals. Many of these same topographic features are sacred shrine sites to which elaborate and often distant pilgrimages were made. Other topographic locations and astronomic positions were incorporated into village planning and ceremonial architecture (see Sofaer chapter, this volume).

In traditional Puebloan worldview, the earth itself is animate. According to Pueblo tradition the people emerged from the underworld womb of "earth mother" at the sacred *Shipap*: hence, the people are said to be "earthborn." The grotto is symbolic of the entrance into the underworld and the home of Corn Mother. All springs and lakes are considered sacred and are believed to lead into a subterranean system of interconnected channels inhabited by the *ka'tsi na,* the spirits of the dead and other supernaturals.

Road Cosmology

A cosmological function for the Anasazi roads is supported by the use of constructed roadways as sacred pilgrimage avenues by historic and modern Pueblo peoples. These include the Acoma and Zuni Salt Lake Trails, the Zuni Barefoot Trail, the Acoma *Wenimats* Trail, and a trail between the Salt Lake and *Kolhu wala wa* (Zuni heaven). All of these historic and modern Pueblo roads appear similar to the Chacoan roads.

The Acoma and Zuni roads are used as annual and quadrennial pilgrimage avenues to sacred landforms and shrines. The underworld shrine near the confluence of the Zuni and Little Colorado Rivers is known to the Zuni as *Kolhu wala wa* or the Village of the Dance Gods (Ladd

1983:177) and to the Acoma as Wenimats (Sterling 1942:16). It is the home of the *ka'tsi na* and the land of the dead (most of the Keres dead first go north to the Shipap and then move westward to Wenimats; see Parsons 1939:1:217). The roads that link this principal shrine to Zuni and Acoma are the avenues over which the *ka'tsi na* visit the pueblos. From Zuni it is also the road down which the spirits of the dead return to the underworld (Cushing 1979:132; Hart 1984; Holmes 1989:23). The forty-five-mile trail to *Kolhu wala wa* from Zuni is called *Wesak'yaya Onnane*, the Barefoot Trail, since the footprints of the dead returning to the underworld are seen along its course. A quadrennial pilgrimage to *Kolhu wala wa* from Zuni Pueblo takes place at about the time of the summer solstice (Hart 1990:1).

The underworld shrine complex at *Kolhu wala wa* incorporates a variety of sacred landforms, including a lake, two mountain pinnacles, and a cave. A constructed path or road and line of cairns leads to a cave entrance on the summit of one pinnacle. This cave is said to pass down four chambers, symbolizing the levels of the underworld, to communicate with the supernaturals in Whispering Lake (Hart 1984:7). The waters of the lake are said to be connected with all sacred springs and lakes by a series of underground channels (Stevenson 1904:157). Another constructed roadway, of north-south orientation, appears to link various features in the shrine complex. It ascends a hill near Whispering Lake and leads to a mesa top that is enclosed by a low wall (T. J. Ferguson May 1991 p.c.).

The Zuni Salt Lake (*Ma'k'yaya*) is the destination of an annual summer pilgrimage. The lake is the home of Salt Mother and the War Gods (Stevenson 1904:354–355) and is an important location in the Zuni and Acoma origin myths (Kelley 1988:2–6). There is also some indication that the Acoman dead inhabit subterranean and heated chambers below the Salt Lake (Allan Minge May 1991 p.c.). The Salt Lake shrine complex includes three cinder cones, two lakes, a variety of shrine offering areas, and a constructed pathway (Stevenson 1904:357). The road to the Salt Lake is said to have been made by Salt Mother when she left her original home near Zuni, since the path of salt she left in the journey prevents the growth of vegetation (Ed Ladd May 1991 p.c.). In this account, the construction of the road is attributed to a god or supernatural.

Archaeological investigation of the Acoma and Zuni roads is very limited, but what evidence there is suggests that all of these avenues were at least partly constructed. Archaeological survey of a section of the east alternate Zuni Salt Lake (Marshall and Kight 1981) revealed a developed corridor with curb construction. Examination of aerial imagery of the Zuni Barefoot Trail has revealed sections that have a signature similar to that of the Chacoan roads (James Ebert April 1991 p.c.), and constructed road segments have been observed in proximity to *Kolhu wala wa* (R. Hart April 1991 p.c.). The Acoma *Wenimats* Trail across the lava flow (Holmes l989:23) also appears to have been constructed in the Cerros de Jaspe area (Dan Hurley April 1991 p.c.). A two-mile long segment of constructed road, located by Dan Hurley, is directly west of the mouth of Cebolleta Canyon. The road, which is two to three meters wide and oriented directly east-west, is the reported approximate entrance of Wenimats Trail into the lava flow.

Crescent-shaped shrine structures, nearly identical to the Chaco road *herraduras* (horseshoes), have been located on the Zuni Salt Lake Trail and are present along the Acoma Salt Lake Trail and the road between the Zuni Salt Lake and *Kolhu wala wa* (Kelley 1988:2–9). A crescent-shaped shrine is also located near the cave entrance on the South Mountain at *Kolhu wala wa* (T. J. Ferguson May 1991 p.c.). The crescent structures along the Zuni Salt Lake road are reported to be shrines where pilgrims made prayer offerings to Sun Father and Moon Mother (Stevenson 1904:355). Shrines are also located along the Zuni Barefoot Trail (Ladd 1983:177).

A series of offering shrines along an unspecified route in the Grants lava flow, perhaps the Wenimats Trail, has been described as beacons, like the lights along an airport runway, which direct the *ka'tsi na* to Acoma (Governor Stanley Patiamo quoted in Stumbo 1987).

Sacred springs appear along the Zuni Barefoot Trail (Hart 1984:7), the Zuni Salt Lake Trail (Kelley l988:2–7), the Acoma Salt Lake Trail (Holmes 1989:25), and the Acoma *Wenimats* Trail (Allan Minge May 1991 p.c.). A large prehistoric ruin near Cerro Techado is associated by the Acoma people with the Salt Lake Trail (Holmes 1989:29). This site is probably located in Horsecamp Canyon ([LA 10983] Fowler and Stein 1987:191), where the trail is believed to have passed (John Roney April 1991 p.c.). A large ruin called Fort Atarque ([LA 55367] Fowler, Stein, and Anyon 1987) located at a spring along the west alternate of the Zuni Salt Lake road is probably the road-associated site of *Kia makia* (Gomolak and Fowler 1989) and was mentioned by Matilda Coxe Stevenson (1904:356).

The Zuni and Acoma Salt Lake and underworld road system was probably developed in the late Pueblo III-early Pueblo IV periods and may have incorporated sections of early Pueblo II great house roadways. The

Zuni Barefoot Trail is also believed to have a prehistoric origin (Hart 1984:8). These roads were used into the historic period, and sections are still in use. For example, the quadrennial Zuni pilgrimage to *Kolhu wala wa* took place in June 1989 and was reportedly well attended (Hart 1990:39). The Acoma road to this shrine is also still in use and is apparently used even more frequently than the Acoma Salt Lake road (Steve Fischer April 1991 p.c.).

A constructed prehistoric road segment in the Atarque Lake area (Marshall and Kight 1981) appears to have been incorporated into the east alternate of the Zuni Salt Lake road. Atarque Lake is twenty-one miles due north of the Zuni Salt Lake. The Atarque Lake road segment is associated with a large Pueblo II great house pueblo called Entremetido, or LA 78187 (Gomolak 1990). This road, three to four meters wide, extends from the area of the great house at Jaralosa Spring due north four kilometers to the edge of Atarque Lake, a large ephemeral playa. The Atarque Lake road thereby incorporates a linkage both to the direction north and to a lake. The linkage of a road to a lake is the common theme in many of the Zuni Plateau avenues. The incorporation of the prehistoric Atarque Lake road into the later Zuni Salt Lake road illustrates the conceptual evolution of the road system from the prehistoric great house period into the historic pueblo era.

Roads to Sacred Lakes and Springs

Springs and lakes are important elements in Puebloan sacred geography and are recognized as the home of supernaturals, the place of emergence and the land of the dead. The Acoma and Zuni peoples both have at least two roads that lead to sacred lakes. A number of Chacoan roads also provide links between great house architecture and lakes or springs.

One of the most prominent is the *Ah-shi-sle-pah* Road, which leads from the pueblo of Peñasco Blanco ten kilometers northwest to an ephemeral pond at Black Lake (Stein 1983:8–9 and C-2). This road incorporates the impressive bedrock pools and shrine enclosures of Los Aguajes and a platform-scaffold stairway at *Ah-shi-sle-pah* Wash. It terminates at a shrine on the south bank of Black Lake (Sofaer and Marshall 1988). The *Ah-shi-sle-pah* Road was probably designed by the Chacoans to open a corridor to the sacred waters of Los Aguajes and Black Lake.

The road may therefore have served to communicate with the water gods and promote rain. It is interesting to observe that the Navajo recognize Black Lake (*Be'ekidd halzhin*) as sacred and use it as an offering place for rain ritual and ceremony (York 1982).

Two Chacoan roads have been found that link the Standing Rock great house pueblo to ponds. One is a double road that extends from the pueblo three kilometers west to Toyee Spring (Wozniak, Ponczynski, and Church 1991:17–20). The other road runs northwest from Standing Rock twelve and a half kilometers to the area of Milk Lake (Marshall et al. 1979:233). These roads resemble the Atarque Lake road in the Zuni district, which leads from the Pueblo II Entremetido great house four kilometers north to Atarque Lake. It is probable that with continued study other examples of Anasazi roads leading to lakes and springs will be found.

Earthwork-Platforms and the Aureola

An important feature of the Chacoan roads and Bonitian architecture is the frequent construction of elaborate earthworks called "great mounds" that parallel the roads as they approach public buildings (Stein and Lekson 1986). In some cases, Chacoan roads encircle a Bonitian great house pueblo and are flanked by a perforated earth mound ring called the aureola (Stein 1987:83). Most aureolas have been located in the southern Chacoan district (Fowler, Stein, and Anyon 1987:82; Marshall and Sofaer 1988; Stein 1987:82; Stein and Lekson 1986; Stein and McKenna 1988:63). The encircling earth mound is perforated by gateway entrances through which a number of roads (three to eight), in an irregular spokelike array, enter the pueblo. A comparative analysis of aureola structures has not been completed. It is known, however, that certain roads entering the aureola are only short sections or elaborated entrances, while others may be more extensive. Aureola structures have been identified at Kin Ya'a, Red Willow Pueblo, Haystack, Kin Hocho'i, Standing Rock, Chambers and Hinkson Ranch, Navajo Springs, Kin Nizhoni, and Lake Valley.

The function or cosmographic implication of the aureola is unclear, but this ring around the great house pueblo and the multiple road entrances may be yet another structural representation of the sacred Middle Place. The roads entering the ring provide directional nexuses that channel the power of sacred landforms and mythic geography into the "center" or Middle Place occupied by the great house. Thus, the great house pueblo, like the pueblos of the modern period, may have represented a multiplicity of centers (Eliade 1957:57; Ortiz 1969:27), each inextricably linked to the surrounding landscape and each fixed as a kind of cardinal Middle Place in the Puebloan universe.

Herraduras and Crescentic Structures

Crescent-shaped structures (3.5 to 18.5 m across) called *herraduras* (horseshoes) are a common and distinctive feature associated with the Chacoan roads (Nials, Stein, and Roney 1987:11). These structures are usually located on elevated divides along roads and most frequently open to the east. Numerous crescent structures have also been identified on isolated pinnacles and mountains in the Chacoan Province by the Solstice Project (Marshall and Sofaer 1988). Crescent structures, for example, are located on Hosta Butte at the end of the South Road, on Cabezon Butte near the Guadalupe Outlier and on the summit of the Hogback above the Hogback Outlier. In the immediate area of Chaco Canyon, most crescent structures are located on the highest summits south of the canyon. Some crescent structures have votive containers in which offerings of turquoise and shell have been found (Hays and Windes 1975). There can be little doubt that the Chacoan crescents represent shrine structures.

Crescent structures have also been located in the Zuni province on the Atarque Lake road and are reported along the Acoma Salt Lake and Salt Lake to *Kolhu wala wa* roads (Kelley 1988:2–9). Modern Pueblo crescent shrines are also common. An important Hopi shrine on the summit of the San Francisco Peaks (Page and Page 1982) is structurally identical to Chaco road and pinnacle-top *herraduras*. The Zuni sun shrine at *Mats'a:kya* (Stevenson 1904:117–118) and the sunhouse shrine at Laguna (Boas 1928:299) are both crescent structures that open to the east. Numerous crescent shrines are also found at Hopi (Fewkes 1906:358, 365, and 367), Cochiti (Goldfrank 1927:70), and elsewhere.

Parallel Roads

Perhaps one of the most curious features of the Chacoan roads is the occasional presence of double or even quadruple parallel roads. Parallel avenues along the Chacoan Great North Road extend over at least a fifteen-kilometer section north of the Pierre's complex to Halfway House (Nials 1983:6–29). Part of this parallel construction, for a distance of one and a half kilometers, actually consists of two sets of parallel roads (Sofaer, Marshall, and Sinclair 1989:369 Fig. 29.4). These quadruple segments appear in proximity to an ephemeral pond three kilometers north of the Pierre's complex. Another impressive double road is the Toyee road, which extends from the Standing Rock great house three kilometers west and ends at Toyee Spring pond (Wozniak, Ponczynski, and Church 1991:19). Other double road segments have been identified at Haystack Site (Nials, Stein, and Roney 1987:23), on the South Road (Nials 1983:6–29), at Muddy Water Outlier (Nials, Stein, and Roney 1987:137–138) and on the Chaco South Gap road (Marshall and Sofaer 1988).

Parallel roads leading to the place of emergence are frequently noted in the ethnographic records. These are called the left and right roads to the underworld (Tyler 1964:71). Double roads leading south from the place of emergence are described over which the Tewan moieties diverged and rejoined in the ancestral journey to Ojo Caliente (Ortiz 1969:16 and 57). In the Jemez origin myths, the ancestors traveled south from the place of emergence along four roads (Parsons 1925:137–138). Reference to four roads leading down to the Middle Place is also made in the origin myths of the Zuni people (Bunzel 1932:717). If certain Chacoan roads are corridors to the underworld, as suggested by Zuni and Acoma road cosmology, then the parallel avenues are possibly the symbolic representation of the multiple paths down which the people traveled in the ancestral journey from the place of emergence to the Middle Place. Pilgrimage down these divergent corridors into parallel paths may have then reactualized and validated the origin myths and opened cosmological channels over which spiritual energy was conducted.

Chacoan Axis Mundi

From the structural organization of the Chacoan buildings and roads it is inferred that Chaco Canyon and in particular the Pueblo Alto-Pueblo Bonito precinct was recognized as the Middle Place or sacred cardinal center of the Chacoan world (see Sofaer chapter and Stein et al. chapter in this volume).

The North and South Roads, which converge on the ceremonial center at Chaco Canyon, describe the great axis mundi of the Chacoan world. Many of the Bonitian buildings that are associated with this axis have cardinal orientations (Fritz 1978:49) or have orientations to solstice and lunar azimuths (Sofaer, Sinclair, and Donahue 1989 and 1991). This axis in the canyon is defined by the north-south position of Pueblo Alto and Tzin Kletzin and by the east-west orientation of numerous walls and buildings in the Pueblo Alto, Pueblo Bonito, Chetro Ketl, and Tzin Kletzin areas. The north axis, defined by the entrance of the North Road into the gate at Pueblo Alto, is continued south by a linear wall and road (Windes 1987:98) to the precise location of the Cave of the Red Hand. This cave, which is thereby the actual southern terminus of the North Road, contains an elaborate roof painting (Marshall and Sofaer 1988).

The Great North Road

The Great North Road is a constructed corridor that extends approximately fifty kilometers north from Chaco Canyon across the empty sagebrush plains to the edge and floor of Kutz Canyon (Kincaid et al. 1983). This road incorporates various elevated kivas and shrines along its course and ends at a high wooden stairway that leads down into Kutz Canyon (Sofaer, Marshall, and Sinclair 1989). The North Road was previously believed to link Chaco Canyon to Aztec or Salmon Ruin on the San Juan river (e.g., Marshall et al. 1979:12). There is, however, no evidence to support this connection, as the road appears to terminate at Kutz Canyon and has a northern orientation well to the east of the San Juan communities. The North Road appears, instead, to be a directional corridor of probable cosmographic function.

North is the primary direction in many of the Puebloan cosmologies (Reyman 1976:112). To the Keres, Tewa, and Jemez, north is the location of the *Shipap* or the place of emergence from which the mythic journey south to the Middle Place began (Benedict 1931:249; White 1960:85). In Keresan myth, a road to the north is described over which the spirits of the dead returned to the underworld: "When the people died their bodies were buried, but their souls returned north to the *Shipapu*, the place of emergence, and returned to their mother in the fourfold womb of the earth" (White 1960:89). The road to the underworld is said to be "crowded with spirits returning to the lower world, and spirits of unborn infants coming from the lower world" (Stevenson 1884:68).

From this ethnographic information (see Sofaer, Marshall, and Sinclair 1989:373–374), it is inferred that the North Road was constructed to provide a formal link or corridor between the mythic *Shipap* entrance to the underworld in the north and the sacred Middle Place, known in Keresan myth as the "White House" in Chaco Canyon. The Great North Road is believed to be the Chacoan avenue of the dead and the metaphoric umbilicus of the Chacoan newborn. As an avenue of the dead, the North Road is similar to the Zuni Barefoot Trail and the Acoma *Wenimats* Trail. The North Road no doubt saw considerable use as a pilgrimage avenue and was probably used for ceremonial events that reactualized the myth of emergence and the search for the Middle Place.

The Great South Road

The opposite pole of the Chacoan axis mundi is the Great South Road, which extends southwest across the San Juan Basin fifty-seven kilometers to the tower kiva of Kin Ya'a (Tall House) and the pinnacle of Hosta Butte (Nials, Stein, and Roney 1987:18 and 32–51; Stein 1983:8–10). Thus, the end of the south axial avenue was a platform to the firmament, in contrast to the chasm of the North Road terminus at Kutz Canyon. A vertical dimension was thereby incorporated into the Chacoan north-south road axis, which metaphorically placed Chaco Canyon in the cardinal Middle Place on the earth's plane between the zenith and nadir.

Conclusion

The Anasazi roads are not an interconnected transportation network. The physical characteristics and destinations of the Chacoan roads fail to support interpretation of the "system" as a transportation-trade network (Roney 1992). A complex array of roads does enter the Chaco Canyon complex, but most of these roads do not systematically link the canyon center to outlying communities. Some of the Chacoan roads interconnect various architectural features, but many of the roads entering Chaco Canyon and others that emanate from outlying great house pueblos appear to have no obvious destination. Recent analysis of the Chaco roads suggests that many of these avenues are cosmological corridors that link ceremonial architecture to various topographic features, horizon markers, and directional-astronomical orientations. This cosmological function for the Chacoan roads is supported by the use of constructed roadways as sacred pilgrimage avenues by historic and modern Puebloan peoples. The construction of roads to lakes and springs and the frequent north-south orientation of roads is a common feature of both historic Zuni-Acoma roads and the Chacoan roads. Ample evidence in the ethnographic records indicates that roads were recognized as corridors of communication between the underworld land of the dead, the home of *ka'tsi nas*, and the place of emergence.

A great deal remains to be learned about the Anasazi roads and architecture. There are many mysteries, and the roads no doubt had a variety of cosmological and integrative functions that we do not understand. The study and interpretation of the Chacoan-Anasazi roads is only in its infancy. However, even at this early date it is clear that many of the Anasazi roads, like the modern Puebloan avenues, had a cosmological function.

References

Benedict, Ruth. 1931. *Tales of the Cochiti Indians.* Bureau of Ethnology Bulletin No. 98. Smithsonian Institution, Washington, D.C. Reprint, University of New Mexico Press, Albuquerque, 1981.

Boas, Franz. 1928. *Keresan Texts.* Publications of the American Ethnological Society, New York.

Bunzel, Ruth L. 1932. "Zuni Ritual Poetry." In *Forty-seventh Annual Report, Bureau of American Ethnology,* pp. 611–835. Smithsonian Institution, Washington, D.C.

Cushing, Frank Hamilton. 1979. *Zuni: Selected Writings of Frank Hamilton Cushing,* ed. Jesse Green. University of Nebraska Press, Lincoln.

Eliade, Mircea. 1957. *The Sacred and the Profane: The Nature of Religion.* Harcourt, Brace and Company, New York.

Fewkes, Jesse Walter. 1906. "Hopi Shrines near the East Mesa, Arizona." *American Anthropologist* n.s. 8:346–375.

Fowler, Andrew P., John R. Stein, and Roger Anyon. 1987. "An Archaeological Reconnaissance of West-Central New Mexico: The Anasazi Monuments Project." Submitted to the New Mexico State Office of Cultural Affairs, Historic Preservation Division, Santa Fe.

Fritz, J. M. 1978. "Paleopsychology Today." In *Social Archeology: Beyond Subsistence and Dating.* Academic Press, Orlando, Fla.

Goldfrank, Esther S. 1927. *The Social and Ceremonial Organization of Cochiti.* Memoirs of the American Anthropological Association No. 33. Lancaster, Penn.

Gomolak, Andrew R., Jr. 1990. Site data forms on LA 78187, JRs Entremetido. Museum of New Mexico, Archeological Records Center, Santa Fe.

Gomolak, Andrew R., Jr., and Andrew Fowler. 1989. Site data form on LA 78187, Atarque Lake Great House. Museum of New Mexico, Archeological Records Center, Santa Fe.

Hart, Richard E. 1984. The Zuni Indian Tribe and Title to Kolh/Wala:wa (Katchina Village).

Hays, Alden C., and Thomas C. Windes. 1975. "An Anasazi Shrine in Chaco Canyon." In *Collected Papers in Honor of Florence Hawley Ellis,* ed. T. R. Frisbie, pp. 143–156. Papers of the Archeological Society of New Mexico No. 2.

Holmes, Barbara E. 1989. *American Indian Land Use of El Malpais.* Office of Contract Archeology, University of New Mexico, Albuquerque.

Kelley, Klara. 1988. *Archeological Investigations in West-Central New Mexico*. Vol. 2, *Historic Cultural Resources*. Bureau of Land Management Cultural Resources Series No. 4.

Kincaid, Chris, Daisy F. Levine, Fred L. Nials, Margaret Senter Obenauf, Benjamin P. Roberson, John R. Stein, and R. Gwinn Vivian. 1983. *Chaco Roads Project, Phase I: A Reappraisal of Prehistoric Roads in the San Juan Basin*. U.S. Department of the Interior, Bureau of Land Management, New Mexico State Office, Albuquerque District.

Ladd, Ed. 1983. "Pueblo Use of High-Altitude Areas: Emphasis on the A'shiwi." In *High-Altitude Adaptations in the Southwest*, ed. J. C. Winter, pp. 168–176. U.S. Forest Service, Southwest Region Report No. 2.

Marshall, Michael P. 1991. "The Ancient Cosmography of Chaco Canyon." In *Chaco Body*, by K. Gittings and V. B. Price. Artspace Press, Albuquerque. Marshall, Michael P., and Bill Kight. 1981. Archeological Survey of the Atarque Lake road segment. Notes on file, Bureau of Land Management, Albuquerque Office.

Marshall, Michael P., and Anna Sofaer. 1988. Solstice Project Archeological Investigations in the Chacoan Province, New Mexico.

Marshall, Michael P., John R. Stein, Richard W. Loose, and Judith E. Novotny. 1979. *Anasazi Communities of the San Juan Basin*. Public Service Company of New Mexico and the Historic Preservation Division, Santa Fe. Reprint 1991.

Nials, Fred. 1983. "Physical Characteristics of the Chacoan Roads." Chapter 6 in *The Chaco Roads Project, Phase I*, ed. C. Kincaid, D. F. Levine, F. L. Nials, et al. U.S. Department of the Interior, Bureau of Land Management, New Mexico State Office, Albuquerque District.

Nials, Fred, John R. Stein, and John R. Roney. 1987. *Chacoan Roads in the Southern Periphery: Results of Phase II of the BLM Chaco Roads Project*. Cultural Resources Series No. 1, New Mexico Bureau of Land Management.

Ortiz, Alfonso. 1969. *The Tewa World: Space, Time, Being and Becoming in a Pueblo Society*. University of Chicago Press.

Page, Susanne, and Jake Page. 1982. *Hopi*. Harry N. Abrams Co., New York.

Parsons, Elsie Clews. 1925. *The Pueblo of Jemez*. Papers of the Phillips Academy Southwestern Expedition, No. 3. Yale University Press, New Haven, Conn.

———. 1939. *Pueblo Indian Region*. Vols. 1 and 2. University of Chicago Press.

Reyman, J. E. 1976. "The Emics and Etics of Kiva Wall Nitch Location." *Journal of Steward Anthropological Society* 7(1):107–129.

Roney, John R. 1992. "Prehistoric Roads and Regional Integration in the Chacoan System." In *Anasazi Regional Organization and the Chaco System*, ed. D. Doyel. Maxwell Museum of Anthropology, Anthropological Papers No. 5. University of New Mexico, Albuquerque.

Sofaer, Anna, Michael P. Marshall, and Rolf M. Sinclair. 1989. "The Great North Road: A Cosmographic Expression of Chaco Culture of New Mexico." In *World Archaeoastronomy: Selected Papers from the Second Oxford International Conference on Archaeoastronomy*, ed. A. F. Aveni. Cambridge University Press, New York.

Sofaer, Anna, Rolf Sinclair, and J. M. Donahue. 1989. "Solar and Lunar Orientations of the Major Architecture of the Chaco Culture of New Mexico." In *Colloquio Internazionale Archeologia e Astronomia*, Venice, 3–6 May 1989. Rivista di Archaeologia, Supplementi 9. Giorgio Bretschneider Editore.

———. 1991. An Astronomical Regional Pattern among the Major Buildings of the Chacoan Culture of New Mexico.

Stein, John R. 1983. "Road Corridor Descriptions." Chapter 8 in *The Chaco Roads Project, Phase I*, ed. C. Kincaid, D. F. Levine, F. L. Nials, et al. U.S. Department of the Interior, Bureau of Land Management, New Mexico State Office, Albuquerque District.

———. 1987. "Architecture and Landscape." Chapter 7 in *An Archeological Reconnaissance of West-Central New Mexico: The Anasazi Monuments Project*, by A. P. Fowler, J. R. Stein, and R. Anyon, pp. 91–103. Submitted to New Mexico State Office of Cultural Affairs, Historic Preservation Division, Santa Fe.

Stein, John R., and Stephen H. Lekson. 1986. "Earthen Architecture and Ritual." Paper presented at the Third Anasazi Symposium, Oljato, Arizona.

Stein, John R., and Peter J. McKenna. 1988. *An Archeological Reconnaissance of a Late Bonito Phase Occupation near Aztec Ruins National Monument, New Mexico*. National Park Service, Southwest Cultural Resources Center, Santa Fe.

Sterling, Matthew W. 1942. *Origin Myth of Acoma and Other Records*. Bureau of Ethnology Bulletin No. 135. Smithsonian Institution, Washington, D.C.

Stevenson, Matilda Coxe. 1884. *The Sia*. Eleventh Annual Report of the Bureau of American Ethnology. Smithsonian Institution, Washington, D.C.

———. 1904. *The Zuni Indians*. Twenty-third Annual Report of the Bureau of American Ethnology. Smithsonian Institution, Washington, D.C.

Stumbo, Bella. 1987. "Tribe Fights to Preserve Sacred Land." *Los Angeles Times* December 26.

Tyler, Hamilton A. 1964. *Pueblo Gods and Myths*. University of Oklahoma Press, Norman.

White, L. A. 1960. "The World of the Keresan Pueblo Indians." In *Culture in History: Essays in Honor of Paul Radin*, ed. S. Diamond, pp. 55–64. Columbia University Press, New York.

Windes, Thomas C. 1987. *Investigations at the Pueblo Alto Complex, Chaco Canyon, New Mexico, 1975–1979*. Vol. 1, *Summary of Test and Excavations at the Pueblo Alto Community*. Publications in Archeology 18F. National Park Service, Santa Fe.

Wozniak, Frank E., John J. Ponczynski, and Tim Church. 1991. *Remote Sensing Studies on the Southern Colorado Plateau*. Office of Contract Archeology, University of New Mexico, Albuquerque.

York, Frederick. 1982. "An Ethnographic Survey of Localities of Significance to the Navajo Populations in the Vicinity of the NMGS Impact Area." In *Quivera Research Publication No. 39*, ed. Carol J. Condie, pp. iv–186.

Part Three

*Stone and Mortar in the
Service of the Imagination*

7 Engineering Feats of the Anasazi

Buildings, Roads, and Dams

Stephen D. Schreiber

Anasazi people throughout the Four Corners area displayed a growing mastery of engineering principles until the area was abandoned in the thirteenth century A.D. As architect Stephen Schreiber's essay makes clear, their expertise in systematically constructing multistoried buildings, meticulously straight roads, elaborate water-collection and irrigation systems, communication networks, and developed outdoor spaces was equaled by no other southwestern people.

The ancient structures of the Anasazi that are scattered throughout much of Arizona, New Mexico, Utah, and Colorado demonstrate the collaboration, perseverance, and engineering expertise of these remarkable people. Using a straightforward, functional technology, these early builders in the American Southwest created enormous urban complexes, sophisticated communication networks, and elaborate water management projects.

Urban Complexes

The most notable Anasazi construction projects—multistoried apartment and religious buildings—punctuate Chaco Canyon, Mesa Verde, Canyon de Chelly, and other sites. The Chacoan "great houses" evolved from common domestic structures into extensive complexes between A.D. 900 and 1200, with an average of more than 200 rooms and over four stories in height. The most famous great house, Pueblo Bonito, contained more than 650 rooms. No apartment complex in North America, if indeed it was that, had more rooms until a larger one was built in New York City in the 1880s (Bassett 1984:100).

These structures reached their enormous sizes through the use of two engineering principles: load-bearing walls (which act simultaneously as structure and enclosure) and post-and-beam skeletons (which enable the supports to be distinguished from the envelope). Anthony Antoniades (1986:191-194) uses two metaphors to describe these systems—the "amoeba" and the "fish."

"Amoeba" buildings employ modest structures that rely on all of their material components, such as adobe bricks or stone blocks, for support. Their load-bearing walls tend to collapse without much resistance—like the amoeba—when they are pressured by external forces. Stronger materials must bridge openings to transfer the weight of the wall material to the ground. This type of architecture, also known as cellular or unit construction, does not distinguish the structure—"the part of the edifice which does the job of bearing all . . . loads to the ground"—from the building itself. The rooms act as the structural grid, and their sizes are limited by the bearing capacity of the roofing material.

In contrast, "fish" structures maintain a clear distinction between the flesh and the skeleton. The bones that support a fish create a three-dimensional frame with a hierarchy of sizes, depending on the loads being carried. In this type of building, the skeleton provides all the structural support while the non-load-bearing walls act as the flesh. Post-and-beam structures, the most common type of architectural skeletons, are limited by the safe span of the beams and the strength of the posts, but the three-dimensional grid can be expanded to create almost limitless room sizes.

Prehistoric builders in the American Southwest primarily used amoeba technology to construct their massive structures. The great houses were built by multiplying and combining the standard Anasazi living modules—the unit pueblo elements—which were made up of cells of from two to twelve rooms, with an adjoining plaza and kiva (Ferguson and Rohn 1987:32). The sizes of the rooms, both in the unit pueblos and in the great houses, were determined by the ability of the stone/clay walls to transfer loads to the ground and by the acceptable span of the roof material. The rectangular rooms could be added to and subdivided with relative ease.

Columnar (fish) structures were used only in a few parts of Anasazi buildings. A twelfth-century masonry colonnade once stood at Chetro Ketl, although no one has determined whether it supported a second floor structure or just a roof (Ferguson and Rohn 1987:32). Other post-and-beam structures supported the roofs of several great kivas (Lekson 1987a:34). The construction technique evolved from the engineering of smaller pit houses and used four columns of masonry or pine to support the heavy roofs. Still other Chacoan masons, during late construction projects, buried wooden pilasters and stringers (cross-members) in rubble core walls to reinforce the stone construction (Hayes, Brugge, and Judge 1987:56).

Anasazi builders used three major materials to construct their buildings: stone, clay, and wood. The proportions of these ingredients in a particular building depended on the size and importance of the structure, the availability of the materials, and the sophistication of the builders. Ratios of mud mortar to stone in masonry walls, for example, varied greatly over time and between different building locations.

The masonry construction of the primary Anasazi great houses employs the sandstone that is indigenous to the Colorado Plateau (see Fig. 7.1). At Chaco Canyon, two types of rock were used in major projects: hard brown, tabular sandstone and bedded, buff-colored sandstone (Ferguson and Rohn 1987:196). The brown stone was quarried, with difficulty, from a bench above the canyon floor. The buff stone came from the cliff itself or was available as talus at the base of the slopes. According to Stephen Lekson, "the tabular sandstone was more easily fractured into usable fragments with at least one flat face" (1987a:11).

Sandstone is a sedimentary rock with a clear, laminated structure. The stone is composed of reconsolidated debris, rocks, or fossil fragments (Wilson 1984:142) that have been melded by intense pressure in the earth. Paul Grillo compares the structure of sandstone to leaf pastry: its layers of soft dough are piled on top of each other, buttered together, flattened, and baked (1960:56). The natural grain of sandstone led to the crisp-edged, flat-surfaced masonry that is characteristic of the Anasazi. Furthermore, sandstone has an inherent tendency to break into easily handled, useful sizes.

The relative weakness of sandstone, especially in tension, favors smaller-scale buildings, because slabs and lintels can span distances of only medium length. In contrast, igneous rocks, such as granite and marble, have a stronger crystallized structure (formed directly from the molten material of the crust of the earth) that can span much greater distances (Grillo 1960:37).

Sandstone blocks are strongest if they are laid in masonry walls the same way that they are found in the quarry, with the bedding planes parallel to the ground (Wilson 1984:142). Early masons at Chaco Canyon sometimes placed the blocks upright as a base course, usually in one-story buildings—a structurally unsound practice.

Fig. 7.1. Distinct, layered courses of Anasazi masonry at Chetro Ketl, Chaco Culture National Historic Park. Photo by Baker H. Morrow

Masonry construction first appeared in Anasazi architecture in the ninth century. Stone was initially used as a replacement for mud in wood-frame buildings. The first masonry walls, generally one stone thick with generous mortar, could not support more than one story (Ferguson and Rohn 1987:32). In late eleventh-century Chaco Canyon, wider walls, with multiple stone thicknesses, allowed rooms to be stacked on top of each other.

Stone construction flourished in the canyon from about A.D. 1070 to 1130. Craftspersons developed several major styles of masonry that varied primarily according to the proportion of rock to mortar, the breadth of the wall, and the specific structural role of the sandstone. Simple walls and double simple walls of masonry relied on one or two "wythes" (or cross-placements) of stone, laid in thick mortar, for their strength

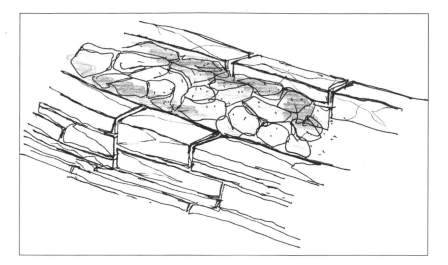

Fig. 7.2. Chacoan three-part core and veneer wall. Illustration by Baker H. Morrow.

(Lekson 1987a:11). Compound walls also used two "wythes," but internal stones interlocked the two sides. The three-part core-and-veneer walls, the hallmark of Chacoan construction, used two facings bound and separated by a load-bearing core of rubble and mortar. Lower walls were made thicker to support the weight of the upper floors and were set back at regular intervals to allow for support of the floors and roofs. The core wall evolved from a Pueblo I use of stone as a veneer on the adobe walls of some buildings (Hayes, Brugge, and Judge 1987:56).

Some authors argue that the development of the rubble core wall precipitated the post-1050 surge of building and remodeling in Chaco Canyon. In fact, the three-part wall had a tendency to split and was less efficient than earlier interlocking block systems (Ferguson and Rohn 1987:196).

Archaeologists classify several types of masonry face styles (Judd 1964). Uncoursed thin slabs of sandstone in thick mortar beds distinguish one type. Another style included small stones in the mortar joints. A third technique used minimal mortar joints and alternated courses of large blocks with several rows of thinner stones. Shaped tabular sandstone with no mortar characterized a fourth type.

Exposed mortar tended to disintegrate under the harsh weather conditions of the canyon. The insertion of smaller stones between the larger blocks, a procedure found around the world, compensates for the shrinkage of the mortar and allows for vertical settling in the wall. Grillo notes that similar patterns can be found on the parts of alligators' bodies that must be flexible, such as the lower jaw (1960:57); small scales bridge larger ones to allow for movement in any direction.

At Chaco Canyon, William Henry Jackson estimated that 315,000 cubic feet of masonry were quarried, dressed, and adapted to build Chetro Ketl alone (Lister and Lister 1987:45). The average room in such structures used more than 100,000 pounds of stone, as well as 35,000 pounds of clay mortar (Lekson 1987b:25). The estimated 50 million pieces of sandstone that were used to build the great houses explains the virtual absence of hard brown tabular sandstone from the benches in the canyon (Lekson 1987a:10).

Chaco builders used platform framing to build the multiple-story room blocks. First, a series of parallel long walls would be built onto substantial rubble and mortar foundations. Cross walls, which according to Lekson were an afterthought, were completed next, followed by individual roofs over each room (Lekson 1987a:15). These rooftops formed platforms for the construction of the next floor. Enormous sandstone disc footings supported the columns in great kivas.

Masonry technology developed later at Mesa Verde, after A.D. 1100. Early stone walls were typically one to three stones thick with faces pecked or ground smooth (Ferguson and Rohn 1987:35). Mortared spaces were often chinked with sandstone spalls or organic refuse.

Anasazi masons built low stone buttresses to hold up the exterior walls of some of the great houses (Lekson 1987a:34). At other sites in Chaco Canyon, Frijoles Canyon, and elsewhere, buildings stood at the base of enormous cliffs—natural buttresses. Many of these cliffs supported delicate walls that have since collapsed.

The combination of cylindrical forms with rectilinear boxes in most buildings also provided lateral stability. The interstitial spaces between the different forms—the "poche"—was reinforced with fill or buttressing. Cylinders are inherently stable shapes that can resist forces in all directions; boxes are strongest in directions parallel to their walls. The marriage of the forms not only served ceremonial purposes but also came from sound structural intuition.

Anasazi builders used clay for non-load-bearing partitions and for simple exterior construction, but in great houses clay primarily bound the stone walls. At Chaco Canyon, the clay for mortar came from alluvial deposits and from the rock-clay found at the base of the cliffs. Particular mixes served different purposes. Lekson notes, "At Chetro Ketl and Pueblo Alto, one type of clay was used for mortar and the scratch coat for wall plaster. A second, sandier mix was used for finish plaster" (1987a:13).

The construction workers in the prehistoric San Juan Basin needed timber mostly to frame the roofs of rooms, but they also used wood as a frame inside some masonry walls, as pilasters and columns in some kiva construction, and as lintels for doors and windows.

The primary ceiling structure of rectangular rooms consisted of pine logs laid horizontally. A secondary system of juniper logs would be laid perpendicular to the primary beams, followed by wood slats or reeds. Clay mortar and sand weatherproofed the roof. This construction method changed only slightly over time, despite the major changes of masonry wall engineering.

Although conventional framing also covered many round rooms, some Chacoan kivas were built with a process of corbeling or cribbing. At Kiva L at Pueblo Bonito, a series of beams forming the perimeter of a hexagon rested directly on low pilasters. A smaller, rotated hexagon rested on that structure. This process continued to the top of the roof level (Lekson 1987a:32). The resulting dome ceiling used a tremendous amount of wood; at Kiva L, 190 timbers were used. This "constructional extravagance" may have had a ritualistic significance (Cordell 1984:248). Rubble filled the area outside of the corbeled structure, providing strength to the construction and a flat platform at the roof level.

The distorted shapes of the local piñon and juniper trees that grew near Chaco Canyon were not useful for constructing rooms (McGuire and Schiffer 1983:293). Stands of ponderosa pine and Douglas-fir from scattered locations provided the best timber. Builders worked with up to a quarter of a million beams to construct the Chaco buildings, with an average of forty beams per room (Brody 1990). This hunger for wood completely depleted stands of fir and pine as far away as fifty miles from specific building sites.

Wooden pilasters, stringers, and cross-bracing strengthened some of the ambitious stone walls of the Anasazi. During the Pueblo III period, the structure of Chacoan kivas was improved by encasing four to ten logs into masonry walls at even intervals, creating low pilasters for the support of cribbing timbers (Hayes, Brugge, and Judge 1987:58). At Spruce Tree House at Mesa Verde, small beams were combined to act as cross-bracing for the weak stone and clay walls (Brody 1990:243).

Sets of short wooden poles served as lintels over door and window openings. The sandstone was generally too weak to carry the weight of the wall above the openings. The Anasazi apparently never used the vertical arch, which is an effective way of spanning openings with small stone members.

Communication

An extensive road network lubricated the vibrant Chacoan economic, political, and religious system. The paths connected the great houses and great kivas in the canyon to distant outlier villages and sacred sites. The elaborate roads were the product of sophisticated engineering, significant planning, and massive labor. Linda Cordell notes, "No other aboriginal land communication system of such magnitude and purpose has been recognized north of Mexico" (1984:257).

Four hundred miles of roads have been discovered in northwestern New Mexico. The longest stretch goes forty miles from Chaco Canyon to the San Juan River. The roads pursued a generally straight course from point to point, skirting major obstacles but not following the overall topography (Cordell 1984:257). Changes in direction were accomplished with sharp turns, much like the vector routing by which commercial airliners navigate. The roads may have been throughways for religious processions, but they also enabled Anasazi laborers to transport a large variety of goods and resources to the canyon (Cordell 1984:255).

Many main roads were thirty feet wide, and secondary roads were often fifteen feet wide, despite the lack of carts and other wheeled vehicles among the Anasazi (Frazier 1986:115). Some were cut (or worn) into the bedrock substructure, often to a depth of five feet. Others were formed just by removing vegetation or by building masonry berms on either side.

Where the earth sloped toward the road, retaining walls leveled the roadbed (Hayes, Brugge, and Judge 1987:46). Ramps, causeways, and footbridges provided access from ledge to ledge or across arroyos. Cliffs were traversed with staircases, which ranged in construction from finger-and toeholds to formal risers and treads cut out of the bedrock.

Communication throughout the San Juan Basin was probably facilitated by a series of shaped stone structures that are located on the high points throughout the outlying Chacoan areas. The buildings were most likely signal stations that could relay messages sent by fire, smoke, or selenite mirrors throughout the region (Cordell 1984:256).

In the canyon itself, the signal stations fell on the north side to facilitate communication between the great houses and the outliers (Cordell 1984:256). At Chetro Ketl, one round tower on the east side of the main room block was three stories tall and had a round room on the upper story. The lofty building, supported by rubble in the interstitial spaces on the lower floor, was probably part of the signal system (Ferguson and Rohn 1987:208).

Possibly a relationship also exists between the line-of-sight signal stations and the configuration of the prehistoric road system. In some cases, such as at the Acropolis site (twelve miles north of Chaco), the building nicknamed "El Faro" falls next to one of the abrupt turns in the otherwise straight roadway (Frazier 1986:122).

Water Management

The Anasazi system of dams, terraces, border gardens, and canals supported populations of several thousand people in a region with a harsh climate (Cordell 1984:202). Most of the effort in water management was directed toward capturing the sparse rainfall runoff from the mesa tops, rather than toward diverting water from Chaco Wash. In one area of the canyon, Rincon 4, runoff from an intercliff zone was diverted by a dam to a canal that carried the water two hundred yards to a headgate. The headgate slowed the water where it was channeled to a border garden along the wash. At least fifteen diversion systems have been documented in the canyon (Cordell 1984:209). The most elaborate border garden network was built near Chetro Ketl. The five-hectare site was divided into two plots, bordered by canals. Each plot sponsored a number of earth-bermed gardens, which were irrigated through temporary openings in the borders. Up to ten thousand gardens may have been cultivated in this way.

One massive dam captures water from a tributary of the Cuentos River at Chaco Canyon (Frazier 1986:101). The structure, which is more than one hundred feet long, six feet thick, and eight feet high, falls just below the top of the South Mesa. Chacoan canals averaged nine feet in width (Frazier 1986:100). Most were lined with stone slab and masonry walls and were built on the north side of the canyon.

At Mesa Verde, some one thousand stone dams checked the runoff and snowmelt from the mesa tops. Furthermore, the prehistoric occupants may have built a stone-lined reservoir—Mummy Lake—which was more than fifty feet in diameter. The lake has no outlets and was probably used for drinking water rather than agricultural irrigation (Jones 1985:33).

Labor

The various engineering projects undertaken by the Anasazi probably resulted from an organized and specialized labor force. Some scholars argue that since the great houses were similar in form and construction to smaller unit pueblos, which were built without a specialized workforce, the great houses, too, may have been built without managed labor. However, the complex formal geometries of the great houses, the precise regular locations of doors, windows and vents, and the overall site location and orientation of these buildings were probably determined by a specialized group of planners and designers (Brody 1990:112). These architects are likely to have worked closely with skilled laborers, much like the master builders who supervised the construction of great Gothic cathedrals. Skilled masons shaped and set stones while laborers hauled stones and mixed mortar. Planners were also responsible for the long-term design of overall construction, for the road and labor system used for obtaining construction materials, and for the standardization of the water management network (Brody 1990:196).

Conclusion

The engineering feats of the Anasazi evolved from patient labor, concentrated effort, and sensible design. Their specific structural and planning techniques were competent but not spectacular. In fact, many pueblo foundations, walls, and roofs were substantially overengineered. This factor of safety probably resulted from an incomplete understanding of static principles, from the cultural significance and general monumentality of the great houses, and from the need for low-maintenance buildings because of the small, intermittent population (Cordell 1984:49).

The Anasazi virtually abandoned the masonry techniques developed in the San Juan Basin after they moved from this sandstone-abundant area in the thirteenth century. Forms of the newer pueblos, particularly in the Rio Grande Valley, reflected the cellular structure of the great houses but utilized locally available materials: tuff, lava, granite, limestone, and clay. Some structures, such as the churches at the Salinas pueblos (Abó, Quarai, and Gran Quivira in and about the Manzano Range), dating from 1630, show the influence of native stone building techniques on colonial architecture (Lekson et al. 1988). In more modern times, many Santa Fe homes now sport the "sharp edged, flat rock" masonry typical of the Anasazi (Brewer 1991). Nevertheless, despite the ancient tradition and the large deposits of bedded sandstone near major cities, modern New Mexican builders rarely incorporate stonework into buildings.

References

Antoniades, Anthony. 1986. *Architecture and Allied Design.* Kendall Hunt, Iowa.

Bassett, Carol. 1984. "Roots of Regionalism: Great Stone Cities." *Architecture* (March 1984):100.

Brewer, Steve. 1991. "Understanding the Anasazi." *Albuquerque Journal*, April 21, p. C-1.

Brody, J. J. 1990. *Anasazi: Ancient People of the Southwest.* Rizzoli, New York.

Cordell, Linda. 1984. *Prehistory of the Southwest.* Academy Press, New York.

Ferguson, William, and Arthur Rohn. 1987. *Anasazi Ruins of the Southwest in Color.* University of New Mexico Press, Albuquerque.

Frazier, Kendrick. 1986. *People of Chaco.* Norton, New York.

Grillo, Paul. 1960. *Form, Function, and Design.* Dover, New York.

Hayes, Alden, David Brugge, and W. James Judge. 1987. *Archaeological Surveys of Chaco Canyon.* University of New Mexico Press, Albuquerque.

Jones, Dewitt. 1985. *Anasazi World.* Graphic Arts Center, Portland.

Judd, Neil. 1964. "The Architecture of Pueblo Bonito." *Smithsonian Miscellaneous Collections* 147, no. 1.

Lekson, Stephen H. 1987a. *Great Pueblo Architecture of Chaco Canyon, New Mexico.* University of New Mexico Press, Albuquerque.

———. 1987b. "Great House Architecture of Chaco Canyon." *Archaeology* 40, no. 3.

Lekson, Stephen H., Thomas C. Windes, John R. Stein, and W. James Judge. 1988. "The Chaco Canyon Community." *Scientific American* (July 1988):100.

Lister, Robert, and Florence Lister. 1987. *Archaeology and Archaeologists.* University of New Mexico Press, Albuquerque.

McGuire, Randall, and Michael Schiffer. 1983. "A Theory of Architectural Design." *Journal of Anthropological Archaeology* 2:293.

Wilson, Forrest. 1984. *Building Materials Evaluation Handbook.* Van Nostrand Reinhold, New York.

8   The Primary Architecture of the Chacoan Culture

A Cosmological Expression

Anna Sofaer

In this trenchant and groundbreaking essay, Anna Sofaer, founder of the Solstice Project, makes an exhaustive case for Anasazi astronomy as the determining factor in the placement and development of the great house structures of Chaco Canyon and outlying pueblos. Her research reinforces the view that Anasazi designers and planners undertook a complex and intricate building project, involving numerous buildings and roadways, and sustained that project over multiple generations without the aid of a written language. Sofaer's work shows that the Anasazi culture of the Chaco Canyon region exhibited a cosmological and administrative sophistication that has been thought to exist in the New World only south of the Rio Grande. This long-term strategy of master-planning at Chaco has impressive implications for urban design in contemporary America. If it was possible to conceive and execute a far-ranging plan to achieve specific social and ecclesiastical goals in the twelfth-century Southwest, it surely must be possible today to hold to an overall urban design that is the product of political consensus.

Recent studies by the Solstice Project indicate that the major buildings of the ancient Chacoan culture of New Mexico contain solar and lunar cosmology in three separate articulations: their orientations, internal geometry, and geographic interrelationships were developed in relationship to the cycles of the sun and moon.

From approximately A.D. 900 to 1130, the Chacoan society, a prehistoric Pueblo culture, constructed numerous multistoried buildings and extensive roads throughout the eighty thousand square kilometers of the arid San Juan Basin of northwestern New Mexico (Cordell 1984; Lekson et al. 1988; Marshall et al. 1979; Vivian 1990)(Fig. 8.1). Recent evidence suggests that expressions of the Chacoan culture extended over a region two to

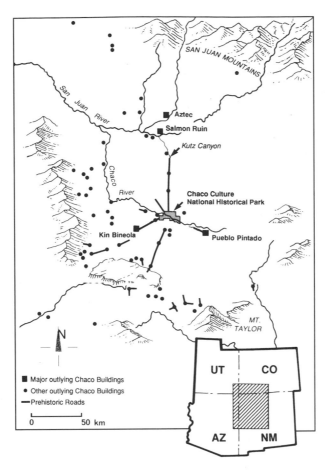

Fig. 8.1. The San Juan Basin and adjoining region, showing the buildings and roads of the Chacoan culture. The inset shows the relation of this region to the present-day states. Suzanne Samuels (By Design Graphics), © The Solstice Project 1995.

four times the size of the San Juan Basin (Fowler and Stein 1992; Lekson et al. 1988). Chaco Canyon, where most of the largest buildings were constructed, was the center of the culture (Figs. 8.2 and 8.3). The canyon is located close to the center of the high desert of the San Juan Basin.

Twelve of the fourteen major Chacoan buildings are oriented to the midpoints and extremes of the solar and lunar cycles (Sofaer, Sinclair, and Donahue 1989). The eleven rectangular major Chacoan buildings have internal geometry that corresponds with the relationship of the solar and lunar cycles (Sofaer, Sinclair, and Donahue 1991). Most of the major buildings also appear to be organized in a solar-and-lunar regional pattern that is symmetrically ordered about Chaco Canyon's central complex of large ceremonial buildings (Sofaer, Sinclair, and Williams 1987). These findings suggest a cosmological purpose motivating and directing the construction and the orientation, internal geometry, and interrelationships of the primary Chacoan architecture.

This essay presents: (1) a synthesis of the results of several studies by the Solstice Project between 1984 and the present; and (2) hypotheses about the conceptual and symbolic meaning of the Chacoan astronomical achievements. For certain details of Solstice Project studies, the reader is referred to several earlier published papers.

Background

The Chacoan buildings were of a huge scale and "spectacular appearance" (Neitzel 1989). The buildings typically had large public plazas and elaborate "architectural earthworks" that formed road entries (Stein and McKenna 1988). The major Chacoan buildings, the subject of the Solstice Project's recent studies (Figs. 8.1, 8.2, 8.3, and 8.4), are noted in particular for their massive core veneer masonry. They were up to four stories high and contained as many as seven hundred rooms, as well as numerous kivas, including great kivas, the large ceremonial chambers of prehistoric Pueblo culture (Lekson 1984; Marshall et al. 1979; Powers, Gillespie, and Lekson 1983).

The construction of the major Chacoan buildings employed enormous quantities of stone and wood. For example, 215,000 timbers—which were transported from distances of more than eighty kilometers—were used in the major buildings in the canyon alone (Lekson et al. 1988). The orderly grid-like layout of the buildings suggests that extensive planning and engineering were involved in their construction (Lekson 1984; Lekson et al. 1988).

No clear topographic or utilitarian explanations have been developed for the orientations of the Chacoan buildings. The buildings stand free of the cliffs, and their specific orientations are not significantly constrained by local topography.[1] While the need to optimize solar heating may have influenced the general orientation of the buildings, it probably did not restrict their orientations to specific azimuths. Similarly, environ-

Fig. 8.2. Aerial view of central area of Chaco Canyon, looking north. The photograph shows three major buildings: Pueblo Bonito (left), Pueblo Alto (above center), and Chetro Ketl (right). Casa Rinconada and New Alto are also shown. Photograph by Adriel Heisey, © Adriel Heisey 1995.

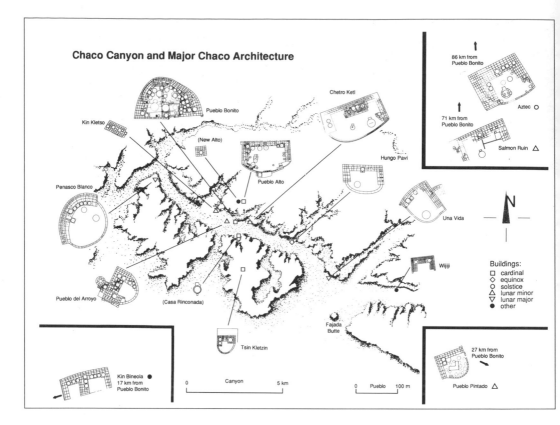

Fig. 8.3. Chaco Canyon, showing the locations and ground plans of ten major buildings (and two minor buildings in parentheses). Four outlying major buildings
are also shown. The astronomical orientations of the buildings are indicated.
Fabian Schmid (Davis, Inc.) and Suzanne Samuels (By Design Graphics),
© The Solstice Project 1995.

mental factors, such as access to water, appear not to have dominated or
constrained the Chacoans' choice of specific locations for their buildings.[2]

The Chacoans also constructed over two hundred kilometers of roads.
The roads were of great width (averaging nine meters wide), and they
were developed, with unusual linearity, over distances of up to fifty kilometers. Their construction required extensive surveying and engineering
(Kincaid 1983) (Fig. 8.1). Recent investigations show that certain of the
roads were clearly overbuilt if they were intended to serve purely utilitarian purposes (Lekson 1991; Roney 1992; Sofaer, Marshall, and Sinclair

PUEBLO BONITO

_N_

PUEBLO DEL ARROYO

0   55m

scale of photos

Fig. 8.4. Aerial photographs of two major buildings in Chaco Canyon, Pueblo Bonito (upper) and Pueblo del Arroyo (lower) with ground plans of these buildings. Photographs by Koogle and Pouls for the National Park Service, graphics by Suzanne Samuels (By Design Graphics), © The Solstice Project 1992.

1989; Stein 1989)[3] and that they may have been constructed as cosmographic expressions (Marshall essay, this volume; Sofaer, Marshall, and Sinclair 1989).

Scholars have puzzled for decades over why the Chacoan culture flourished in the center of the desolate environment of the San Juan Basin. Earlier models proposed that Chaco Canyon was a political and economic center where the Chacoans administered a widespread trade and redistribution system (Judge 1989; Sebastian 1992). Recent archaeological investigations show that major buildings in Chaco Canyon were not built or used primarily for household occupation (Lekson et al. 1988). This evidence, along with the dearth of burials found in the canyon, suggests that, even at the peak of the Chacoan development, there was a low resident population. (The most recent estimates of this population range from 1,500 to 2,700 [Lekson 1991; Windes 1987]). Evidence of periodic large-scale breakage of vessels at key central buildings indicates, however, that Chaco Canyon may have served as a center for seasonal ceremonial visitations by great numbers of residents of the outlying communities (Judge 1984; Toll 1991).

Many aspects of the Chacoan culture—such as the transport of thousands of beams and pots—have struck archaeologists as having a "decided aura of inefficiency" (Toll 1991). Other findings—such as "intentionally destroyed items in the trash mounds," "plastered-over exquisite masonry," and strings of beads "sealed into niches" in a central great kiva—indicate esoteric uses of Chacoan constructions. Recent speculation suggests that, in the "absence of any evidence that there is either a natural or societal resource to which Chaco could control access by virtue of its location" (Toll 1991), Chaco Canyon was the center of exchange of information and knowledge (Sebastian 1991). One archaeologist suggests that Chaco Canyon was a "central archive for esoteric knowledge, such as maintenance of the region's ceremonial calendar" (Crown and Judge 1991).

Scholars have commented extensively on the impractical and enigmatic aspects of Chacoan buildings, describing them as "overbuilt and overembellished" and proposing that they were built primarily for public image and ritual expression (Lekson et al. 1988; Stein and Lekson 1992). Some observers have thought that the Chacoan buildings were developed as expressions of the Chacoans' "concepts of the cosmos" (Stein and Lekson 1992) and that their placement and design may have been determined in part by "Chacoan cosmography" (Marshall and Doyel 1981). One report proposes that "Chaco and its hinterland are related by a canon of shared design concepts" and that the Chacoan architecture is a "common ideational bond" across a "broad geographic space" (Stein and Lekson 1992). That report suggests that the architectural characteristics of Pueblo Bonito, one of the two largest and most central buildings of the Chacoan system, are rigorously repeated throughout the Chaco region. Thus, important clues to the symbology and ideology of the Chacoan culture may be embedded in its central and primary architecture and expressed in the relationship of this architecture to primary buildings in the outlying region.

Numerous parallels to the Chacoan expressions of cosmology appear in the astronomically and geometrically ordered constructions of Mesoamerica—a region with which the Chacoans are known to have had cultural associations (Aveni 1980; Broda 1994). Moreover, traditions of the descendants of the prehistoric Pueblo people who live today in New Mexico and Arizona also suggest parallels to the Chacoan cosmology and give us insight to the general cosmological concepts of the Chacoan culture.

Previous Work

Solstice Project studies, begun in 1978, documented astronomical markings at three petroglyph sites on Fajada Butte, a natural promontory at the south entrance of Chaco Canyon (Fig. 8.3). Near the top of the butte, three rock slabs collimate light so that markings of shadow and light on two spiral petroglyphs indicate the summer and winter solstices, the equinoxes, and the extreme positions of the moon, that is, the lunar major and minor standstills (Sofaer, Zinser, and Sinclair 1979; Sofaer, Sinclair, and Doggett 1982; Sinclair, Sofaer, McCann, and McCann 1987). At two other sites on the butte, shadow and light patterns on five petroglyphs indicate solar noon and the solstices and equinoxes (Sofaer and Sinclair 1987).

A 1989 Solstice Project study showed astronomical significance in the Chacoans' construction of the Great North Road (Sofaer, Marshall, and Sinclair 1989). This nine-meter wide, engineered road extends from Chaco Canyon north fifty kilometers to a badlands site, Kutz Canyon (Fig. 8.1). The purpose of the road appears to have been to articulate the north-south axis and to connect the canyon's central ceremonial complex with distinctive topographic features in the north.

Prior to the Solstice Project studies of the Chacoan constructions, others had reported cardinal orientations in the primary walls and the great kiva of Pueblo Bonito, a major building located in the central complex of

Chaco Canyon, and in Casa Rinconada, an isolated great kiva (Williamson et al. 1975; Williamson, Fisher, and O'Flynn 1977)(Figs. 8.2, 8.3). In addition, researchers have shown that certain features in Pueblo Bonito and Casa Rinconada may be oriented to the solstices (Reyman 1976; Williamson, Fisher, and O'Flynn 1977; Zeilik 1984).[4]

Certain early research also highlighted astronomically related geometry and symmetry in the Chacoan architecture. One scholar describes "geometrical/astronomical patterns" in the extensive cardinal organization of Casa Rinconada (Williamson 1984). This report notes that these patterns were derived from the symmetry of the solar cycle, rather than from the observation of astronomical events from this building. Similarly, other research describes a symmetric, cardinal patterning in the geographic relationships of several central buildings; and it further suggests that other major buildings—outside of the center and out of sight of the center—were organized in symmetric relationships to the cardinal axes of the center (Fritz 1978).

These previous findings led the Solstice Project to examine and analyze the orientations, internal geometry, and interrelationships of the major Chacoan buildings for possible astronomical significance. The Solstice Project's study regarded as important both orientations to visible astronomical events and expressions of astronomically related geometry. In the following analysis, the Solstice Project considers the orientations of the major Chacoan buildings, and of their inter-building relationships, to astronomical events on both the sensible and the visible horizons.[5]

Solar and Lunar Orientations
of the Major Chacoan Buildings

The Solstice Project asked if the fourteen major buildings were oriented to the the sun and moon at the extremes and mid-positions of their cycles, i.e., the meridian passage, the solstices and the equinoxes, and the lunar major and minor standstills. The rising and setting azimuths for these astronomical events at the latitude of Chaco Canyon are given in Fig. 8.5. (The angles of the solstices, equinoxes, and lunar standstills are expressed as single values taken east and west of north; as positive to the east of north and negative to the west of north.)

In the clear skies of the high desert environment of the San Juan Basin, the Chacoans had nearly continuous opportunity to view the sun and the moon, to observe the progression of their cycles, and to see the changes

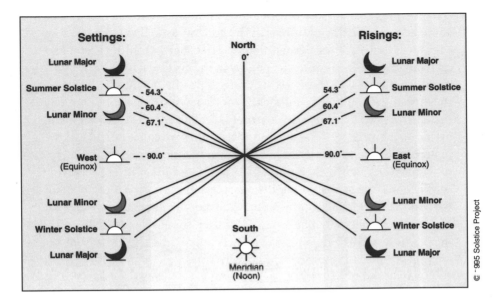

Fig. 8.5. Azimuths of the rising and setting of the sun and moon at the extremes and mid-positions of their cycles, at the latitude (36° north) of Chaco Canyon. The meridian passage of the sun is also indicated. The lunar extremes are the northern and southern limits of rising or setting at the major and minor standstills. Fabian Schmid (Davis, Inc.) and Suzanne Samuels (By Design Graphics), © The Solstice Project 1995.

of their relationships to the surrounding landscape and in patterns of shadow and light.

The sun: The yearly cycle of the sun is evident by its excursions to the extreme positions: rising in the northeast at the summer solstice and in the southeast at the winter solstice; setting in the northwest at the summer solstice and in the southwest at the winter solstice (Fig. 8.5). At equinox, in the middle of these excursions, it rises and sets east and west. At solar noon, in the middle of its daily excursion, the sun is on the meridian—i.e., aligned with the north-south axis.

The cardinal directions (0°, 90°) are regarded in this paper as having the solar associations of equinox and meridian passage.[6] In a location surrounded by significantly elevated topography, however, the equinox sun can also be observed on the visible horizon in sunrise and sunset azimuths that are not the cardinal east-west axis of the sensible horizon.

The moon: The moon's standstill cycle is longer (18.6 years) and more complex than the sun's cycle, but its rhythms and patterns also can be observed in its shifting positions on the horizon, as well as in its relationship to the sun (see also Aveni 1980:Ch. III)(Fig. 8.5). In its excursions each month it shifts from rising roughly in the northeast to rising roughly in the southeast and from setting roughly in the northwest to setting roughly in the southwest, but a closer look reveals that the envelope of these excursions expands and contracts through the 18.6-year standstill cycle. In the year of the major standstill, this envelope is at its maximum width, and at the latitude of Chaco, the moon rises and sets approximately 6.1° north and south of the positions of the rising and setting solstice suns. These positions are the farthest to the northeast and northwest and southeast and southwest that the moon ever reaches. In the year of the minor standstill, nine to ten years later, the envelope is at its minimum width, and the moon rises and sets approximately 6.7° within the envelope of the rising and setting solstice suns.

The progression of the sun and the moon in their cycles can also be quite accurately observed in their changing heights at meridian passage and in the accompanying shifts in shadow patterns.

A number of factors, such as parallax and atmospheric refraction, can shift and broaden the range of azimuth where the risings and settings of the solstice suns and the standstill moons appear on the horizon. In addition, judgments in determining a solar or lunar event introduce uncertainties. These judgments involve determining which portion of the object to sight on and what time to sight it in its rising or setting, as well as identifying the exact time of a solstice or a standstill. Calculations for the latitude and environment of the Chaco region show the standard deviation developed from these sighting conditions and uncertainties: 0.5° in locating a solstice event; 0.5° in locating the minor standstill; and 0.7° in locating the major standstill (Sinclair and Sofaer 1994; see also Hawkins 1973:287–288).

The Solstice Project surveyed the orientations of the fourteen largest buildings of the Chaco cultural region as ranked by room count (Powers, Gillespie, and Lekson 1983)(Figs. 8.1 and 8.3). The group comprises twelve rectangular and two crescent-shaped buildings that contained 115 to 695 rooms and were one to four stories high (Powers, Gillespie, and Lekson 1983). Ten buildings are located in the canyon, and four are located outside of the canyon.

The buildings in the survey represent the Chacoans' most elaborate architecture. They include all of the large buildings in the canyon and the only outlying buildings that share the massive scale and impressive formality of the large buildings in the canyon (Lekson 1991; Roney 1992).[7]

All of the buildings in the Solstice Project's studies were developed between the late A.D. 800s and 1120s (Lekson 1984; Marshall et al. 1979; Powers, Gillespie, and Lekson 1983). Although the earlier buildings were modified and whole new buildings were constructed within this period, all the buildings that the Solstice Project surveyed were in use and most were being extensively worked on in the last and most intensive phase of Chacoan construction A.D. 1075 to about 1115 (Lekson 1984).

Six teams, working with the Solstice Project between 1984 and 1989, surveyed the orientations of most of the exterior walls of the twelve rectangular buildings. (The teams did not survey three short exterior walls of the rectangular buildings because the walls were too deteriorated.) The Solstice Project also surveyed the long back wall and the exterior corners of Peñasco Blanco, as well as the two halves of the exterior south wall and the primary interior wall of Pueblo Bonito, which approximately divides the plaza. In addition, the Solstice Project surveyed the dimensions of most of the exterior walls of the fourteen buildings. The teams established references at the sites by orienting to the sun, Venus, Sirius, or Polaris, or by ranging to existing Class I and Class II monumentation.

Most of the walls are quite straight and in good condition at ground level and can be located within a few centimeters. Ten to thirty points were established along the walls which were measured in relation to the established references. These values were averaged to calculate the orientations of the walls. The Solstice Project was able to estimate from having multiple surveys of several walls that most of its measurements are accurate to within +/- 0.25° of the orientation of the original walls. (Table 8.1 indicates where the survey was less accurate.)

The survey defined the orientations of the twelve rectangular buildings as either the direction of the longest wall (termed here the "principal" wall)[8] or the perpendicular to this wall. In all but one of the rectangular buildings, this perpendicular represents the "facing" direction of the building, the direction that crosses the large plaza. With respect to the crescent-shaped buildings, the orientation of Pueblo Bonito is defined as: (1) the primary interior wall that approximately divides the plaza; and (2) the perpendicular to that wall, which corresponds closely in its orientation to that of a major exterior wall.[9] The orientation of Peñasco Blanco is defined by its symmetry as: (1) the line between the ends of the crescent; and (2) the perpendicular to this line (Fig. 8.6).

TABLE I

Building	Number of Rooms	Area (m²)	Length of Principal Wall or Axis (m)	Orientations of:		
				Princ. Wall or Axis	Perp.	Diagonals
Pueblo Bonito	695	18,530	65	0.21° 0.14°	-89.79° ± 0.14°	
Chetro Ketl	580	23,395	140	69.60° ± 0.50°	-20.40° ± 0.50°	-86.4°
Aztec	405	15,030	120	62.47° ± 0.33°	-27.53° ± 0.33°	86.6° 37.2° -81.4° 24.8°
Pueblo del Arroyo	290	8,990	80	24.79° ± 0.25°	-65.21° ± 0.25°	-1.6° 49.9°
Kin Bineola	230	8,225	110	78.7° ± 3.2°	-11.3° ± 3.2°	-77.6° 54.2°
Penasco Blanco	215	15,010	100	36.8° ± 1.3°	-53.2° ± 1.3°	
Wijiji	190	2,535	53	83.48° ± 0.15°	-6.52° ± 0.15°	-62.0° 49.2°
Salmon Ruin	175	8,320	130	65.75° ± 0.15°	-24.75° ± 0.15°	88.4° 43.3°
Una Vida	160	8,750	80	-35.18° ± 0.15°	54.82° ± 0.15°	
Hungo Pavi	150	8,025	90	-85.24° ±0.15°	4.76° ±0.15	-61.4° 70.7°
Pueblo Pintado	135	5,935	70	69.90° ±0.15°	-20.10° ± 0.15°	31.4°
Kin Kletso	135	2,640	42	-65.82° ± 0.64°	24.18° ± 0.64°	87.38° -38.09°
Pueblo Alto	130	8,260	110	88.9° ±1.3°	-1.1° ± 1.3°	-68.6° 64.8°
Tsin Kletzin	115	3,552	40	89° ± 2°	-1° ± 2°	-66° 51°

Numbers of rooms and area from R.P. Powers et al,. "The Outlier Survey" (National Park Service, Albuquerque, 1983), Table 41.

Numbers of rooms and area from R. P. Powers et al., "The Outlier Survey" (National Park Service, Albuquerque, 1983), Table 41, © The Solstice Project 1994.

Note: Positive azimuths are east of north; negative azimuths are west of north. ©The Solstice Project 1995

The results of the survey show that the orientations of eleven of the fourteen major buildings are associated with one of the four solar or lunar azimuths on the sensible horizon (Tables 8.1 and 8.2 and Fig. 8.6).[10] Three buildings (Pueblo Bonito, Pueblo Alto, and Tsin Kletzin) are associated with the cardinal directions (meridian and equinox). One building (Aztec) is associated with the solstice azimuth. Five buildings (Chetro Ketl, Kin Kletso, Pueblo del Arroyo, Pueblo Pintado, and Salmon Ruin) are associated with the lunar minor standstill azimuth, and two buildings (Peñasco Blanco and Una Vida) are associated with the lunar major standstill (Fig. 8.7).[11]

The orientations of the eleven major buildings that are associated with solar and lunar azimuths fall within 0.2° and 2.8° of the astronomical azimuths on the sensible horizon. Of these eleven, nine fall within 0.2° and 2.1° of the astronomical azimuths. The remaining two buildings, Chetro Ketl and Pueblo Pintado, are oriented respectively within 2.5° and 2.8° of the azimuth of the lunar minor standstill. (The wider differences in the orientations of these latter buildings from the lunar minor standstill are in the direction away from the solstice azimuth, which reinforces the conclusion that these buildings are associated with the moon rather than the sun.)

A number of factors (together or separately) could account for the divergence of the actual orientations of the major Chacoan buildings from the astronomical azimuths. These may include small errors in observation, surveying, and construction and a desire by the Chacoans to integrate into their astronomically oriented architecture symbolic relationships to significant topographic features and/or other major Chacoan buildings.(See for example the discussion in this essay of solar-lunar regional pattern among the major Chacoan buildings.)[12]

The Solstice Project found that the eleven buildings that are oriented to astronomical events on the sensible horizon are also oriented to the same events on the visible horizon. The reason for this is that the topography introduces no significant variable in the observation of the rising or the setting astronomical events from these buildings. The divergence of the orientations of these buildings from the azimuths of astronomical events in one direction on the visible horizon (0.5° to 2.5°) is approximately the same as the divergence described above of their orientations from the azimuths of the same astronomical events on the sensible horizon.[13] The differences between the orientations to the sensible and those to the visible horizon are so small as to not clearly indicate to which of

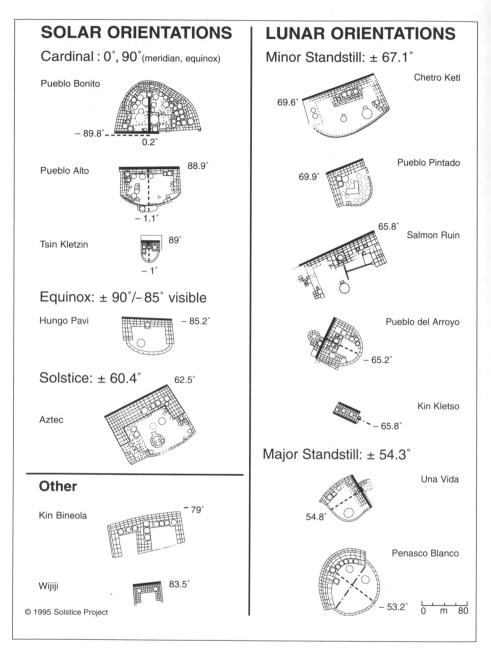

SOLAR ORIENTATIONS

Cardinal : 0°, 90° (meridian, equinox)

Pueblo Bonito

− 89.8° - - - - - - - - - -
0.2°

Pueblo Alto

88.9°

− 1.1°

Tsin Kletzin

89°

− 1°

Equinox: ± 90°/− 85° visible

Hungo Pavi — − 85.2°

Solstice: ± 60.4°

62.5°

Aztec

Other

Kin Bineola — ~ 79°

Wijiji

83.5°

© 1995 Solstice Project

LUNAR ORIENTATIONS

Minor Standstill: ± 67.1°

Chetro Ketl

69.6°

Pueblo Pintado

69.9°

65.8°

Salmon Ruin

Pueblo del Arroyo

− 65.2°

Kin Kletso

− 65.8°

Major Standstill: ± 54.3°

Una Vida

54.8°

Penasco Blanco

− 53.2°

0   m   80

Fig. 8.6. Orientations of the fourteen major Chacoan buildings shown in relation to
the astronomical azimuths on the sensible horizon. For one building, Hungo Pavi,
the orientation to the equinox sunrise on the visible horizon also is indicated.
Suzanne Samuels (By Design Graphics), © The Solstice Project 1995.

TABLE II

	Principal Wall or Axis	Perpendicular	
Pueblo Bonito	0.2°	- 89.8°	
Pueblo Alto	88.9°	- 1.1°	} 0°, 90° Cardinal (meridian, equinox)
Tsin Kletzin	89.0°	- 1.0°	
Hungo Pavi	- 85.2°		} - 85° Equinox/visible
Aztec	62.5°		} 60.4° Solstice
Penasco Blanco		- 53.2°	} 54.3° Lunar Major Standstill
Una Vida		54.8°	
Pueblo del Arroyo		- 65.2°	
Kin Kletso	- 65.8°		
Salmon Ruin	65.8°		} 67.1° Lunar Minor Standstill
Chetro Ketl	69.6°		
Pueblo Pintado	69.9°		
Wijiji	83.5°		
Kin Bineola	~ 79.0°		

Note: Positive azimuths are east of north; negative azimuths are west of north. © The Solstice Project 1995

Fig. 8.7. The moonrise seen through two doorways of Pueblo del Arroyo on April 10, 1990, when the moon rose at minus 67.5° on the visible horizon, close to the 67.1° azimuth of the lunar minor standstill. Although it cannot be known whether an exterior wall, which is now deteriorated, blocked this view, the photograph illustrates the framing of the minor standstill moon by other exterior doorways and it conveys the perpendicular direction of the building toward the minor standstill moon (see Fig. 8.6). Photograph by Crawford MacCallum, © The Solstice Project 1990.

these horizons the architects of Chaco oriented their buildings. The Solstice Project finds no evidence that the Chacoans were interested in making such a distinction in the case of eleven buildings.

Hungo Pavi, the twelfth building, appears to be oriented too far (4.8°) from the equinox rising or setting sun on the sensible horizon to qualify as an orientation associated with the solar azimuths on that horizon. It is, however, oriented to within one degree of the visible equinox sunrise.[14] Because of the topography, there is no corresponding visibility from Hungo Pavi to the equinox setting sun.

With respect to Wijiji and Kin Bineola, there appear to be no solar or lunar events associated with either the sensible or the visible horizon.[15] To conclude, orientation to the extremes and mid-positions of the solar and lunar cycles apparently played a significant role in the construction of the primary Chacoan architecture. No utilitarian reasons appear to explain the astronomic orientations of twelve of the fourteen major buildings.

Other researchers of prehistoric Pueblo buildings report solar and lunar orientations and associations (Malville et al. 1991; Malville and Putnam 1989; Williamson 1984). At Hovenweep, in southern Utah, the orientations and locations of port holes of certain tower-like structures appear to be related to the solar cycle. Chimney Rock, an outlying Chacoan building in southern Colorado, appears to have been situated for its view of the major northern standstill moon rising between natural stone pillars, "chimney rocks." The relationship of this building to the lunar major standstill moon is underscored by the close correspondence of the tree ring dates of its timbers with the occurrences of the lunar major standstill (A.D. 1075 and 1094) at the peak of the Chacoan civilization. These findings in the outlying region of the Chacoan culture, as well as earlier findings of solar and lunar light markings in Chaco canyon, support the phenomenon of solar and lunar orientations in the primary Chacoan buildings.

Solar-Lunar Geometry Internal to the Major Chacoan Buildings

The Solstice Project's survey of the eleven rectangular major Chacoan buildings found strictly repeated internal diagonal angles and a correspondence between these angles and astronomy.

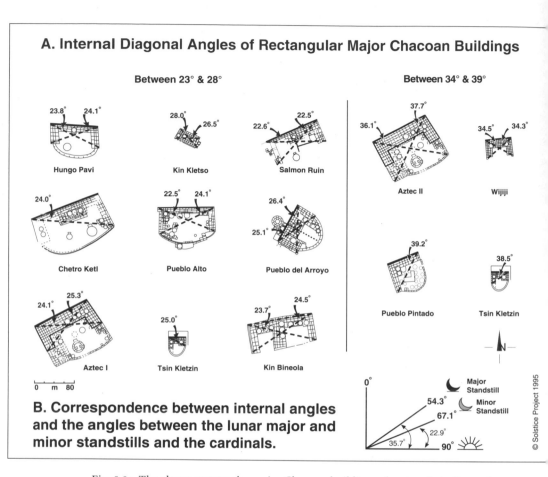

A. Internal Diagonal Angles of Rectangular Major Chacoan Buildings

Between 23° & 28°

Between 34° & 39°

23.8° 24.1°
Hungo Pavi

28.0° 26.5°
Kin Kletso

22.6° 22.5°
Salmon Ruin

36.1° 37.7°
Aztec II

34.5° 34.3°
Wijiji

24.0°
Chetro Ketl

22.5° 24.1°
Pueblo Alto

26.4° 25.1°
Pueblo del Arroyo

39.2°
Pueblo Pintado

38.5°
Tsin Kletzin

24.1° 25.3°
Aztec I

25.0°
Tsin Kletzin

23.7° 24.5°
Kin Bineola

0   m   80

B. Correspondence between internal angles and the angles between the lunar major and minor standstills and the cardinals.

0°
54.3° Major Standstill
67.1° Minor Standstill
22.9°
35.7°
90°

© Solstice Project 1995

Fig. 8.8a. The eleven rectangular major Chacoan buildings, showing their diagonals and internal diagonal angles. (Two building phases of Aztec are shown.) Suzanne Samuels (By Design Graphics), © The Solstice Project 1995.

Fig. 8.8b. The correspondence of these angles with the angles between the lunar standstill azimuths and the cardinal directions. Suzanne Samuels (By Design Graphics), © The Solstice Project 1995.

The internal angles formed by the two diagonals and the long back walls of the rectangular buildings cluster in two groups (Fig. 8.8a):

16 angles in nine buildings[16] are between 23° and 28°; six angles in four buildings are between 34° and 39°.

(One of the buildings, Aztec, was constructed first as a rectangular building with shorter side walls [Aztec I] that were extended in a later building stage [Aztec II] [Ahlstrom 1985]. It is of interest that when the side walls of Aztec I were extended to form Aztec II, the builders shifted from one preferred angle to the other.)

At the latitude of Chaco, the angles between the lunar standstill azimuths on the sensible horizon and the east-west cardinal axis, are 22.9° and 35.7° (Fig. 8.8b). The correspondence between these angles of the solar-lunar relationships and the internal diagonal angles is intriguing. It suggests that the Chacoans may have favored these particular angles in order to incorporate a geometry of the sun and moon in the internal organization of the buildings.[17]

In addition, three rectangular buildings (Pueblo Alto, Salmon Ruin, and Pueblo del Arroyo) are oriented on the sensible and visible horizons along one or both of their diagonals, as well as on their principal walls or perpendiculars, to the lunar minor standstill azimuth and to one of the cardinals (Table 8.1). The Chacoans may have intended that the two phenomena—internal geometry and external orientation—be so integrated that these three rectangular buildings would have both solar and lunar orientation.

Results of a recent study by the Solstice Project suggest that a similar solar-lunar geometry guided the design of all of the major Chacoan buildings (Sofaer 1994).[18] Furthermore, as with the three rectangular buildings discussed above, it appears that certain other of the major buildings also contain both solar and lunar orientations.

Solar-Lunar Regional Pattern between the Major Chacoan Buildings

Having seen that the Chacoans oriented and internally proportioned their major buildings in relationship to astronomy, the Solstice Project asked if the geographical relationships between the major buildings likewise expressed astronomical significance.

One scholar observed that four key central buildings are organized in a cardinal pattern (Fritz 1978). The line between Pueblo Alto and Tsin Kletzin is north-south; the line between Pueblo Bonito and Chetro Ketl is east-west. This work also showed that these cardinal interrelationships of four central buildings involved a symmetric patterning. The north-

TABLE III

Astronomically Oriented Buildings	Astronomical Bearings to Other Buildings			
	Buildings	Azimuth (degrees)	Differences between astronomical azimuth and interbuilding bearings (degrees)	Distance (km)
Cardinal Buildings associated azimuths 90°/0°				
Pueblo Bonito	Chetro Ketl	-88.7	-1.3	0.72
	Aztec	-2.2	2.2	86.3
Pueblo Alto	Tsin Kletzin	0.6	-0.6	3.7
	Aztec	-2.5	2.5	86.0
Hungo Pavi	- -	- -	- -	- -
Tzin Kletzin	Pueblo Alto	0.6	-0.6	3.7
	Aztec	-2.3	2.3	89.0
Solstice Building associated azimuth ±60.4°				
Aztec	- -	- -	- -	- -
Lunar Minor Buildings associated azimuth ±67.1°				
Chetro Ketl	Kin Bineola	69.3	-2.2	17.1
	Pueblo Pintado	-69.9	2.8	27.2
	Kin Kletso	-69.9	2.8	1.5
Pueblo del Arroyo	Hungo Pavi	-69.3	2.2	3.4
	Kin Bineola	67.8	-0.7	16.2
	Wijiji	-65.9	-1.2	8.4
Salmon Ruin	- -	- -	- -	- -
Pueblo Pintado	Chetro Ketl	-69.9	2.8	27.2
	Peublo Bonito	-70.3	3.2	27.9
	Penasco Blanco	-68.6	1.5	32.1
	Pueblo Alto	-68.0	0.9	27.8
	Kin Kletso	-69.9	2.8	28.7
Kin Kletso	Chetro Ketl	-69.9	2.8	1.5
	Pueblo Pintado	-69.9	2.8	28.7
	Wijiji	-64.5	-2.6	9.0
	Peublo Alto	65.8	-1.3	1.3
	Kin Bineola	65.9	-1.2	16.0
	Hungo Pavi	-65.2	-1.9	4.0
Lunar Major Buildings associated azimuth ±54.3°				
Penasco Blanco	Pueblo Bonito	-55.9	1.6	4.2
	Pueblo del Arroyo	-55.8	1.5	4.1
	Una Vida	-56.7	2.4	9.8
	Kin Bineola	55.0	0.7	14.3
Una Vida	Chetro Ketl	-51.3	-3.0	4.8
	Pueblo Bonito	-55.8	1.5	5.4
	Penasco Blanco	-56.7	2.4	9.8
	Pueblo del Arroyo	-55.8	3.0	5.7
	Kin Kletso	-55.8	1.4	6.3

Note: Positive azimuths are east of north; negative azimuths are west of north

© 1995 Solstice Project

Note: Positive azimuths are east of north; negative azimuths are west of north.

© The Solstice Project 1995

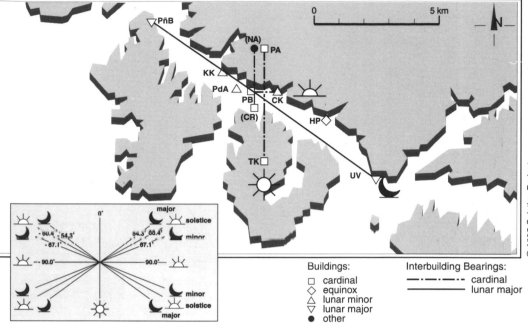

Fig. 8.9. The locations and orientations of the buildings in Chaco Canyon. The diagram shows the inter-building bearings that correlate with the orientations of individual buildings to the cardinal directions and to the lunar major standstill azimuths. Fabian Schmid (Davis, Inc.), © The Solstice Project 1995.

south line between Pueblo Alto and Tsin Kletzin evenly divides the east-west line between Pueblo Bonito and Chetro Ketl.

The Solstice Project observed, from its own survey, that three of the four buildings involved in these cardinal inter-building relationships are also cardinal in their individual building orientations (Table 8.3; Figs. 8.2, 8.9, 8.10a, and 8.10b).[19] These findings suggested that the Chacoans coordinated the orientations and locations of several central buildings to form astronomical inter-building relationships. The Project then asked if there were other such relationships between the major buildings.

As Table 8.3 and Figs. 8.9 and 8.11 show, numerous bearings between thirteen of the fourteen major buildings align with the azimuths of the solar and lunar phenomena associated with the individual buildings.[20] Only one major building, Salmon Ruin, is not related in this manner to

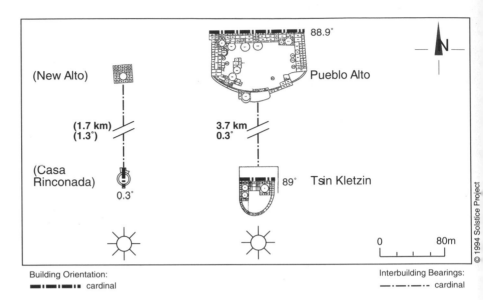

Fig. 8.10a. The relationships between two pairs of Chacoan buildings in the central complex that are connected by north-south astronomical inter-building bearings. Fabian Schmid (Davis, Inc.), © The Solstice Project 1995.

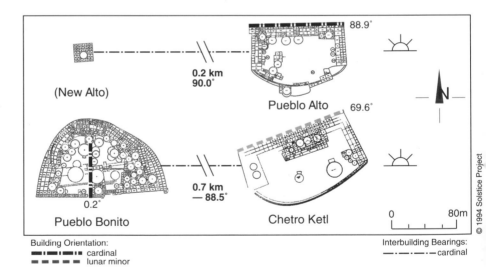

Fig. 8.10b. The relationships between two pairs of Chacoan buildings in the central complex that are connected by east-west astronomical inter-building bearings. Fabian Schmid (Davis, Inc.), © The Solstice Project 1995.

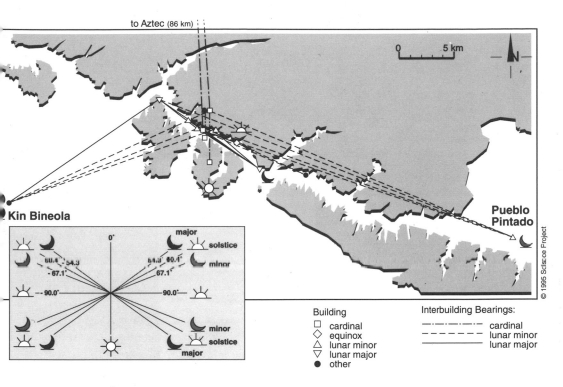

Fig. 8.11. The locations and orientations of twelve of the major Chacoan buildings
of this study. The diagram shows inter-building bearings that correlate with the
orientation of the individual buildings to the cardinal directions and the lunar
major and minor standstill azimuths. Fabian Schmid (Davis, Inc.),
© The Solstice Project 1995.

another building. In questioning the extent to which these astronomical
inter-building relationships were intentionally developed by the Chacoans, the Solstice Project examined the pattern formed by them.

In a manner similar to the central cardinal patterning, the bearings between the lunar-oriented buildings and other buildings appear to form
lunar-based relationships that are symmetric about the north-south axis
of the central complex (Fig. 8.11).

The two isolated and remote outlying buildings, Pueblo Pintado and
Kin Bineola, twenty-seven kilometers and eighteen kilometers respectively from the canyon center, are located on lines from the central complex that correspond to the bearings of the lunar minor standstill. As in

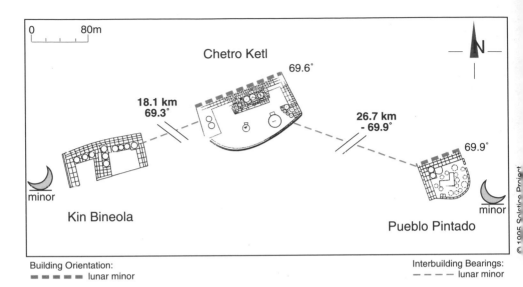

Fig. 8.12a. The relationships between three major Chacoan buildings connected by astronomical inter-building bearings aligned to the lunar minor standstill. Fabian Schmid (Davis, Inc.), © The Solstice Project 1995.

the cardinal patterning, these lunar-based inter-building relationships are underscored by the fact that they involve buildings that also are oriented individually to the lunar standstills (for one example see Fig. 8.12a). Specifically, Chetro Ketl, Pueblo del Arroyo, and Kin Kletso—the three buildings in the central complex that are oriented to the lunar minor standstill—also are related to Pueblo Pintado and Kin Bineola on bearings oriented to the lunar minor standstill. It is of interest that Pueblo Pintado also is oriented to the lunar minor standstill (Figs. 8.11, 8.12a).[21] In addition, two major buildings, Wijiji and Hungo Pavi, located outside of the central complex but within the canyon, also are on the bearing from the central complex to Pueblo Pintado and to the lunar minor standstill (Fig. 8.11).[22]

The relationship of the central complex to Pueblo Pintado (southeast of the canyon) is to the rising of the southern minor standstill moon; the relationship of the central canyon complex to Kin Bineola (southwest of the canyon) is to the setting of this same moon. Thus the north-south axis of the central complex is the axis of symmetry of this moon's rising, meridian passage, and setting, as well as the axis of the ceremonial center and of the relationships of these significant outlying structures to that center.

It is of further note that Pueblo Pintado and Kin Bineola are regarded as having particularly significant relationships with the buildings in the canyon. One archaeologist reports that these two buildings are more like the canyon buildings than they are like other outlying buildings, and he suggests, because of their positions to the southeast and southwest of the canyon, that they could be viewed as the "gateway communities" (Michael P. Marshall 1990 p.c.).

This lunar-based symmetrical patterning about the north-south axis of the central ceremonial complex also is expressed in the relationships of the lunar major-oriented buildings, Una Vida and Peñasco Blanco, to that complex (Fig. 8.9). Without knowing the astronomical associations of these buildings, other scholars had observed the symmetrical relationship of Una Vida and Peñasco Blanco to the north-south axis, as described above, between two major buildings in the central complex, Pueblo Alto and Tsin Kletzin; and one of these scholars described this relationship as, along with the cardinal relationships of the central complex, "establishing the fundamental symmetry of the core development of Chaco Canyon" (Fritz 1978; Stein and Lekson 1992).

From the central complex, bearings to the major standstill moon are also the bearings to Una Vida and Peñasco Blanco, the only major Chacoan buildings that are oriented to the lunar major standstill (Fig. 8.12b). This correspondence of the inter-building relationships with the individual building orientations is again what is found with the cardinal and lunar minor relationships of the major buildings. Here it also is striking that the two buildings are equidistant from the north-south axis of the central complex. It is of further interest that the bearing from Peñasco Blanco to Kin Bineola also corresponds with the bearing to the lunar major standstill (Fig. 8.11).[23] Una Vida, Peñasco Blanco, and Kin Bineola, along with Pueblo Bonito, share the earliest dates among the major Chacoan buildings (Lekson 1984; Marshall et al. 1979).

Thus, from the central complex of Chaco Canyon, in the year of the major standstill moon, there was a relationship to that moon, as it rose farthest south in its full cycle, that also incorporated a relationship to Una Vida; and, in that same year, as the moon made its excursion to setting farthest north in its full cycle, it was on a bearing from the central complex that incorporated a relationship with Peñasco Blanco. Furthermore,

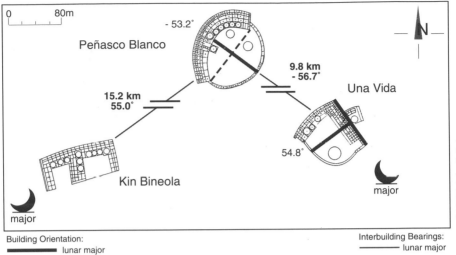

Fig. 8.12b. The relationship between three major Chacoan buildings connected by astronomical inter-building bearings aligned to the lunar major standstill.
Fabian Schmid (Davis, Inc.), © The Solstice Project 1995.

in that year, the southern major standstill moon that rose on the bearing from Peñasco Blanco to Una Vida and the central complex would set on the bearing from Peñasco Blanco to the outlying major building, Kin Bineola. This phenomenon may have been intended to draw Kin Bineola into a lunar major relationship with Peñasco Blanco and with Peñasco Blanco's lunar major connection with Una Vida and the central canyon complex.

At the other end of the lunar standstill cycle, nine to ten years later, in the year of the minor standstill moon, two outlying buildings, Kin Bineola and Pueblo Pintado, would be drawn into relationship with the central complex by their locations on bearings from the central complex that are to the rising and setting of the southern minor standstill moon.

Finally, in the face of the evidence that the Chacoans oriented and proportioned their major buildings in relationship to the solar and lunar cycles—and also interrelated their cardinally oriented buildings in a cardinal and symmetrical pattern—it is difficult to dismiss as coincidental the lunar-based inter-building relationships, which are based on the same principles.[24] The recurring correlation of the inter-building lines with the astronomical phenomena associated with the individual Chacoan build-ings, and the centrally and symmetrically organized design of these lines, suggest that the Chacoan culture coordinated the locations and orienta-tions of many of its major buildings to form an inter-building regional pattern that commemorates and integrates the cycles of the sun and the moon.[25]

Most of the buildings related by astronomical inter-building lines are not intervisible. In general, this is because the canyon and other topo-graphic features block the views between the buildings, especially those related over long distances. Thus the astronomical inter-building lines could not have been, in general, used for astronomical observations or predictions.[26] It is of interest that the Chacoan roads, which are typified by their rigorous straight course, frequently appear to ignore topographic obstacles and connect sites that are great distances apart and are not in-tervisible.

Consideration of the Evolution of Astronomical Expression in Chacoan Architecture

The evidence of a conscious effort by the Chacoans to orient and interrelate their buildings on astronomical bearings raises a number of questions for further study. Were the building locations selected because they fell on astronomical bearings from other buildings? Were the inter-building bearings developed from a plan? Were some buildings originally located for reasons other than astronomy and later drawn into the astro-nomical regional pattern?

It will probably never be known how great a role astronomy played in the decisions regarding the placement of the Chacoan buildings. Nor does it appear possible to know the extent of planning that preceded the de-velopment of the astronomical expressions in Chacoan architecture.[27] The data presently available on the chronology of the construction of the major buildings, however, does provide some insight to the history of the development of astronomical orientations and interrelationships among the major Chacoan buildings.

This data shows that astronomical orientation appears to have played a part in Chacoan architecture from the earliest to the latest phases of its construction. Pueblo Bonito's north-south axis was incorporated in a major interior wall in the building's earliest design in the late A.D. 800s (Stein, Suiter, and Ford in this volume); and this north-south axis was extended and elaborated in the construction of the primary interior wall during the building's last phase of construction, in the late A.D. 1090s. The cardinal orientations of Pueblo Alto and Tsin Kletzin were developed in the early A.D. 1000s and the early A.D. 1100s, respectively. The lunar orientations were developed from the mid A.D. 900s (in Una Vida) through the early A.D. 1100s (in Kin Kletso).

Presently available data on the evolution of individual buildings shows that for most of the fourteen major buildings the walls that are revealed today—and that were the subject of this study—are the original walls of these buildings, or that they follow closely the orientation of the buildings' prior walls. This data indicates that the orientation of two of the fourteen buildings changed significantly from one building phase to another.

It is also of interest that three of the four buildings in which the earliest dates were found among the fourteen major buildings (Peñasco Blanco, Una Vida, and Kin Bineola) are involved in the lunar major standstill inter-building bearings.(Curiously, Peñasco Blanco is one of the two buildings that shifted from an earlier orientation [of minus 67°, in A.D. 900–915] to a later orientation [of minus 53.2° in A.D. 1050–65.])

With further dating information it may be possible to know more of the evolution of astronomical expression in the Chacoan buildings. Such information could also shed light on the intriguing possibility that there may be, as there was found to be at Chimney Rock, correlations between the building phases of the major Chacoan buildings and the astronomical cycles (Malville and Putnam 1989).

Speculations on the Chacoans' Experience

Many of the major buildings appear to incorporate interesting views and experiences of the sun and moon at the extremes and mid-positions of their cycles. For example, each day at meridian passage of the sun, the mid-wall which approximately divides the massive structure of Pueblo Bonito casts no shadow. Similarly, the middle of the sun's yearly passage is marked at Pueblo Bonito as the equinox sun is seen rising and setting closely in line with the western half of its south wall. Thus, the middle of the sun's daily and yearly journeys are visibly in alignment with the major features of this building which is at the middle of the Chacoan world.[28]

From many of the other major buildings, the sun and moon at the extreme positions of their cycles would be seen rising and/or setting along the long back walls or across the plazas at angles perpendicular to the back walls. In buildings oriented in their facing directions to the lunar standstill azimuths, the rising or setting moon, near its extremes, would be framed strikingly by the doorways (Fig. 8.7).

Also visually compelling would have been the view from Peñasco Blanco of the moon rising at the major standstill position. This building is located 5.4 kilometers to the northwest of Pueblo Bonito near the top of West Mesa. From it, one would view the southern major standstill moon rising in line with the mid-axis of the building's crescent, and also on a bearing to Pueblo Bonito and to the central complex of the canyon. The bearing would appear to continue through the valley of the canyon to the rising moon on the horizon. This event marked the time when the moon rises farthest south in its full cycle, once every eighteen to nineteen years.

This dramatic view of the major standstill moonrise also embodied astronomical and symmetrical relationships to non-visible objects. Out of sight, but on the alignment between the viewer at Peñasco Blanco and the rising moon, is Una Vida, the one other of the Chacoan buildings that is oriented to the major standstill moon. Some viewers would likely have known of this non-visible building's position on the bearing from Peñasco Blanco to the major rising moon, and may also have known of Una Vida's and Peñasco Blanco's symmetrical relationship with the north-south axis of the central complex; i.e., that the two buildings are located the same distance from the north-south axis. Seeing the southern major standstill moon set on the mesa rise behind Peñasco Blanco would have conveyed to some Chacoans that as it set, out of view, on the sensible horizon it was on a bearing with Kin Bineola, out of view, 14.3 kilometers to the southwest. Thus the experience of viewing the moon rising and setting at its southern major standstill from Peñasco Blanco would have involved seeing certain visible—and knowing certain non-visible—aspects of the building's relationships with astronomy and with other major Chacoan buildings.

In the sculptured topography of the southern Rockies, at a location one hundred and fifty kilometers north of Chaco, the Chacoans witnessed a spectacular view of the moonrise at its major standstill. From their building situated high on an outcrop at Chimney Rock, once every eighteen to nineteen years, the Chacoans watched the moon rise between two nearby massive stone pillars.

Thus, while certain aspects of Chacoan architecture embed relationships on astronomical bearings to nonvisible objects, others appear to have been designed and/or located to frame, or to align to, bold displays of astronomy. Furthermore, some Chacoan astronomical expressions are on bearings that ignore topographic features, while others use topography dramatically to reinforce the visual effects of the architectural alignments to the sun and moon.

Concluding Discussion

Peoples throughout history and throughout the world have sought the synchronization and integration of the solar and lunar cycles. For example, in times and places not so remote from Chaco, the Mayans of Mesoamerica recognized the nineteen-year metonic cycle—the relationship of the phase cycles of the moon to the solar cycle—and noted elaborately, in the Dresden Codex, the pattern of lunar eclipses (Aveni 1980).[29] The Hopi, a Pueblo people living today in Arizona, are known to have synchronized the cycles of the sun and moon over a two-to-three-year period in the scheduling of their ceremonial cycle (McCluskey 1977). At Zuni Pueblo in northwestern New Mexico, the joining of Father Sun and Mother Moon is sought constantly in the timing of ceremonies (Tedlock 1983).

Each of the Chacoan expressions of solar and lunar cosmology contains within it this integration of the sun and the moon. For example, at the three-slab site on Fajada Butte, the sunlight in a dagger-like form penetrates the center of the large spiral at summer solstice near midday, the highest part its cycle (Sofaer, Zinser, and Sinclair 1979); and, as though in complement to this, the moon's shadow crosses the spiral center at the lowest point of its cycle, the minor standstill (Sofaer, Sinclair, and Doggett 1982). In the same way, the outer edges of the spiral are marked by the sun in light patterns at winter solstice, and the moon's shadow at its maximum extreme is tangent to the left edge.

This integration of the sun and the moon is in the three expressions of solar-lunar cosmology in Chacoan architecture. Five major buildings commemorate the solar cycle: three in their cardinal orientations, one in its equinox orientation, and one in its solstice orientation. Seven of the other nine major buildings commemorate the lunar standstills: five the minor standstill, and two the major standstill. And the overall patterning of the buildings joins the two sets of lunar-oriented buildings into rela-

118 *Anna Sofaer*

tionship with the cardinal-solar center in a symmetrically organized design. The geometry of the rectangular buildings again expresses the joining of sun and moon; the internal angles related to the cardinal and lunar azimuths bring a consciousness of each of these cycles into the layout of the buildings.

Commemoration of these recurring cycles appears to have been a primary purpose of the Chaco phenomenon. Many people must have been involved over generations in the planning, development, and maintenance of the massive Chacoan constructions. The work may have been accomplished in relatively short periods of time (Lekson 1984) and perhaps in episodes timed to the sun and moon. This activity would have unified the Chacoan society with the recurring rhythms of the sun and moon in their movements about that central ceremonial place, Chaco Canyon.[30]

There are many parallels to the cosmological patterning of the Chacoan culture in the architectural developments of the Mesoamerican cultures. These developments occurred in the region to the south of Chaco, for several centuries before, during, and after Chaco's florescence.

It is observed that "the coordination of space and time in the Mesoamerican cosmology found its expression in the orientations of pyramids and architectural complexes" (Broda 1982) and in the relationships of these complexes to outlying topography and buildings (Broda 1994). Ceremonies related to the dead and timed to the astronomical cycles occurred in Mesoamerican centers (Broda 1982). In central structures of the ceremonial complexes, light markings commemorated the zenith passage of the sun (Aveni 1980). Certain of the ceremonial centers were organized on axes close to the cardinal directions (Aveni 1980; Broda 1982). It is stated that cosmological expression in Mesoamerica "reached an astonishing degree of elaboration and perfection," and that its role was "to create an enduring system of order encompassing human society as well as the universe" (Broda 1994). A Mesoamerican archaeoastronomer comments that "a principle of cosmic harmony pervaded all of existence in Mesoamerican thought" (Aveni 1980).

The parallels between Mesoamerica and Chaco illustrate that the Chacoan and Mesoamerican peoples shared common cultural concerns. In addition, the several objects of Mesoamerican origin that were found in Chacoan buildings indicate that the Chacoans had some contact with Mesoamerica through trade.

In the complex cosmologies of the historic Pueblo peoples, descendants of the Chacoans, there is a rich interplay of the sun and moon.[31] Time and space are integrated in the marking of directions that order the ceremonial structures and dances, and in the timing of ceremonies to the cycle of the sun and the phases of the moon. The sun and the moon are related to birth, life, and death.[32] Commemoration of their cycles occurs on some ceremonial occasions in shadow-and-light patterns. For instance, sunlight or moonlight striking ceremonial objects or walls of ceremonial buildings may mark the solstices, as well as the meridian passage of the solstice sun and the full moon, and time the beginning and ending of rituals.

In many Pueblo traditions, the people emerged in the north from the worlds below and traveled to the south in search of the sacred middle place. The joining of the cardinal and solstice directions with the nadir and the zenith frequently defines, in Pueblo ceremony and myth, that sacred middle place. It is a center around which the recurring solar and lunar cycles revolve. Chaco Canyon may have been such a center place and a place of mediation and transition between these cycles and between the worlds of the living and the dead (F. Eggan 1990 p.c.).[33]

For the Chacoans, some ceremonies commemorating the sun and the moon must have been conducted in relatively private settings, while others would have been conducted in public and monumental settings. A site such as the three-slab site would have been visited probably by no more than two or three individuals, who were no doubt highly initiated, specialized, and prepared for witnessing the light markings (Ortiz 1982). By contrast, the buildings would have been visited by thousands of people participating in ceremony.

The solar and lunar cosmology encoded in the Chacoans' massive architecture—through the buildings' orientations, internal geometry, and geographic relationships—unified the Chacoan people with each other and with the cosmos. This order is complex and stretches across vast reaches of the sky, the desert, and time. It is to be held in the mind's eye, the one that sees into and beyond natural phenomena to a sacred order. The Chacoans transformed an arid empty space into a reach of the mind.

Acknowledgments

The generous help and disciplined work of many individuals made possible the research presented here. We are particularly indebted to Rolf M. Sinclair (National Science Foundation) for his help in the rigorous collection and reduction of large amounts of data, for his thoughtful analysis of naked-eye astronomical observations, and for his help in organizing numerous and complicated surveying trips. We most especially appreciate his dedication to pursuing the truth through thousands of hours of discussion and analysis of the Chacoan material.

We wish to express a special thanks to John Stein (Navajo Nation) for sharing with us, over fifteen years, his many insights to the non-material side of the Chaco phenomenon. To our knowledge, John was the first scholar to speak of Chacoan architecture as "a metaphoric language" and to express the view that the Chacoan roads were built for purposes other than utilitarian functions. He early on saw geometric complexity in the individual buildings and their inter-relationships.

Phillip Johnson Tuwaletstiwa (Ohio State University and the Hopi Tribe), the late Fred Eggan (Santa Fe), and Jay Miller (Chicago) helped us move from the confines of an engineering and surveying perspective, to think of the rich and complex dualities of Pueblo cosmology and their analogies with the Chacoan developments. Alfonso Ortiz (University of New Mexico), when first viewing our material on the patterning of Chacoan roads and major buildings, observed that these complex constructions were developed as though they were to be seen from above.

Phillip Johnson Tuwaletstiwa was also responsible for initiating the surveys that form the basis of our studies. Most of the surveys were carried out by Richard Cohen (National Geodetic Survey), assisted by Phillip Johnson Tuwaletstiwa, and supplemented recently by William Stone (National Geodetic Survey). Other surveys were conducted by Robert and Helen Hughes and E. C. Saxton (Sandia National Laboratories); C. Donald Encinias and William Kuntz, with the cooperation of Basil Pouls (Koogle and Pouls Engineering, Inc.); James Crowl and associates (Rio Grande Surveying Service); Scott Andrae (La Plata, N. M.), assisted by Dabney Ford (National Park Service) and Reid Williams (Rensselaer Polytechnic Institute); and William Mahnke (Farmington, N. M.).

Michael Marshall (Cibola Research Consultants) shared with us his comprehensive knowledge of Chacoan archaeology, and his keen insights to the Chacoans' use of topography. Stephen Lekson's (Crow Canyon Center for Archaeology) extensive knowledge of the major buildings in Chaco Canyon was invaluable to us. We also benefitted from many helpful discussions regarding Chacoan archaeology with John Roney (Bureau of Land Management), Dabney Ford, and Thomas Windes (National Park Service). LeRoy Doggett (U.S. Naval Observatory), Bradley Schaefer

(Goddard Space Flight Center), and Gerald Hawkins (Washington, D.C.) assisted with a number of points concerning the naked-eye astronomical observations. Crawford MacCallum (University of New Mexico) photographed the moonrise under unusual lighting conditions.

We thank J. McKim Malville (University of Colorado) for a number of interesting discussions and a tour of several northern prehistoric Pueblo building complexes, where he has identified astronomical building orientations and inter-building relationships, and Murray Gell-Mann (Santa Fe Institute) for joining us for a tour of several major Chacoan buildings and contributing stimulating and encouraging comments on our early analysis of possible astronomical significance in the Chacoan architecture.

William Byler (Washington, D.C.) once more gave us extremely generous and thoughtful assistance in editing the final manuscript. The graphics were prepared by Suzanne Samuels (By Design Graphics) and by Fabian Schmid with the cooperation of Davis, Inc. (Washington, D.C.).

The field work in Chaco Canyon was done with the helpful cooperation of former superintendents, Thomas Vaughan and Larry Belli, with the thoughtful guidance of National Park Service archaelogist Dabney Ford, and with the general assistance of many others of the staff of Chaco Culture National Historical Park.

Notes

1. It should be noted that the long back walls of five of the ten major building which are located in Chaco Canyon are somewhat parallel to local segments of the north canyon wall. Since there are innumerable locations along this canyon wall where significantly different orientations occur and where these buildings could have been placed, this approximate parallel relationship does not appear to have been a constraint on the orientations of these five buildings.

2. In the literature of Chacoan studies, we find one suggestion of a utilitarian reason for the location of the major buildings, and it applies to only one building. Specifically, it has been suggested that Tsin Kletzin was placed to optimize the direct sight lines to six other buildings (Lekson 1984:231). A suggestion by Judge (1989) that three major buildings "functioned primarily as storage sites to accompany resource pooling and redistribution within the drainage systems they 'controlled'" locates them only generally.

3. For an example of a non-utilitarian Chacoan road, see Dabney Ford's recent finding of a road connecting the canyon floor with the three-slab site on Fajada Butte (Ford 1993).

4. In addition, the relationship of Pueblo Bonito's design to the solar cycle appears to be symbolically represented in a petroglyph on Fajada Butte in Chaco Canyon. (Sofaer and Sinclair 1989:499; Sofaer 1994).

5. "Sensible horizon" describes the circle bounding that part of the earth's surface if no irregularities or obstructions are present. "Visible horizon" describes the horizon that is actually seen, taking obstructions, if any, into account.

6. It would seem unlikely that the Chacoans, who incorporated cardinal orientations in their architecture, and who also marked the equinoxes and meridian passage in light markings, did not associate the north-south axis with the sun's meridian passage and the east-west axis with the sun's rising and setting positions at equinox.

7. See also Lekson 1991: "Using intrinsic criteria, one could argue that only the Big Four (Salmon Ruin, Aztec, Pueblo Pintado, and Kin Bineola) . . . were identical to Pueblo Bonito and Chetro Ketl." Eventually, the Solstice Project will also study the "medium" size (Powers et al. 1983) and the more remote Chacoan buildings for possible astronomical significance.

8. In most cases the longest wall is obvious. For the orientation of Pueblo Pintado, values were taken for the longer of the two walls and the perpendicular to it. For Kin Kletso, the orientations of the two long walls of equal length, which differed in orientation by only 0.8° , were averaged. Kin Bineola's principal wall is not a straight wall, but three sections, which vary by several degrees. The sections were averaged in the value given here, and the error quoted (+ or –3°) reflects the differences in the sections.

9. The Solstice Project notes that other scholars have described the cardinal orientation of Pueblo Bonito by the direction of this primary interior wall and the direction of this western half of the south wall (Williamson et al. 1975; Williamson et al. 1977). The eastern half of the south wall, which is not perpendicular to the primary interior wall and is oriented to 85.4°, is a curious departure from these perpendicular relationships.

10. The orientation of Hungo Pavi as reported here corrects an error in an earlier paper (Sofaer, Sinclair, and Donahue 1990). The orientations of nine other major Chacoan buildings are also reported here with slightly different values than those reported in the earlier paper. These changes are the result of certain recent refinements in the reduction of the Solstice Project's survey data, which will be presented in a forthcoming report by Rolf Sinclair on the Solstice Project's survey of the major Chacoan buildings. These changes, unlike in the case of Hungo Pavi, are so slight (from 0.1° to 0.7°) that they do not affect the conclusions.

11. It is of interest that a unique and extensive construction of the Chacoan culture, the Chetro Ketl "field," which is a grid of low walls covering over twice the land area of the largest Chacoan building, appears also to be oriented to the azimuth of the lunar minor standstill. This construction was reported to have an orientation of minus 67° (Loose and Lyons 1977). It should be further noted that the Solstice Project's survey found that the orientation of the perpendicular of Kin Klizhin, a tower kiva located ten

The Primary Architecture of the Chacoan Culture 123

kilometers from Chaco Canyon, is minus 65°, an azimuth also close to
the azimuth of the lunar minor standstill.

12. In certain of the Solstice Project's earlier studies of Chacoan constructions, an emphasis was given to substantiating claims of accurate alignments. The present author believes that this focus sometimes blinded us in
our search for the significance of the orientations and relationships developed by this prehistoric and traditional society, to whom symbolic incorporation of astronomical relationships would have been at least as important
as the expression of optimal accuracy. In addition, in several instances, the
Project's studies have shown that alignments (such as the north orientation
of the Great North Road) are adjusted off of precise astronomical direction in order to incorporate other symbolic relationships (Sofaer, Marshall,
and Sinclair 1989).

13. The preliminary results of the Solstice Project's current study of elevated
horizons that are near certain of the major buildings show that from eight
of these eleven buildings both the rising and setting of astronomical events
occur within 1° to 3° of the building orientations.

14. The preliminary results of the Solstice Project's current study show that no
other of the fourteen buildings is oriented, as Hungo Pavi is, to an astronomical event on only the visible and not the sensible horizon.

15. The Solstice Project finds that the orientation of Wijiji, which is approximately 6.5° off of the cardinal directions, is also close to the orientation
of New Alto, Aztec East, and the east and north walls of the great kiva of
Pueblo Bonito, as well as the orientation of several inter-building relationships. Although there is no obvious astronomical reason for the selection
of this azimuth for building orientations and inter-relationships, its repetition indicates that it may have been significant to the Chacoans. In addition, it was recently observed (J. M. Malville and G. B. Cornucopia, p.c.)
that at Wijiji at winter solstice the sun is seen rising in a crevice on the horizon. The Solstice Project survey shows that the alignment from Wijiji to
this event is also the diagonal of the building. Other instances of astronomical orientation of the diagonals of the buildings are discussed in the
next section of this chapter.

16. Because of the deterioration of one of its short walls, Chetro Ketl has only
one measurable diagonal angle.

17. The Chacoans may have had additional reasons to choose angles of approximately 23° and 36° consistently. It has been suggested that these angles were used by a Mesoamerican culture (Clancy 1989; Harrison 1989).

It is of interest that only at locations close to the latitude of Chaco Canyon (i.e., 36°) do the angles of 23° and 36° correspond with the relationships
of the cardinal directions and the lunar major and minor standstill azimuths. In addition, at the latitude of 36° at solar noon on equinox day, the
shadow of a stick or other vertical object cast on a flat surface forms a
right angle triangle that has the internal angles of 36° and 54°. The correspondence of the internal angles of the major Chacoan buildings with angles apparently favored by a Mesoamerican culture, as well as with the an-

gles evident in the solar and lunar astronomy that occurs only close to the latitude of Chaco, raises intriguing questions. It may be that Chaco Canyon was selected as the place, within the broader cultural region of Mesoamerica, where the relationships of the sun and the earth, and the sun and the moon, could be expressed in geometric relationships that were considered particularly significant.

Of further interest is one archaeologist's recent discussion of the location of Chaco Canyon and Casas Grandes, a postclassic Mesoamerican site, on the same meridian. He suggests that this correspondence may have been an intentional aspect of the locating of Casas Grandes (Lekson 1996). Casas Grandes is 630 kilometers south of Chaco Canyon.

18. The Solstice Project's recent further study of the internal design of the major Chacoan buildings suggests that one of the solar-lunar related angles found in the rectangular buildings, 36°, is also incorporated in the design of three other major buildings (Pueblo Bonito, Peñasco Blanco, and Una Vida) and that Kin Bineola's design (like Aztec I and II) incorporates 36° as well as 24°. In addition, in several of these buildings the solar-lunar geometry is combined with orientational relationships to both the sun and the moon. It also is of interest that three great kivas in Chaco Canyon are organized in geometric patterns of near-perfect squares and circles. This further geometric study of Chacoan architecture will be presented in work that is in preparation by the Solstice Project.

19. The Solstice Project also found that cardinal inter-building lines relate two minor buildings located in the central canyon to each other and to one of the major central buildings involved in the central cardinal patterning. The line between Casa Rinconada, the cardinally oriented great kiva, and New Alto aligns closely with the north-south axis of Casa Rinconada; and New Alto lies directly west of the cardinally oriented Pueblo Alto (Figs. 8.2, 8.3, 8.9, 8.10a, and 8.10b). An internal feature of Casa Rinconada appears to mark the kiva's north-south relationship with New Alto. The south stairway of Casa Rinconada is positioned slightly off the axis of symmetry of the kiva, and this stairway also is offset in the south doorway. The effect of the offset placement of this stairway is that from its center one sees New Alto over the center of the north doorway on a bearing of 1.3°. (While the construction of Casa Rinconada was completed before the construction of New Alto, it is possible that the position of the stairway within the south doorway of Casa Rinconada was modified at the time of New Alto's construction.)

Three long low walls extending from Pueblo Alto (surveyed by the Solstice Project) are also cardinally oriented and they appear to further elaborate the cardinal pattern of the central complex (Windes 1987).

20. The astronomical inter-building bearings shown in Table 8.3 and in Figs. 8.9 and 8.11 are defined as the bearings between two buildings that align (within 3°) with the rising or setting azimuths of the astronomical phenomena associated with one of the two buildings.

The Solstice Project identified the locations of the fourteen major buildings from the coordinates of the 7.5′ topographic survey maps of the United States Geological Survey. The relative locations for certain of the central buildings were confirmed by direct surveying and by the use of existing aerial photography. The bearings of the inter-building lines were taken from estimated centers of the buildings. (The close relationship of two very large buildings, Pueblo Bonito and Chetro Ketl, introduced the only uncertainty. In this case, however, it was observed that each point in Chetro Ketl is due east of each point in Pueblo Bonito.) The relative locations of the buildings could be identified to within 15 meters on the maps. The Solstice Project estimates that its measurements have a typical uncertainty in the bearing of an inter-building line of 0° 12′ at an average separation of 4.7 kilometers for the ten buildings within the canyon, and much less uncertainty in the bearings of inter-building lines extending outside the canyon.

21. The orientation of the perpendicular of Pueblo Pintado is to the azimuth that corresponds with a bearing to Salmon Ruin, eighty-five kilometers distant from Pueblo Pintado; furthermore, the azimuth of the orientation of the perpendicular of Salmon Ruin also corresponds with this bearing. Perhaps these relationships were deliberately developed by the Chacoans to join two outlying major buildings that are oriented to the minor standstill moon on a bearing perpendicular to the azimuth of the minor standstill moon and to draw Salmon Ruin into connection with the central complex of Chaco Canyon, to which Pueblo Pintado is related by lunar minor standstill relationships (as is suggested elsewhere in this chapter).

22. It is of interest that the two other Chacoan constructions, the Chetro Ketl "field" and Kin Klizhin (a tower kiva), that are oriented to the lunar minor standstill are also on the lunar minor standstill inter-building bearings from the central complex to Kin Bineola and to Pueblo Pintado, respectively (see note 11).

23. The Solstice Project's preliminary investigations of several C-shaped, low-walled structures (Windes 1978) and three sets of cairns located in and near Chaco Canyon show that the bearings between these sites are oriented to the lunar major standstill. It is also of interest that several recent findings by others suggest astronomical relationships among sites within prehistoric pueblo building complexes, including one Chacoan building complex, in southwestern Colorado (Malville 1991; Malville and Putnam 1989).

24. Certain of the astronomical inter-building relationships within the canyon, such as that between Una Vida and Peñasco Blanco, appear to correspond roughly with the topography of the canyon. While this correspondence suggests the possibility that the relationship between these buildings could have fallen into lunar alignment by coincidence, it does not explain the other interlocking aspects of these buildings, which suggest an intentional marking of the lunar major relationship between them. The relationships of the central complex to Pueblo Pintado and Kin Bineola on the lunar minor bearings are not affected by the canyon topography, because these

buildings are located beyond the canyon. The lunar minor relationships of the central complex to Hungo Pavi and Wijiji could have been affected in part by accommodation to the canyon topography. This would not discount the possibility that these relationships had lunar significance for the Chacoans.

25. Although the Solstice Project cannot be certain that all of the astronomical inter-building bearings that are shown in Table 8.3 and Fig. 8.11 were intentionally developed by the Chacoans, it seems important at this stage in our study to present all the inter-building bearings that meet the criterion described above (see note 20).

One astronomical inter-building bearing which has not been discussed in the text deserves particular note. Aztec, eighty-six kilometers north of Pueblo Bonito, is located on a bearing from the central complex of Chaco that could have been regarded by the Chacoans as a continuation of the north-south axis of the central buildings and their inter-building relationships (Table 8.3 and Fig. 8.11). Certain recent analysis suggests that the north-south bearing between Chaco and Aztec had particular significance to the Chacoans. Aztec, itself a massive architectural complex, is regarded as an important late center of the Chacoan culture. An architectural study shows that Aztec appears to be "modeled on standards fixed in Pueblo Bonito" (Stein and McKenna 1988). An author of this latter study further notes that the core activity of the Chacoan culture moved in the late A.D. 1100s from Chaco Canyon to Aztec (Fowler and Stein 1992), and that this center maintained an active relationship with the canyon through the A.D. 1100s and 1200s (Stein 1996 p.c.). Furthermore, a recent study suggests that a north-south alignment between Chaco Canyon and Casas Grandes (a Mesoamerican site 630 kilometers south of Chaco), which was developed in the A.D. 1300s, extended the earlier north-south axis from Aztec through Chaco (Lekson 1996).

26. Preliminary results of the Project's current study of elevated horizons in the views to astronomy from certain major buildings suggest that the orientations of most of the inter-building bearings to astronomical events on the sensible horizon (as shown in Table 8.3) are within 3° of the same astronomical events on the visible horizon. Exceptions to this generality appear to be the inter-building bearings from Pueblo del Arroyo and Peñasco Blanco to Kin Bineola, from Kin Kletso to Pueblo Alto, and from Chetro Ketl to Kin Kletso.

27. In respect to the techniques used for orienting and inter-relating buildings on astronomical bearings, the Solstice Project's experiments have shown that the cardinal directions can be determined with shadow and light to within one quarter of a degree (Solstice Project, pre-published report 1988; see also Williamson 1984:144). Recordings of the shadows cast by a vertical object onto a flat surface during several hours of the sun's midday passage indicate the cardinal directions. If this were done at a site with flat horizons toward the lunar standstills, at the time of the lunar standstills on that same surface where the cardinal directions would be recorded, the azi-

muths of the rising and setting standstill moons could also be recorded. It is possible that the Chacoan architects and planners used such a recording of the solar-lunar azimuths for incorporating lunar orientations in their buildings and in the inter-relationships of their buildings, instead of waiting for the recurrence of the lunar events on the local horizons. The wait for the reccurence of the lunar major standstill would be 18 to 19 years. The Solstice Project has also shown that inter-relating the buildings which are not inter-visible could have been done with quite simple inter-site surveying techniques.

28.   See note 4.

29.   It has recently been suggested that the Mayans' interest in the lunar eclipse cycle may have involved knowledge of the lunar standstill cycle (Dearborn 1992). Floyd Lounsbury expressed a similar opinion a number of years ago (1982 p.c.).

30.   J. M. Malville and W. J. Judge speculate on Chaco as a center for lunar eclipse prediction (Malville and Judge 1993), and Malville and N.J. Malville suggest that ceremonial pilgrimage to Chaco Canyon was scheduled to the solar and lunar cycles (Malville and Malville 1995).

31.   For ethnographic reports on the cosmology of the historic Pueblo Indians, see Sofaer, Marshall, and Sinclair (1989); Sofaer and Sinclair (1987); Sofaer, Sinclair, and Doggett (1982); Sofaer, Zinser, and Sinclair (1979); and Williamson (1984).

32.   M. C. Stevenson (1894:143): "The moon is father to the dead as the sun is father to the living."

33.   Fred Eggan's studies of the Hopi "roads" suggested to him several parallels with the Chacoans' use of roads. Eggan noted that at Hopi the spirits of the dead emerge from the world below and travel on symbolic roads to visit with the living, and that the Great North Road of Chaco appears to have been built to join the ceremonial center symbolically with the direction north and with the world below (Eggan 1990 p.c.).

References

Ahlstrom, Richard Van Ness 1985. "Interpretation of Archeological Tree-Ring Dates." Ph.D. dissertation, University of Arizona, Tucson.

Aveni, Anthony F. 1980. *Skywatchers of Ancient Mexico.* University of Texas Press, Austin.

Broda, Johanna 1982. "Astronomy, 'Cosmovision,' and Ideology in Prehispanic Mesoamerica." In *Ethnoastronomy and Archaeoastronomy in the American Tropics,* ed. Anthony F. Aveni and Gary Urton, pp. 81–110. Annals of the New York Academy of Sciences.

———. 1994. "Archaeoastronomical Knowledge, Calandrics, and Sacred Geography in Ancient Mesoamerica." In *Astronomies and Culture,* ed. C. Ruggles and N. Saunders. University Press of Colorado, Niwot.

Clancy, Flora S. 1989. "Spatial Geometry and Logic in the Ancient Mayan Mind:

Monuments." In *Seventh Palenque Round Table 1989*, The Palenque Round Table Series, Vol. 9, ed. Merle Greene, pp. 237–242.

Cordell, Linda S. 1984. *Prehistory of the Southwest*. Academic Press, Orlando, Fla.

Crown, Patricia L., and W. James Judge, Jr. 1991. "Synthesis and Conclusions." In *Chaco and Hohokam: Prehistoric Regional Systems in the American Southwest*, ed. Patricia L. Crown and W. James Judge, Jr. pp. 293–308. School of American Research Press, Santa Fe.

Dearborn, David D. 1992. "To the Limits." In *Archaeoastronomy and Ethnoastronomy News, The Quarterly Bulletin of the Center for Archaeoastronomy* 3:1, 4.

Ford, Dabney. 1993. "The Spadefoot Toad Site: Investigations at 29SJ 629."In *Marcia's Rincon and the Fajada Gap Pueblo II Community, Chaco Canyon, New Mexico*, Vol. I, ed. Thomas C. Windes, Appendix H. Reports of the Chaco Center, No. 12.

Fowler, Andrew P., and John Stein. 1992. "The Anasazi Great House in Time, Space, and Paradigm." In *Anasazi Regional Organization and the Chaco System*, ed. David E. Doyel. Maxwell Museum of Anthropology, Anthropological Papers No. 5. University of New Mexico, Albuquerque.

Fritz, John M. 1978. "Paleopsychology Today: Ideational Systems and Human Adaptation in Prehistory." In *Social Archeology, Beyond Subsistence and Dating*, ed. Charles L. Redman et al. Academic Press, New York.

Harrison, Peter D. 1989. "Spatial Geometry and Logic in the Ancient Mayan Mind: Architecture." In *Seventh Palenque Round Table 1989*, The Palenque Round Table Series, Vol. 9, ed. Merle Green, pp. 243–252.

Hawkins, Gerald S. 1973. *Beyond Stonehenge*. Harper and Row, New York.

Judge, W. James, Jr. 1989. "Chaco Canyon—San Juan Basin." In *Dynamics of Southwest Prehistory*, ed. Linda S. Cordell and George J. Gumerman, pp. 209-262. Smithsonian Institution Press, Washington, D.C.

Judge, W. James, Jr. 1984. "New Light on Chaco Canyon." In *New Light on Chaco Canyon*, ed. David G. Noble, pp. 1–12. School of American Research, Santa Fe.

Kincaid, Chris, ed. 1983. *Chaco Roads Project Phase I: A Reappraisal of Prehistoric Roads in the San Juan Basin*. Bureau of Land Management, Albuquerque.

Lekson, Stephen H. 1984. *Great Pueblo Architecture of Chaco Canyon*. National Park Service, Albuquerque.

———. 1991. "Settlement Patterns and the Chacoan Region." In *Chaco and Hohokam: Prehistoric Regional Systems in the American Southwest*, ed. P. L. Crown and W. J. Judge, pp. 31–56. School of American Research Press, Santa Fe.

———. 1996. "Chaco and Casas." Paper presented at the 61st Annual Meeting of the Society of American Archeology.

Lekson, Stephen H., Thomas C. Windes, John R. Stein, and W. James Judge, Jr. 1988. "The Chaco Canyon Community." *Scientific American* (July 1988):100-109.

Loose, Richard W., and Thomas R. Lyons. 1977. In *Remote Sensing Experiments in Cultural Resource Studies*, ed. Thomas R. Lyons, pp. 133–153. Reports of the Chaco Center No. 1, National Park Service, Washington, D.C.

Malville, J. McKim. 1993. In *Proceedings of the Anasazi Symposium, 1991*, eds. Art

Hutchinson and Jack E. Smith, pp. 155–66. Mesa Verde Museum Association.

Malville, J. McKim, Frank W. Eddy, and Carol Ambruster. 1991. "Moonrise at Chimney Rock." In *Archeoastronomy* (Supplement to the *Journal for the History of Astronomy*), No. 1b, S34–S50.

Malville, J. McKim, and W. James Judge, Jr. 1993. "The Uses of Esoteric Astronomical Knowledge in the Chaco Regional System." Paper presented at the Fourth Oxford International Conference on Archaeoastronomy (1993). Stara, Zagora, Bulgaria. In press.

Malville, J. McKim, and Nancy J. Malville. 1995. "Pilgrimage and Astronomy at Chaco Canyon, New Mexico." Paper presented at the National Seminar on Pilgrimage, Tourism, and Conservation of Cultural Heritage, Allahabad, India, January 21–23, 1995.

Malville, J. McKim, and Claudia Putnam. 1989. *Prehistoric Astronomy in the Southwest.* Johnson Books, Boulder.

Marshall, Michael P. 1997. "The Chacoan Roads—A Cosmological Interpretation." In *Anasazi Architecture and American Design,* ed. Baker H. Morrow and V. B. Price, University of New Mexico Press, Albuquerque.

Marshall, Michael P., and David E. Doyel. 1981. "An Interim Report on Bis sa'ni Pueblo, with Notes on the Chacoan Regional System." Manuscript on file, Navajo Nation Cultural Resource Management Program, Window Rock, Ariz.

Marshall, Michael P., John R. Stein, Richard W. Loose, and Judith E. Novotny. 1979. *Anasazi Communities of the San Juan Basin.* Public Service Company of New Mexico, Albuquerque.

McCluskey, Stephen C. 1977. "The Astronomy of the Hopi Indians." *Journal for the History of Astronomy* 8:174–95.

Neitzel, Jill 1989. "The Chacoan Regional System: Interpreting the Evidence for Sociopolitical Complexity." In *The Sociopolitical Structure of Prehistoric Southwestern Societies,* ed. Steadman Upham, Kent G. Lightfoot, and Roberta A. Jewett, pp. 509–556. Westview Press, Boulder, Colo.

Ortiz, Alfonso. 1982. In the film *The Sun Dagger.* Solstice Project.

Powers, Robert P., William B. Gillespie, and Stephen H. Lekson. 1983. *The Outlier Survey: A Regional View of Settlement in the San Juan Basin.* National Park Service, Albuquerque.

Reyman, Jonathan E. 1976. "Astronomy, Architecture, and Adaptation at Pueblo Bonito." *Science* 193:957–962.

Roney, John R. 1992. "Prehistoric Roads and Regional Integration in the Chacoan System." In *Anasazi Regional Organization and the Chaco System,* ed. David E. Doyel. Maxwell Museum of Anthropology, Anthropological Papers No. 5. University of New Mexico, Albuquerque.

Sebastian, Lynne. 1991. "Sociopolitical Complexity and the Chaco System." In *Chaco and Hohokam: Prehistoric Regional Systems in the American Southwest,* ed. Patricia L. Crown and W. James Judge, Jr., pp. 107–134. School of American Research Press, Santa Fe.

———. 1992. "Chaco Canyon and the Anasazi Southwest: Changing Views of Sociopolitical Organization." In *Anasazi Regional Organization and the Chaco System,* ed. David E. Doyel. Maxwell Museum of Anthropology, Anthropological Papers No. 5. University of New Mexico, Albuquerque.

Sinclair, Rolf M., and Anna Sofaer. 1993. "Limits on the Accuracy of Naked-Eye Locations of Astronomical Events." In *Archaeoastronomy in the 1990s,* ed. Clive Ruggles. Group D Publications, Ltd., Loughborough, U. K.

Sinclair, Rolf M., Anna Sofaer, John J. McCann, and John J. McCann, Jr. 1987. "Marking of Lunar Major Standstill at the Three-Slab Site on Fajada Butte." In *Bulletin of the American Astronomical Society,* 19:1043.

Sofaer, Anna. 1994. "Chacoan Architecture: A Solar-Lunar Geometry." In *Time and Astronomy at the Meeting of Two Worlds,* ed. Stanislaw Iwaniszewski et al. Warsaw University, Warsaw. Poland.

———. "Pueblo Bonito Petroglyph on Fajada Butte: Solar Aspects." In *Celestial Seasonings: Connotations of Rock Art, Papers of the 1994 International Rock Art Congress,* ed. E. C. Krupp. In press.

Sofaer, Anna, Michael P. Marshall, and Rolf M. Sinclair. 1989. "The Great North Road: A Cosmographic Expression of the Chaco Culture of New Mexico." In *World Archaeoastronomy,* ed. A. F. Aveni, pp. 365–76. Cambridge University Press, Cambridge, U. K.

Sofaer, Anna, and Rolf M. Sinclair. 1989. "An Interpretation of a Unique Petroglyph in Chaco Canyon, New Mexico." In *World Archaeoastronomy,* ed. Anthony F. Aveni. Cambridge University Press, Cambridge, U. K.

———. 1987. "Astronomical Markings at Three Sites on Fajada Butte." In *Astronomy and Ceremony in the Prehistoric Southwest,* ed. John Carlson and W. James Judge, pp. 43–70. Maxwell Museum of Anthropology, Albuquerque.

Sofaer, Anna, Rolf M. Sinclair, and LeRoy Doggett. 1982. "Lunar Markings on Fajada Butte, Chaco Canyon, New Mexico." In *Archaeoastronomy in the New World,* ed. Anthony F. Aveni, pp. 169–181. Cambridge University Press, Cambridge, U. K.

Sofaer, Anna, Rolf M. Sinclair, and Joey B. Donahue. 1991. "Solar and Lunar Orientations of the Major Architecture of the Chaco Culture of New Mexico." In *Colloquio Internazionale Archeologia e Astronomia,* ed. G. Romano and G. Traversari. Rivista di Archaeologia, Supplementi 9, ed. Giorgio Bretschneider, Rome, Italy.

Sofaer Anna, Rolf M. Sinclair, and Reid Williamson. 1987. "A Regional Pattern in the Architecture of the Chaco Culture of New Mexico and its Astronomical Implications." In *Bulletin of the American Astronomical Society,* 19:1044.

Sofaer, Anna, Volker Zinser, and Rolf M. Sinclair. 1979. "A Unique Solar Marking Construct." *Science* 206:283–291.

Stein, John R. 1989. "The Chaco Roads—Clues to an Ancient Riddle?" *El Palacio* 94:4–16.

Stein, John R., and Stephen H. Lekson. 1992. "Anasazi Ritual Landscapes." In *Anasazi Regional Organization and the Chaco System,* ed. David E. Doyel. Maxwell Museum of Anthropology, Anthropological Papers No. 5. University of New Mexico, Albuquerque.

Stein, John R., and Peter J. McKenna. 1988. *An Archaeological Reconnaissance of a*

Late Bonito Phase Occupation near Aztec Ruins National Monument. National Park Service, Southwest Cultural Resource Center, Santa Fe.

Stein, John R., Judith E. Suiter, and Dabney Ford. 1997. "High Noon in Old Bonito: Sun, Shadow, and the Geometry of the Chaco Complex." In *Anasazi Architecture and American Design*, ed. Baker H. Morrow and V. B. Price. University of New Mexico Press, Albuquerque.

Stevenson, Mathilda Coxe. 1894. The Sia 11th Annual Report of the Bureau of Ethnology. Smithsonian Institution, Washington, D.C.

Tedlock, Barbara. 1983. "Zuni Sacred Theater." *American Indian Quarterly* 7:93–109.

Toll, Henry Walcott. 1991. "Material Distributions and Exchange in the Chaco System." In *Chaco and Hohokam: Prehistoric Regional Systems in the American Southwest,* ed. Patricia L. Crown and W. James Judge, Jr. pp. 77–108. School of American Research Press, Santa Fe.

Vivian, R. Gwinn 1990. *The Chacoan Prehistory of the San Juan Basin.* Academic Press, San Diego.

Williamson, Ray A. 1984. *Living the Sky.* Houghton Mifflin, Boston.

Williamson, Ray A., Howard J. Fisher, and Donnel O'Flynn. 1977. "Anasazi Solar Observatories." In *Native American Astronomy*, ed. Anthony F. Aveni, pp. 203–218. University of Texas Press, Austin.

Williamson, Ray A., Howard J. Fisher, Abigail F. Williamson, and Clarion Cochran. 1975. "The Astronomical Record in Chaco Canyon, New Mexico." In *Archaeoastronomy in Pre-Columbian America*, ed. Anthony F. Aveni, pp. 33-43. University of Texas Press, Austin.

Windes, Thomas C. 1978. *Stone Circles of Chaco Canyon, Northwestern New Mexico.* National Park Service, Albuquerque.

———. 1987. *Investigations at the Pueblo Alto Complex, Chaco Canyon, New Mexico, 1975–1979.* Vol. 1, *Summary of Test and Excavations at the Pueblo Alto Community.* Publications in Archeology 18F. National Park Service, Santa Fe.

Zeilik, Michael 1984. "Summer Solstice at Casa Rinconada: Calendar, Hierophany, or Nothing?" *Archaeoastronomy* 7:76–81.

9 High Noon in Old Bonito

Sun, Shadow, and the Geometry of the Chaco Complex

John R. Stein, Judith E. Suiter, and Dabney Ford

In this lively and surprising essay, archaeologists John Stein, Judith Suiter, and Dabney Ford widen our perspectives on Chaco Canyon's Pueblo Bonito, arguably the most famous prehistoric structure in North America. The authors contend that Pueblo Bonito's overall form arose from concerns other than physical or aesthetic function.

During the excavations of Pueblo Bonito in the 1920s, the stump of a "great pine tree" was unearthed in a trench near the south wall of the west plaza (Fig. 9.1). A widely held assumption at the time was that a pine forest had once existed in Chaco Canyon and that this forest had been ruthlessly stripped to supply the hundreds of thousands of logs needed to build the "great houses" of the Canyon Complex. The tree in the west plaza of Pueblo Bonito figures prominently in artists' reconstructions of the period, but as an environmental object lesson and not as architecture (Fig. 9.2). Temporarily sheltered behind the walls of Pueblo Bonito, this lone survivor of the Chaco forest anticipates doom as it overlooks a bleak and desiccated landscape.

We now know that a forest capable of supplying the species, numbers, and uniformly dimensioned timbers used in the construction of the "great houses" had not existed in Chaco Canyon for many thousands of years. In the mid ninth century A.D., when the first blocks were placed in Pueblo Bonito, the Chaco region was primarily a pinyon-juniper woodland supporting only isolated stands of ponderosa pine (Bentancourt et al. 1986). Local trees were certainly harvested; however, many would have been passed over in favor of the superior and abundant timber available in the upland forests that border the San Juan Basin.

If the Pueblo Bonito pine was a unique tree in Chaco Canyon, perhaps it was a factor in the selection of the site for that important building. A clue to the significance of the tree lies in the cardinal orientation of

Fig. 9.1. The stump of the great pine from Judd (1954:plate 2)

Pueblo Bonito (see Sofaer et al. 1990 and Sofaer essay, this volume). Such an orientation is "solar" in the sense that true north-south always coincides with the azimuth of the sun at midday. Similarly, east-west coincides with the azimuth of the rising or setting sun at mid-year, the vernal and autumnal equinox. To establish these orientations would have required a gnomon, and the great pine would have naturally served this purpose.

Fig. 9.2. Reproductions of Pueblo Bonito produced in 1926 for the National Geographic Society by Dr. Kenneth J. Conant of Harvard's School of Architecture. Fig. 9.2(A) is reproduced in Lister and Lister (1981:figure 34);

The configuration of Pueblo Bonito as we know it results from a series of epic construction events over the course of approximately three hundred years beginning in the mid ninth and ending in the mid twelfth century A.D.(Lekson 1984:109–44; Windes and Ford 1996)(Fig. 9.3). From the evidence of the tree-ring record, the great pine tree would have been over a century old when the first construction event was initiated (see description for Fig. 9.1). A common perception of Pueblo Bonito excludes much of its architecture (Judd 1964; Lekson 1984; Stein and Lekson 1992). Fig. 9.4 illustrates the familiar ground plan of the building but includes the platform mounds and the enigmatic foundation complex.

A question often pondered by archaeologists regards the purpose of the earliest construction at Pueblo Bonito: was Old Bonito always a "great house" or was it a common structure that grew to great house proportions? This is a very important question because it tacitly recognizes fundamentally different design processes at work in the Canyon (see Stein and Lekson 1992) and wonders aloud about the circumstances and criteria for the siting of Old Bonito. From the architecture of the structure we draw two conclusions: one, that the scale and configuration of Pueblo Bonito result from planned large-scale construction events and not a

High Noon in Old Bonito 135

Fig. 9.2(B) is adapted from Judd (1964:plate 1).

gradual accretion of individual households; and two, that the axes of orientation, symmetry, basic internal geometry, and proportional relationships that dictate the form of the final structure are clearly established in the earliest section of the building.

Fig. 9.5 illustrates the geometrical relationship between the earliest and latest construction at Pueblo Bonito, showing the common north-south axis of symmetry, the articulation with the great pine tree, and the "wedges" of architecture formed within a configuration of opposing triangles. A common misconception, and an idea that has been carried forward from the earliest to the most recent reconstructions of this building, is that the oldest section of Pueblo Bonito was ultimately buried beneath a mass of late construction. In Fig. 9.6, stripping away the nonexistent massing above the level of the original platform illustrates the continuity of this surface down the elevated causeway that formalizes the structure's old north-south axis and onto the late platform that contains great kiva "A." It is worth reminding ourselves that architecture is three dimen-

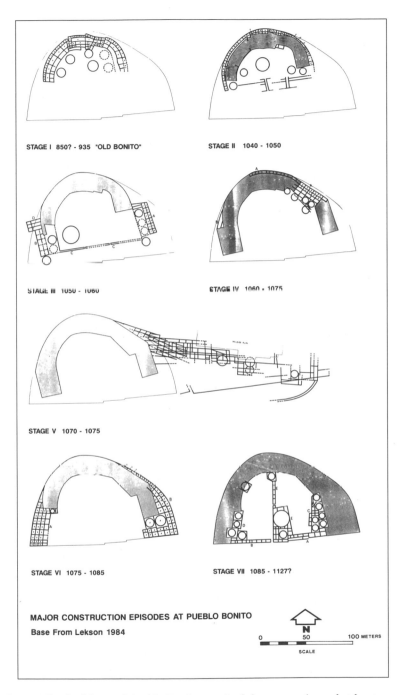

Fig. 9.3. The final form of Pueblo Bonito required three centuries and at least seven major construction episodes. Note the wedge shape of the earliest construction. From Lekson (1984:figure 4.20, pp 114–117)

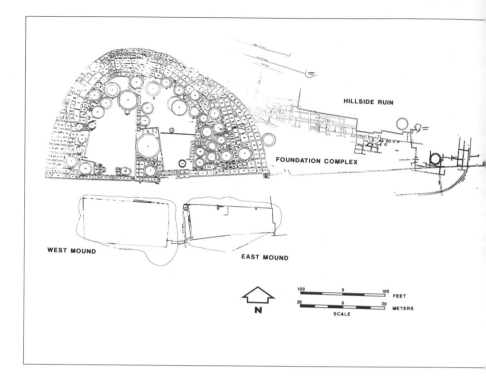

Fig. 9.4. Composite plan view of Pueblo Bonito from Judd (1964, figs. 2, 11, and 23) showing the architecture of the mounds and the foundation complex

sional, and that we should expect to find that the plan and elevation of a structure are determined by a common set of rules. Archaeological as well as architectural evidence indicate that the old platform was maintained and used throughout the life of the building. Windes and Ford (1992:77) found that "some of the latest repair/remodeling dates came from around this (earliest) core, which served as a pivotal point for subsequent construction." The cells beneath the surface of the platform contained the ritual and high-status materials that were apparently stored so as to be accessible. Among these materials was the cache of cylinder jars, with examples of vessels dating from the early, middle, and late construction periods. The reversed geometrical relationship of the early and late sections of Pueblo Bonito suggest the completion of a calendrical cycle, and the closure or ritual retirement of the structure (see Fowler and Stein [1992] for a discussion of similar phenomena in community based ritual landscapes).

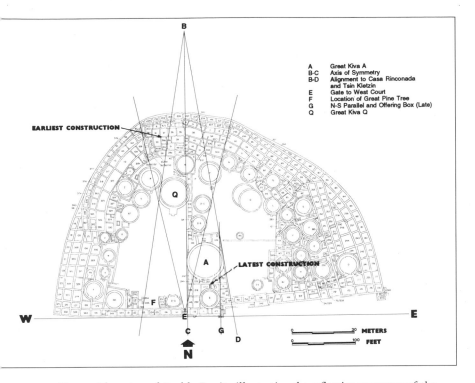

Fig. 9.5. Plan view of Pueblo Bonito illustrating the reflective geometry of the
opening and closing construction episodes at Pueblo Bonito. Note the location
of the ponderosa pine and the rotated position of the early (Kiva Q) and
late (Kiva A) great kivas along the axis of symmetry.

The internal structure of Pueblo Bonito incorporates the geometries
of a much larger composition. Thus, if the scale of one's analytical perspective is limited to this one building, there may be no apparent meaning
in certain angles, alignments, or position of architectural elements. Figs.
9.7–9.9 illustrate some of the more obvious geometrical and proportional
relationships between the major architectural elements of the core of the
canyon development, an area of approximately one square mile that includes Pueblo Bonito, Chetro Ketl, Pueblo del Arroyo, and Kin Kletso.
Note that many significant points of the geometry of the core are not architecturally acknowledged, at least not with masonry and mortar. Although it remains to be investigated, we speculate that during the time
of Pueblo Bonito, a dominant architectural element of the core may have
been an elaborate gridwork of high poles.

High Noon in Old Bonito 139

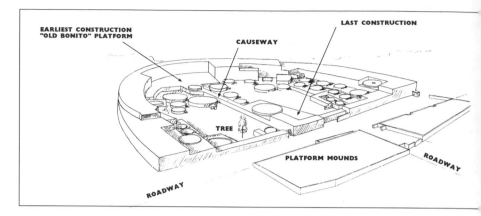

Fig. 9.6. Perspective reconstruction of Pueblo Bonito modified
from Townsend (1986)

Expanding our view from the core area to include the principal "great houses" of the Canyon Complex (Fig. 9.10), we find the earliest structures of the complex, Peñasco Blanco, Pueblo Bonito, and Una Vida, aligned on the axis of the lunar major (see also Sofaer essay this volume). This axis is sufficiently coincident with the trend of the canyon to allow Peñasco Blanco, elevated on the south rim, and Una Vida, located in the canyon floor at the base of the north cliff, to be intervisible by way of a narrow window framed by the canyon walls. These two structures address one another even though they are separated by a distance of six miles. As the Canyon Complex evolved, later development in the core area continued to emphasize the solar/cardinal orientation established at Old Bonito; however, as can be seen from the juxtaposition of Pueblo Bonito and Pueblo del Arroyo, there is also a clear intent to accommodate the Peñasco Blanco-Una Vida axis. A principal north-south axis is established between Pueblo Alto, located on the crest of the north canyon rim and Tsin Kletzin, located on the crest of South Mesa (Fritz 1978). These buildings also address one another and are intervisible at a distance of slightly over two miles. The alignment between Pueblo Alto and Tsin Kletzin marks the mid-point between Peñasco Blanco and Una Vida as well as the mid-point between Pueblo Bonito and Chetro Ketl. The dramatic interplay between cosmic and terrestrial topography is a critical factor in the configuration of the Chaco Complex but it is an aspect of design that is difficult to measure and describe.

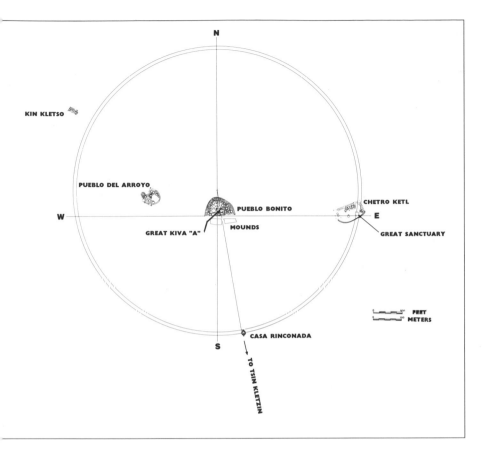

Figs. 9.7–9.9. Design relationship of the principal architectural elements
of the core of the Chaco Complex

Visualizing Pueblo Bonito as a monumental sundial is a point of departure for reexamining its architecture and, by extension, the purpose
of the Chaco Complex. However, it is unlikely that a structure such as
Pueblo Bonito would have functioned to simply mark the passage of
time. While the solar component of Pueblo Bonito is a dominant organizing theme, it is but one of many layers of geometrical and architectural relationships not directly related to the sun cycle. The manifestation
of these "other" geometries is analogous to "dial furniture" (Waugh
1973:122–49). The massive envelope and liberal use of exotic materials at
Pueblo Bonito indicate "temple architecture" (Stein and Lekson 1992);

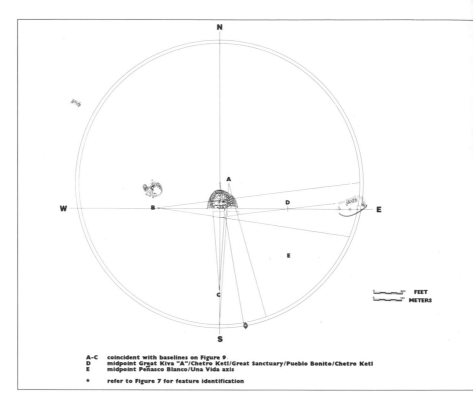

Fig. 9.8

thus, we expect that the layers of esoteric meaning embedded in the configuration and the finish and material content of the internal structure will derive from the historical as well as the ideational realm.

If Pueblo Bonito was not simply a sundial then the great pine tree was not simply a gnomon; attached to such a tree would have been the symbolism of the "tree of life" or "world tree" as the cosmic vertical axis (axis mundi) that unites the lower, middle, and upper worlds in the spatial dimension as well as the past, present, and future in the temporal dimension (Cook 1988: 9–12, Reyman 1971:103, 155, Schele and Freidel: 66–77). It is apt that the world tree should be viewed as the center of the universe, for it is relative to this axis that sacred time, the heavenly rhythm reflected by the play of light and shadow, becomes the geometry and symmetry of sacred space.

From the schematic diagram (Fig. 9.10) of the Chaco Complex, we find the origin/articulation of the principal solar and lunar axes to be located

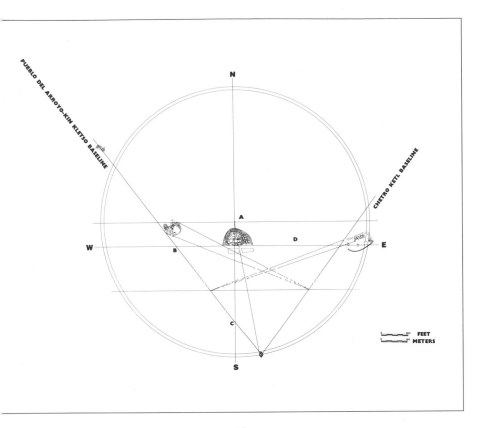

Fig. 9.9

at Pueblo Bonito in the vicinity of the great pine tree. We suggest that the principal structures of the Chaco Complex functioned as calendrical machinery with a geomantic purpose, and that Pueblo Bonito, located in the center of this device, functioned as the solar balance cogwheel or escapement where the individual strands of the celestial and historical cycles were woven into an intricate fabric of ritual time and sacred space.

Acknowledgments

This paper would not have been possible without the accurate placement of the principal great houses in Chaco Canyon. The base for our reconstruction was produced by Scott Andrae of Scott Andrae Surveying Inc. of La Plata, New Mexico. We thank Tom Windes and Dr. Jeff

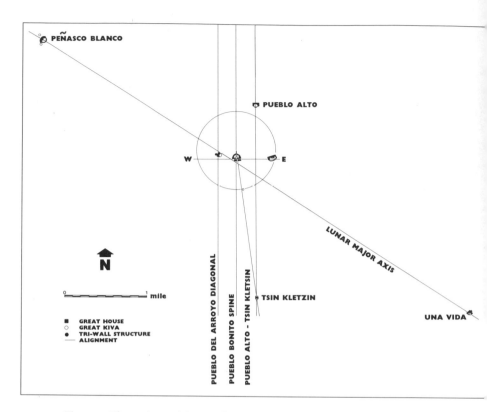

Fig. 9.10. The major architectural components of the Chaco Complex.

Dean for taking the time to reexamine JPB-99 and Dick Duman and J. R. Gomolak for their comments on the earliest draft of this paper. Finally, the ideas expressed herein expand only slightly on the work of Anna Sofaer, whose tenacious dedication has made the reexamination of the monuments of Chaco both possible and credible.

Notes to Figures

Fig. 9.1. The specimen was cataloged by the Laboratory of Tree-Ring Research as JPB (Judd Pueblo Bonito) No. 99 (see Judd 1954:plate 2). Bannister (1964:181) records the dating of JPB-99 as A.D. +/-983+vv (vv indicates that an undetermined number of rings beyond A.D. 983 are missing). The specimen was recently reexamined by Dr. Jeffrey Dean, director of the Laboratory of Tree-Ring Research and Tom Windes, archaeologist for the National Park Service. Windes (1994 p.c.) summarized their findings: the tree was indeed a ponderosa pine; the diameter at the base of the trunk was an estimated 52cm; forty to seventy rings are estimated to be missing. The tree began its life in the early A.D. 700s and no later than A.D. 732; thus, it was approximately a century old when the first stones were laid in Pueblo Bonito. A date of A.D. 981+vv was derived from the actual surviving rings (because of the poor condition of the specimen, outer rings may have been lost since the first dating). Taking into account the estimated number of missing rings, Dean and Windes concluded that the tree expired between A.D. 1020 and 1050. According to Judd (1924), the tree "obviously had grown" at the location where it was discovered. The rings of JPB-99 indicate that the tree was stressed, as would be expected if the tree were growing in the floor of Chaco Canyon.

Fig. 9.2. Based on detailed surveys conducted for the National Geographic Society by Oscar B. Walsh in 1925 and 1926, Conant's drawings accurately include details such as the location of the ponderosa pine tree. However, Conant's massing is more fanciful and does not always agree with the information presented in cross sections of the structure. Interestingly, the location of the stump was omitted from final published versions of the plan views.

Fig. 9.6. The Townsend reconstruction was selected for this illustration because it includes the platform mounds. Both the Conant and Townsend reconstructions err in placing the highest structural mass upon the footprint of the oldest section of Pueblo Bonito. Here we have removed this mass to the level of the surface of the early platform. This platform was maintained throughout the use life of Pueblo Bonito and apparently was "concealed" by high curtain walls but never buried under later construction. Note how this early surface is extended across the causeway to the platform of Great Kiva "A" and ultimately to the paved surfaces of the platform mounds.

Fig. 9.7. Begin by projecting the north-south axis of Pueblo Bonito and the axis of the east wall of the Great Kiva "A" platform to a point of intersection at the base of the cliff, approximately forty meters north of the back wall of Pueblo Bonito. Looking to the south, the alignment is acknowledged by a notch in the retaining wall of the west mound. At approximately one half mile distant from the intersection with the north-south axis behind Pueblo Bonito, the alignment intersects the western edge of Casa Rinconada. The absolute center of the alignment between Una Vida and Peñasco Blanco is coincident with the absolute center of the distance between Pueblo Bonito and Chetro Ketl, which, if projected north-south will describe the central north-south axis of Pueblo Alto and Tsin Kletzin (see Fig. 9.8). Projecting the alignment of the east wall of the housing of Great Kiva "A" at Pueblo Bonito, beyond Casa Rinconada, it will intersect with the central north-south axis at Tsin Kletzin. From the orientation of the west wall of the east mound, we infer a formalized avenue thirteen meters (forty-three feet) in width passing between the mounds and connecting Pueblo Bonito with Casa Rinconada. Note that despite the obvious and purposeful visual as well as formalized architectural reference to Casa Rinconada, there is no gate into the east plaza of Pueblo Bonito.

Fig. 9.8. Casa Rinconada is located 769 meters (2,500 feet) from the point of intersection of the north-south axis of Pueblo Bonito and the alignment of the east housing wall of Great Kiva "A". We have drawn a circle with this radius (approximately one mile in diameter) and have discovered that the Great Sanctuary at Chetro Ketl is located on this arc at the point where it intersects the east-west alignment projected from the front wall of the West Court of Pueblo Bonito. Thus we find that Great Kiva "A" at Pueblo Bonito, Casa Rinconada, and the Great Sanctuary at Chetro Ketl may be articulated by alignment and distance relationships. The north wall of the housing of Great Kiva "A" is an artifact of the alignment of the front (south) wall of the middle eleventh century (stage II) structure of Pueblo Bonito. Extending this alignment to the point where it intersects with the east-west base line creates a triangle similar in proportion to the Pueblo Bonito north-south axis-Casa Rinconada triangle. These triangles lie at right angles and have the Great Kiva "A" platform in common.

Many odd angles and alignments occur in the internal structure of Pueblo Bonito. Projecting some of the more obvious alignments, we find that they converge on points on a cardinal grid or address the center point of the Chaco Complex.

Fig. 9.9. The importance of the orientation of the axis of a great house measured diagonally from corner to corner has been demonstrated by Sofaer et. al. (1990) and Sofaer (this volume). In this illustration, we project the diagonal of Kin Kletso to the central hearth of Casa Rinconada. We reference this alignment as the "Pueblo del Arroyo Base Line" because of its articulation with the south-west corner of that structure. The point where the base line crosses the east-west line projected from the front (south) wall of the west plaza at Pueblo Bonito is coincident with the intersection of the alignment projecting the north wall of the Great Kiva "A" platform.

The "Chetro Ketl Base Line" is a line drawn from the central hearth of Casa Rinconada to the northwest corner of Chetro Ketl. Projecting a north-south axis through the center of Casa Rinconada (not drawn) creates two identical triangles, thus the Chetro Ketl alignment is a mirror image of the Pueblo del Arroyo-Kin Kletso alignment. Many interesting things begin to happen within the geometry bounded by the base lines. The base of the triangle formed by projecting the north and south walls of the Great Kiva "A" platform converges with the Chetro Ketl base line at a point coincident with the intersection with the east-west line passing through the point of origin for the north-south Bonito axis—Casa Rinconada triangle. Projected west, this same alignment addresses the southeast corner of Pueblo del Arroyo, forms the diagonal of the north section of that structure, and intersects the Pueblo del Arroyo base line so as to create an equilateral triangle with the Pueblo del Arroyo tri-wall at its center.

As geometrically pure as the great houses may appear, the alignment of the exterior walls may be oriented slightly askew to accommodate a larger hidden geometry or, more obviously, to address other architectural pieces of the overall composition. Projecting the alignment of the north outside wall of Pueblo del Arroyo, we find that it addresses the SW corner of Pueblo Bonito and defines the diagonal of the west mound. Not shown is the axis between Una Vida and Peñasco Blanco that passes between Pueblo Bonito and Pueblo del Arroyo. Projecting the alignments of the outside walls of Chetro Ketl and Pueblo del Arroyo, we find that they converge on the base lines on a common east-west axis.

Fig. 9.10. Peñasco Blanco, Una Vida, and Pueblo Bonito, structures with construction histories beginning in the ninth century A.D., are located upon and oriented to the axis of the lunar major. The juxtaposition of Pueblo Bonito and Pueblo Del Arroyo creates a narrow window that accommodates this axis. Pueblo Bonito lies slightly northwest of the halfway point between Peñasco Blanco and Una Vida. The halfway point is marked by the intersection with the north-south line connecting Pueblo Alto with Tsin Kletzin. The midpoint between Pueblo Bonito and Chetro Ketl is where this line intersects the east-west line extended from the south wall of the west plaza at Pueblo Bonito. We have shown the one mile diameter circle shown on Fig. 9.7–9.9 as a means of comparing the scale of the Canyon Complex with that of the core development.

References

Bannister, Bryant 1964. "Tree-Ring Dating of the Archaeological Sites in the Chaco Canyon Region." In *New Mexico. Southwest Monuments Association Technical Series*, Vol.6, Part 2.

Betancourt, Julio, Jeffery S. Dean, and Herbert M. Hull 1986. "Prehistoric Long-Distance Transport of Construction Beams, Chaco Canyon, New Mexico," *American Antiquity* 51(2):370–375.

Cook, Roger 1974. *The Tree of Life; Image for the Cosmos.* Thames and Hudson, New York.

Fowler, Andrew P. and John R. Stein 1992. "The Anasazi Great House in Space, Time, and Paradigm." In *Anasazi Regional Organization and the Chaco System*, ed. David D. Doyel. Maxwell Museum of Anthropology, Anthropological Papers No. 5. University of New Mexico, Albuquerque.

Fritz, John M. 1978. "Paleopsychology Today: Ideational Systems and Human Adaptation in Prehistory." In *Social Archeology, Beyond Subsistence* and *Dating*, ed. Charles L. Redman et al. Academic Press, New York.

Judd, Neil M. 1924. Notes: West Court, Card 3. Copy on file, Chaco Culture National Historical Park.

———. 1954. *The Material Culture of Pueblo Bonito.* Smithsonian Miscellaneous Collections 124 (1). Washington D.C.

————. 1964. *The Architecture of Pueblo Bonito.* Smithsonian Miscellaneous Collections 147(1). Washington D.C.

Lister, Robert H. and Florence C. Lister 1981. *Chaco Canyon: Archaeology and Archaeologists.* University of New Mexico Press, Albuquerque.

Reyman, Jonathan Eric 1971. "Mexican Influence on Southwestern Ceremonialism." Ph. D. Dissertation, Southern Illinois University.

Schele, Linda and David Freidel 1990. *A Forest of Kings; The Untold Story of the Ancient Maya.* William Morrow and Company Inc., New York.

Sofaer, Anna, Rolf M. Sinclair, and Joey B. Donahue 1990. "An Astronomical Regional Pattern Among the Major Buildings of the Chaco Culture of New Mexico." Paper presented at the Third International Conference on Archaeoastronomy, University of St. Andrews, Scotland.

Stein, John R. and Stephen H. Lekson 1992. "Anasazi Ritual Landscapes." *In Anasazi Regional Organization and the Chaco System,* ed. David E. Doyel. Maxwell Museum of Anthropology, Anthropological Papers No. 5. University of New Mexico, Albuquerque.

Townsend, Lloyd K. 1986. "Artists Reconstruction of Pueblo Bonito." In *Mysteries of the Ancient Americas, The New World Before Columbus.* Readers Digest Association, Inc., Pleasantville, New York.

Waugh, Albert E. 1973. *Sundials; Their Theory and Construction.* Dover Publications, Inc., New York.

Windes, Thomas C, and Dabney Ford 1992. "The Nature of the Early Bonito Phase. *In Anasazi Regional Organization and the Chaco System,* ed. David E. Doyel. Maxwell Museum of Anthropology Anthropological Papers No. 5. University of New Mexico, Albuquerque.

————. 1996. "The Chaco Wood Project: The Chronometric Reappraisal of Pueblo Bonito." *American Antiquity* 61(2). In press.

10 Prehistoric Architecture with Unknown Function

Ian Thompson, Mark Varien, and Susan Kenzle, with a Puebloan Perspective by Rina Swentzell

Many subtle features of Anasazi construction have gone unnoticed until quite recently. Authors Ian Thompson, Mark Varien, Susan Kenzle, and Rina Swentzell examine landscape architectural elements such as enclosing walls, aligned stones, and rock circles. Santa Clara Pueblo art historian Rina Swentzell sheds light on constructions of "unknown function" by describing the differences between the European and the Puebloan view of architecture and its relationship to the natural environment.

The architecture of thirteenth-century Puebloan hamlets and villages in southwestern Colorado and southeastern Utah is dominated by residential room blocks, kivas, and towers. Because archaeologists are concerned with such questions as site population, site function, site use-life, and site dating, they have tended to focus on these more apparent architectural features.

Yet the Anasazi world of the thirteenth-century hamlets and villages is also characterized by more subtle forms of architecture. Low stone walls, for instance, connect and enclose structures that, in turn, create enclosed interior plazas. Stone circles and rectangles appear in the landscape, and aligned stones, which are not walls, surround parts or all of certain pueblos—alignments sometimes containing boulders weighing a ton or more. Site reports sometimes give passing mention to these features but may refer to them as terraces, retaining walls, water control devices, or defensive features. In some cases, they could not have served any of these functions.

At the Crow Canyon Archaeological Center, where such subtle forms of architecture are now the subject of attention, they are referred to as architecture with unknown function, or AWUF. From the perspective of archaeological research, such features may help us better understand human interaction within and between communities. From the perspective of Puebloan cosmology, they may help place built communities in the larger natural and spiritual world.

A first encounter with AWUF is often surprising. Two of the authors of this essay were shown how the boundaries of an archaeological site can extend into the landscape beyond the rubble of rooms, kivas, towers, and middens. They stood on a low, eroded bench overlooking the Rio Puerco, surrounded by a vast and brilliant sweep of northeastern Arizona. With them were archaeologists John Stein and Andrew Fowler. It was these authors' first visit there; for Stein and Fowler, it was one more weekend there pursuing a project to which they had given thousands of hours of their own time (Fowler and Stein 1990; Fowler, Stein, and Anyon 1987). What we saw at the remains of a twelfth-century pueblo was a distinct mound of masonry rubble that had once been a tall public structure or great house with associated blocks of rooms set in a place of arroyos and eroded red earth.

Stein and Fowler proceeded to expand our initial perception of the site by pointing out more subtle architectural features extending into the surrounding landscape. They began by pointing out a series of low, curving, subtle earthen berms nearly encircling the rubble mounds and adjacent areas. From one opening in the encircling berm, another long, linear berm and swale, which they referred to as a road, extended eastward several hundred meters. The eastward-running berm, we were told, pointed toward another great house that lay beyond the horizon. Other such features radiated out in various directions from the great house. Suddenly an archaeological site that we had viewed only moments before as covering only a few hundred meters extended over thousands of square meters, encompassing much more than the obvious rubble mound.

We returned home wondering whether similar features were associated with archaeological sites in southwestern Colorado. We began by looking at large thirteenth-century pueblos in Montezuma County, where Mesa Verde National Park is located, and found that they did include architecture extending beyond room blocks, kivas, and towers, albeit of stone rather than earth; casual surveys in San Juan County, Utah, supported the preliminary conclusion that stone AWUF occurs at some, but not all, late sites located in the two counties.

At about the time that stone AWUF began appearing, other changes were occurring in the Puebloan world. The Puebloans were coming together from small hamlets scattered across fertile mesa tops into larger villages, some of which were newly located in the rockier environment of canyon rims, slopes, and bottoms.

The Archaeological Setting

To place AWUF in an archaeological setting we will look briefly at settlement patterns in the Mesa Verde region—that is, at the distribution of sites across the landscape. In discussing the AWUF that we have documented, we will focus on continuity and change during the Pueblo II and III (A.D. 900-1300) periods.

Many changes occurred during the Pueblo II to III periods. If we focus on buildings and sites, some of the important changes include a change in site size, more use of stone masonry, an increase in the diversity of site layout, and a change in site location. If we expand our field of vision and focus on the region, we see another important change: a dramatic shift in the way *communities* were organized. These changes in community organization are a key to explaining the changes in buildings and sites listed above.

At the beginning of the Pueblo II period, the archaeological landscape was dotted with small, remarkably similar habitation units (Fig. 10.1). Most consist of a group of contiguous surface rooms, a subterranean kiva, and a midden containing discarded artifacts, ashy sediments, and human burials. The buildings on sites of the early Pueblo II period are usually made from earth and timber (Kuckelman and Morris 1988) and not masonry. The layout of these sites is so remarkably standard that a researcher at the turn of the century labeled them "unit pueblos" (Prudden 1903), and archaeologists continue to refer to these sites as unit pueblos or Prudden-units.

At first glance, these small sites might appear to be evenly distributed across the landscape. However, archaeological surveys (Adler 1990) that record the location of sites reveal that the settlement pattern is not evenly dispersed. On a regional scale, clusters of numerous small sites are separated by areas with relatively few sites. We believe these clusters of small sites represent communities.

By the late Pueblo II period many of these dispersed communities included some type of public architecture, usually a great kiva or a great house. We define these buildings as public architecture because of their size, the details of their construction, and the fact that they occur less frequently than buildings interpreted as habitation sites. The great kivas

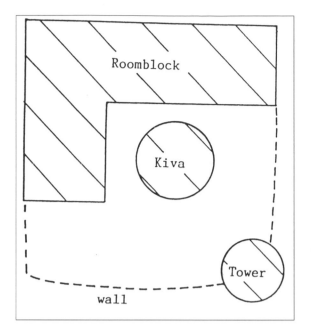

Fig. 10.1. Unit pueblo with enclosing wall

are too large to have been used by just a few families, and the great houses are constructed with different techniques and materials that make them seem monumental when compared to the habitation sites (Bradley 1988). This public architecture is interpreted as being the location for community ritual activity that helped integrate the surrounding small habitation sites (Breternitz, Doyel, and Marshall 1982:1228).

From Pueblo II to Pueblo III, two interesting things happened to these communities. First, the small sites became bigger. Instead of one or two kivas, they began to have three or four or more kivas. Second, individual unit pueblos began to be located closer together (Adler 1990; Fetterman and Honeycutt 1987; Neily 1983). This process resulted in clusters of small sites so closely spaced that archaeologists record them as a single aggregated site. Some of these aggregated sites became large enough to be villages and represent a single prehistoric community. These aggregated sites became most common in the A.D. 1200s, when we see the peak of population density in the Mesa Verde region (Adler 1990; Fetterman and Honeycutt 1987; Neily 1983; Rohn 1983, 1989). We first began to notice AWUF at these aggregated sites.

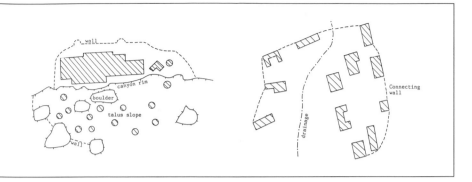

Fig. 10.2. Left. Canyon-rim site with enclosing wall. Right.
Canyon-head site with connecting wall

Architecture with Unknown Function

Low Stone Walls

These features are found at sites of varying size usually located on canyon rims and around canyon heads. Sites at these locations generally stretch along the top of the cliff and continue for varying distances from the bottom of the cliff down onto the talus slope below. The low stone walls, constructed of rough-hewn rectangular sandstone blocks, enclose the architecture at the top of the cliff (Fig. 10.2). In a few cases the feature may be traced across the talus below, but frequently it either has been erased from the talus by erosion or was never there at all. At cliff-edge and canyon-head sites, low stone walls sometimes connect room blocks, towers, and public architecture (Fig. 10.2). At many of these sites the low stone enclosing wall juts outward to form a semicircular arc, never more than two meters across, and the linear wall resumes (the wall in Fig. 10.2, left, contains two such features).

Preservation of these walls varies from site to site and within sites. Some of the sites include short segments of fully standing perimeter walls, and from these intact remnants one can draw inferences about the general appearance and construction of the low walls at other sites. From research done in the Mesa Verde region, it appears that the perimeter walls were similar from site to site. This, in turn, leads to the inference that they served a similar function at all sites where they occur.

The majority of the perimeter walls in the Mesa Verde region were relatively low; most of them stood between 0.5 and 1.5 meters high. In addition, most of the fully enclosing perimeter walls have openings or gates that allowed entry into the enclosed area from outside. These entries allowed outsiders access into public areas such as plazas. In effect, it appears that these walls served to channel visitors into public areas where they would have been visible to inhabitants. A similar conclusion was reached about the long, low walls found at sites in Chaco Canyon (Lekson 1986:77).

The relatively sudden and widespread appearance of low stone walls at sites built in the Pueblo III period is important to our understanding of social relations in the final decades preceding abandonment. It is possible that these low walls served social convention and functioned like the fences around houses in North America today. However, these walls were probably multifunctional in nature. In some cultures, perimeter walls function not only to define a community's boundaries, but also as mundane physical embodiments of cosmological boundaries (Oliver 1987).

Enclosed Cracks

Access between cliff-top and talus structures is frequently through cracks in the cliff wide enough to allow human passage. The tops of these cracks are often enclosed by low towers or low, circular stone walls.

Aligned Stones

These are not walls but unworked stones and boulders aligned to enclose part or all of a site. They are present in at least three canyon-bottom sites built in association with buttes or natural monoliths (Fig. 10.3). In some cases the boulders weigh a ton or more. At two sites built adjacent to and atop buttes in southeastern Utah, the stone alignments are found along the edge of the caprock on top of the butte as well as around structures at the base of the butte (Fig. 10.3, site on right side). At another canyon-bottom site, currently the subject of test excavations by the Crow Canyon Archaeological Center, the aligned stones completely enclose structures at the south base of a natural monolith but are not, except for a few short segments, apparent around structures at the north base of the monolith (Fig. 10.3, site on left side).

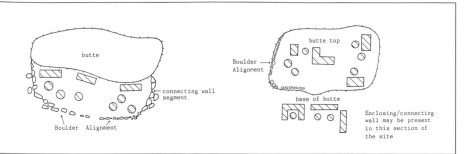

Fig. 10.3. Left. Butte site with boulder enclosing wall. Right.
Butte site with boulder alignment

Large Stone Circles

These are circles, usually four to five meters in diameter, formed of unworked stone. Some such circles are found within the perimeters of sites, but they can be isolated, at some distance from residential sites, as well.

Small Stone Rectangles

These are immediately outside the site perimeter and usually measure about a meter across and one and a half meters long. Such rectangles are present at several sites; three of them are clustered just outside a site being tested by the Crow Canyon Archaeological Center.

A Puebloan Perspective

These "constructions" or AWUF went unnoticed by earlier archaeologists because Puebloan "architecture" has been defined not by Puebloans but by Western peoples who look for what *they* define as architecture. Puebloans do not view their own architecture the way it is viewed by Western peoples.

In the Western world, architecture is altogether contained within the human landscape: it considers only the human context. In fact, Western architecture is about human genius and ego. It does not often consider any larger contexts—particularly the natural context. Architecture in the Western world is really about human constructions, with great attention

Prehistoric Architecture with Unknown Function 155

paid to the types of construction materials used and the manipulation of those materials. It focuses on the walls or that which defines space rather than on the contained space. It is very material-oriented.

"Architecture" is a misnomer where applied to the constructions of the Pueblo people over the last fifteen hundred years because the word does not capture the full scope of space definitions or the symbolic nature of building. Here, the human landscape is meaningless outside the natural context—human constructions are not considered out of their relationship to the hills, valleys, and mountains. Buildings and structures, and their walls, are not the primary focus. They are extensions of the natural world and therefore do not call attention to themselves or their makers. They are meaningful only as containers—for the function served by the described spaces and for the cosmic relationships that they reiterate.

For instance, at one site in Montezuma County the relationship of one naturally paved plaza has direct reference to the canyon space below. A smaller naturally paved area, bounded by house structures and low walls, leads into the plaza space, which then opens, drops, into the canyon. The focus of the plaza space on the canyon space acknowledges the larger feminine space of the canyon while also establishing a visual relationship with another pueblo across the canyon, a peak in the distance, and the sky beyond.

Puebloan constructions are significant parts of a highly symbolic world. Bears, rainbows, and rain can be pulled out of walls. Lakes are contained within house and kiva structures. In this world human beings live, on a daily and intimate basis, with the movement in the sky and acknowledgment of simultaneous existences in the underworld. Human existence is *not* contained within the material form of the human village; the human village is but one of the places where people make contact with movement in the sky and the underworld existences. Many other such places, spaces, described by hills, concavities, rock outcroppings, naturally paved areas, and human built walls extend throughout this defined "world."

Even today, that defined "world" is bounded by the far mountains and includes the hills, valleys, lakes, and springs. These natural boundaries define the space within which the people live. Points or places within the natural environment that connect with the region beyond or with worlds below or the sky above are often marked by a single stone, piles of stone, circles of stone, stones placed on end, or concavities in the ground or bedrock. Often, human constructions are a part of natural formations such as cliffs, stone outcroppings, or natural concavities.

In several thirteenth-century sites in Montezuma County, there are circular areas defined by loose alignments of stones. These areas are similar to those found around modern pueblos; they are where the living people meet the cloud beings. These are places visited by the people of this fourth world to make connections with the breath of the cosmos, with the underworld, and with the cloud people/spirits, the deer/buffalo people/spirits, or the water serpent.

The entire "world" is intimately known, acknowledged, and used. Spatial use and organization is not limited to the village area. The material village is one of the concentric rings about the symbolic center of the world. It is not given more weight or focus than the area of the fields, hills, or mountains. It constitutes one place within the whole. The web of human existence is interlaced with what happens in the larger natural context and therefore flows into the adjacent spaces, hills, and mountains. All constructions within that context, including AWUF, acknowledge the intertwining life forces within which human existence happens.

Conclusion

The most significant characteristic of AWUF, when contrasted with the residential and large public structures at archaeological sites, is its subtlety. It is easily overlooked in studying and interpreting sites. Indeed, according to some accounts, a substantial amount of AWUF was hauled away from Aztec National Monument and used for roadfill, thus ensuring that that pueblo will never be fully understood.

We are a long way from understanding the functions of AWUF; thus, the name stands. We can safely say, however, that it offers the promise of better understanding human movement toward and within communities and of the place of the human community in the natural world.

References

Adler, Michael A. 1990. "Communities of Soil and Stone: An Archaeological Investigation of Population Aggregation among the Mesa Verde Region Anasazi A.D. 900–1300." Ph.D. dissertation, Department of Anthropology, University of Michigan, Ann Arbor.

Bradley, Bruce A. 1988. "Wallace Ruin Interim Report." *Southwestern Lore* 52 (2):8–33.

———. 1991. "Planning, Growth, and Functional Differentiation at a Prehistoric Pueblo: A Case Study in Southwestern Colorado." *Journal of Field Archaeology*

Breternitz, Cory Dale, David E. Doyel, and Michael P. Marshall. 1982. *Bis sa'ani: A Late Bonito Phase Community on Escavada Wash, Northwest New Mexico.* Navajo Nation Papers in Anthropology, No. 14. Navajo Nation Cultural Resource Management Program, Window Rock, Ariz.

Fetterman, Jerry, and Linda Honeycutt. 1987. *The Mockingbird Mesa Survey, Southwestern Colorado.* Cultural Resource Series No. 22. Bureau of Land Management, Colo.

Fowler, Andrew P., and John R. Stein. 1990. "The Anasazi Great House in Time and Space." Paper presented at the 55th Annual Meeting of the Society for American Archaeology, Las Vegas, Nevada.

Fowler, Andrew P., John R. Stein, and Roger Anyon. 1987. "An Archaeological Reconnaissance of West-Central New Mexico: The Anasazi Monuments Project." Submitted to State of New Mexico Office of Cultural Affairs, Historic Preservation Division, Santa Fe.

Kuckelman, Kristin A., and James N. Morris. 1988. *Archaeological Investigations on South Canal,* vols. 1 and 2. Four Corners Archaeological Project, No. 11. Prepared for Cultural Resource Program, Bureau of Reclamation, Upper Colorado Region, Salt Lake City, Utah. Contract No. 4-CS-40–01650. Complete Archaeological Service Association, Cortez, Colo.

Lekson, Stephen H. 1986. *Great Pueblo Architecture of Chaco Canyon, New Mexico.* University of New Mexico Press, Albuquerque.

Neily, Robert B. 1983. "The Prehistoric Community on the Colorado Plateau: An Approach to the Study of Change and Survival in the Northern San Juan Area of the American Southwest." Ph.D. dissertation, Department of Anthropology, Southern Illinois University, Carbondale.

Oliver, Paul. 1990. *Dwellings: The House across the World.* University of Texas Press, Austin.

Prudden, T. Mitchell. 1903. "The Prehistoric Ruins of the San Juan Watershed in Utah, Arizona, Colorado, and New Mexico." *American Anthropologist,* n.s. 5 (2):224–88.

Rohn, Arthur H. 1983. "Budding Urban Settlements in the Northern San Juan." In *The Proceedings of the Anasazi Symposium, 1981,* ed. J. E. Smith, pp. 175–80. Mesa Verde Museum Association, Mesa Verde National Park, Colo.

———. 1989. "Northern San Juan Prehistory." In *Dynamics of Southwestern Prehistory,* ed. L. S. Cordell and G. J. Gumerman, pp. 149–77. Smithsonian Institution Press, Washington, D.C.

11 Notes on the Landscape Architecture of Anasazi Communities

Baker H. Morrow

Until recently, not much serious consideration had been given to the open space and landscape architecture of Anasazi communities. In this essay, landscape architect Baker Morrow invites us to imagine Chaco Canyon as a single community, punctuated by great houses amid fields of irrigated crops, waterworks, and welcoming public meanders. Morrow gives an overview of the varied and complex forms of landscape architecture that was a regular part of Anasazi town planning.

The Anasazi people were extraordinary masons; this is a general cultural characteristic. There is a relationship among the carefully trimmed and laid small building stones of the great houses, the wonderful geometry of the individual buildings, and the open spaces and structures arranged in careful D's and E's to make a town. These people understood that to create a place, or a "space," you must manipulate both mass and void. Without the careful planning and articulation of the void, the mass has no meaning.

Perhaps that is why the connected towns, or town parts, of Chaco Canyon remain to this day so stunning. The *mass* of these remarkable little cities plays well against the great voids of the San Juan uplands, perhaps because it is made from them, from their stones, with a lot of patience and care; and within the towns themselves, the voids are put to good use as plazas, patios, and even the cool recesses of ramada or shade structures. In Chaco, there is a grasp of not just how to site a building but of how to place a town in its landscape to the best effect.

At Mesa Verde, the process was reversed. Here, the green mass of the pine-juniper forest was selectively cleared to make hamlets, towns, fields,

Fig.11.1. Central Plaza with modern footpaths, Tyuonyi,
Bandlier National Monument. Photo by Baker H. Morrow

and irrigation works. The voids of the open landscape spaces created among the architectural structures were essential to the everyday life of the people in these settlements.

The painstakingly constructed grid gardens of the Chacoan towns correspond to the green open space of modern southwestern city planning. These gardens lay between such towns or town parts as Chetro Ketl and Una Vida, and they represent an important *urban* kind of space. In high summer, just before harvest, they would have been delightful places to stroll in—green, sweet-smelling, pleasant reminders of the bounty of the earth.

How did people move through and use these places? To understand the choreography of motion on Mesa Verde and in the open spaces of Chaco and its surrounding settlements, it is important to analyze the potential range of human motion, or movements, that might have taken place in them. Anasazi landscape architecture was entirely oriented, after all, to pedestrians—the people had no pressing need to make a place for carts, horses, oxen, or wagons, since there were none. So how would a society in motion but completely afoot use its outdoor "rooms"?

Movement and Activities

Simple Casual Walking

This would have been the most universal type of informal motion in and around the towns of Chaco and Mesa Verde. Most routine daily activities would have involved casual walking.

Trade Trekking

This must have been an extremely common form of motion. It would have involved not simply hiking to random villages but the organized transport by cooperative effort of materials and goods ranging from logs and stones (these perhaps in baskets); to grain (corn, dropseed), beans, squash, and additional foodstuffs; to textiles, pottery, and other trade items. This kind of motion is likely not to have been ritualistic, but it is quite likely to have been highly organized and systematic, especially in the Chaco country. It supported a great complex of towns, hamlets, and their satellites.

Dancing

This type of ritualized and repetitive motion likely took place frequently in the plazas and patios and perhaps in the great and ordinary kivas. It is an important determinant of the quality and form of outdoor space. Areas for musicians (flutists, drummers, etc.), singers, dancers, and observers must be carefully laid out, and in an organized town this demands a thoughtful analysis and design of outdoor space.

Children's Play

This involves walking, crawling, leaping, jumping, running, climbing, and other strenuous activities. It is best carried on where adults may observe and perhaps supervise the children but still follow their own daily tasks. Rooftops are not good areas for children's play because they are dangerous; perhaps ground-level patios, areas under or near ramadas, or plaza segments with a bit of shade are the likeliest candidates for this specialized activity.

Religious Observance Other Than Dancing

This might include processions, seasonal rites, and other activities that would require organized movement through a dramatic or centrally organized outdoor space. It might also incorporate formal entry into or exit from kivas.

Everyday Activities

Conversing with friends, food preparation (milling, processing, and cooking), eating, weaving and clothing manufacture, ceremonies and entertainment, storytelling, and stargazing are several of the likely activities that would have been carried out in the open. All these activities generally involve limited or circumscribed motion, and all would have required successful planning of landscape architectural space, including areas shaded by walls from the morning or afternoon sun or beneath planted or volunteer trees or the leafy branches of ramadas, common in southwestern villages since Basketmaker times.

Footracing

Perhaps the predecessors of modern Pueblo people also enjoyed this popular pastime. Racing may have been conducted along approach trails near walled towns, with the races beginning and ending in a plaza. Thus the open space may well be said to have been used for organized athletics—one of the traditional primary design objectives of landscape architecture.

Terrace Use

Life in well-constructed masonry buildings would have offered a number of advantages, including relatively good climate control, a strong sense of cultural cohesion, and the opportunity to participate in a rich and complex urban social life. But murky apartment rooms are not the most pleasant places in which to spend a long day (or night), and it is likely that common, everyday domestic activities took place on the roofs of Anasazi towns, which would have easily doubled as terraces. These highly geometric "spaces" also would have served as main entries to Anasazi living and storage rooms, as viewing and seating areas, and perhaps as cool sleeping spots on warm nights. In this respect, perhaps many Anasazi roofs can be said to have been "porches."

Use of Architectural Space

People tend to move about in more formal or constrained ways inside buildings, if only because they are afraid of bumping their heads or stubbing their toes. They do not often swing their arms, they do not jump, and they do not gyrate wildly unless they have been drinking odd liquids. Indoor motion is frequently more constrained, less free, more orderly. Outdoor movement is, by contrast and in general, freer, more casual, and more often athletic or recreational. Indoor design and outdoor design reflect these basic differences, and the Anasazi appear to have understood this very well indeed. The impression that the modern traveler develops in visiting, say, Mesa Verde, Aztec, Chaco, and the Pajarito pueblos in sequence is that their designers and builders engaged in very thoughtful site selection, in well-reasoned town construction for defense and agriculture, in tight clustering and stacking of living and storage rooms for building economy and social comfort, and in the rational development of village open space as a well-orchestrated series of outdoor rooms. Their open space is not just leftover space: it is simply the well-designed void that complements in a sophisticated way the elegant masses of the nearby buildings and walls, to which it contributes its own urban meaning.

A people as sophisticated as the eleventh-and twelfth-century Anasazi certainly had the technical knowledge to develop and refine a series of outdoor plantings, including trees, shrubs, ground covers, vines, and flowers, had they wished to do so. Their near-contemporaries, the Aztecs of the Valley of Mexico, had done exactly this—including parks and botanical gardens—by the early 1400s. These kinds of ornamental plantings are often thought to be one of the hallmarks of traditional Western landscape architecture, and they are intimately connected to advances in agriculture. In fact, rarely do you have the one without the other. And the Anasazi were an agriculturally accomplished people.

But there are two points to be considered here. The first is that great landscape architectural space does not necessarily require plants. Landscape architects have long thought the Piazza San Marco in Venice to be perhaps the greatest of Western squares. The Piazza della Signoria, in Siena, is another high-water mark in Western outdoor design. Yet these spaces, late medieval contemporaries of the great plazas in Pueblo Bonito and Chetro Ketl, have no plants at all: no trees, no shrubs, no flowers. They have wonderful pavements with curious patterns, and their proportions are uncommonly good. It is fun to be in them. They derive their form and the outline quality of their space from the buildings that surround them and from the surrounding sea or countryside—and then give it back. The great buildings at their edges would not be what they are without the plazas, because these squares put the buildings in the proper context. And people use them all the time, and enliven them. They would be nothing without their people.

We must conclude that the Chacoan towns, and the towns in the cliffs of Mesa Verde, with their tighter patios and courtyards that never waste a fraction of a square foot, must have been much the same.

A second point in regard to planting is this: no plants from medieval cities anywhere in the world have survived into the twentieth century, so the modern absence of trees or shrubs in the Anasazi towns of the Southwest means little. Perhaps we have not taken pollen samples from

Fig. 11.2. Hungo Pavi, with section of plaza, old fields beyond the standing walls, and Fajada Butte in the distance (Chaco Canyon). Photo by Baker H. Morrow

the right spots or have missed opportunities to make plaster casts of ancient root systems in key areas that would tell a tale.

At any rate, it is probably safe to say that landscape archaeology in the country of the Anasazi is for this and a number of other reasons in its infancy. The Anasazi certainly used plants for food, textiles, dyes, and other everyday domestic purposes. But the use of various plant species for what we would call today landscape architectural or ornamental horticultural purposes is poorly known. It is a challenging field of inquiry for the future.

So here we have people very much in love with the cryptic geometry of their buildings, excellent masons, capable of constructing multistoried apartments, complicated reservoirs, strikingly beautiful ceremonial chambers, friendly courtyards, graceful plazas, intricate grid gardens, and wide, smooth roads to propel themselves over the distant horizon. And they were a restless people, for whatever reasons, moving far and wide across their landscape, planning and constructing clusters of new buildings and plazas with skill and terrific effort only to abandon them after a few short generations for greener pastures.

Their outdoor space—outdoor rooms, really—was very frequently carefully planned and beautifully executed. I would argue simply that what we are looking at here is the classic landscape architecture of the Southwest— indeed, of the United States as a whole. And in an irony that probably would not be lost on the Anasazi themselves, modern visitors to ancient Anasazi towns continue to use these classic man-made landscapes as landscape architectural spaces have always been intended: on foot, in the company of their families and friends, and for recreation, socializing, and fun.

For Further Reading

Castañeda, Pedro de, et al. 1990. *The Journey of Coronado,* trans. and ed. George Parker Winship. Dover Publications, New York.
Cordell, Linda S., ed. 1980. *Tijeras Canyon: Analyses of the Past.* University of New Mexico Press, Albuquerque.
———. 1984. *Prehistory of the Southwest.* Academic Press, San Diego.
Lekson, Stephen H. 1984. *Great Pueblo Architecture of Chaco Canyon, New Mexico.* University of New Mexico Press, Albuquerque.
Lipe, W. H., and Michelle Hegmon. 1989. *The Architecture of Social Integration in Prehistoric Pueblos.* Crow Canyon Archaeological Center, Cortez, Colo.

Lister, Robert H., and Florence C. Lister. 1987. *Aztec Ruins on the Animas: Excavated, Preserved, and Interpreted*. University of New Mexico Press, Albuquerque.

Morrow, Baker H. 1985. "Old Landscapes, New Ideas." *New Mexico Architecture* (September-October 1985).

———. 1987a. *A Dictionary of Landscape Architecture*. University of New Mexico Press, Albuquerque.

———. 1987b. "Stone and Spring in Torrance County: Three Classic New Mexico Landscapes." *Mass: Journal of the School of Architecture and Planning, University of New Mexico* (fall 1987).

———. 1988. "New Deal Landscapes of New Mexico." *New Mexico* (April 1988).

———. 1992. "A Southwest Legacy of Trees and Stone: New Mexico's Historic Manmade Landscapes." *Landscape Architect and Specifier News* [Santa Ana, Calif.] (April 1992).

———, trans. and ed. 1995. *A Harvest of Reluctant Souls: The Memorial of Fray Alonso de Benavides, 1630*. University Press of Colorado, Niwot.

Nabokov, Peter, and Robert Easton. 1989. *Native American Architecture*. Oxford University Press, New York.

Riley, Carroll L. 1987. *The Frontier People: The Greater Southwest in the Protohistoric Period*. University of New Mexico Press, Albuquerque.

Wills, W. H. 1988. *Early Prehistoric Argriculture in the American Southwest*. School of American Research, Santa Fe.

Part Four   *Regional Tradition and*
                 Architectural Meaning

12 Pueblo Indian and Spanish Town Planning in New Mexico

The Pueblo of Isleta

Theodore S. Jojola

In a remarkably fresh and penetrating account, urban planner and scholar Theodore Jojola of Isleta Pueblo reviews Spanish and Native American town planning practices in sixteenth-and seventeenth-century New Mexico. He shows how Spanish and Puebloan peoples adapted to each other's design strategies and traditions. Jojola also puts his finger on a curiosity of Franciscan mission construction at the ruins of the Tompiro pueblo of Abó that may well be the symbolic origin of the modern Santa Fe regional style.

When the Spanish entered the hinterlands of New Mexico in the mid 1500s and began to establish relations among the native people, they organized not so much under their own volition but carried the dispatch of other Spanish colonial regimes that had preceded them. Correspondingly, the Pueblo Indians who were indigenous to the major river basins of New Mexico also had a long and sustaining tradition of community interrelations. In both instances, each society was solidly entrenched in its own civilization but was also aware that it could not survive in isolation. The interrelations between the Spanish and the Pueblo Indians became indicative of settlement patterns that were cross-assimilative and reciprocal, rather than ones of dominance and conquest.

The early Spanish colonial period among the Pueblo Indians of New Mexico is an ideal setting for examining the sustaining impacts of community transformation. The result of such interaction is the fact that both cultures were profoundly affected in significant ways. Moreover, these transformations have lasted into contemporary times, and they can still be evidenced in the planning and building styles of the greater Southwest. In this essay, I will explore only one aspect of these earliest traditions: the events leading to the transformation of one Pueblo Indian community—Isleta Pueblo—into a context of Spanish colonial settlement.

The History of New World Settlements

The discussion of transformation must necessarily find its foundation in the earliest attempts at New World occupation. Although the first attempts at exploration in the New World were diminutive and unregulated, the need for authority and control eventually required that an overall plan be emplaced for the earliest Spanish explorers, the *conquistadores.* The conquistadors were ill equipped to settle the frontier. Their exploration parties often consisted of military commanders who were versed in the art of warfare. They commanded soldiers who were afforded the opportunity to accompany the exploration as a reprieve from untold misdemeanors and crimes. The exploration party was rounded out with the inclusion of a few chroniclers, who were also the priests, as well as native vassals from other regions who served as translators.

The earliest attempts by the Spanish at conquest and domination resulted in the widespread genocide of many indigenous societies and peoples. These forays were made with the intent of usurping all material wealth and enslaving all natives. Only when the plan of Spanish occupation was expanded to include Spanish settlement did the framework of Iberian conquest include reform. By then, it became a raging debate among clerics as to whether enslavement for the purposes of personal servitude was ethical. The first set of reforms that came from these debates was directed at preventing Spanish atrocities not simply against an Indian, but against the whole of what would constitute the Indian settlement.

The New World was already extensively settled at the time of first contact. This required that Spanish settlements be developed under the aegis of a master plan. Although the ideal Spanish settlement emerged from the transformation of Old World traditions and the adaptation of New World experiences, the underlying principles for the execution of the authoritative town plan were the cultural and social ideals of the Iberian Hispanics. The overall result of this legacy was a decidedly standardized and authoritative township, alongside a decidedly indigenous and regional style of town planning and community settlement.

Spanish ideals were predicated on the belief that human benevolence and divine intervention were one and the same. The Spaniards held the conviction that the natives could be transformed through the efforts of a "humane nation," which as in the instance of Spain was considered to be "excellent in every kind of virtue" (Hanke 1971:47). The "proper kind of rule," therefore, was to transform native people in such a way that the more civility they exhibited, the more liberties they were to be given. The Spaniards fully expected that the natives would, of their own volition, become more subservient toward the occupiers. The role of the clergy was to proselytize but, more strategically, to wean the native congregation away from their "pagan" beliefs; as enlightened converts, they would come to accept their dictated roles. Eventually it became a colonial convention that Indian converts were to apportion a minimum of nine months of the year toiling for the benefit of the Spanish benefactors.

Eventually, Spanish subjugation became regulated by the theory that "civilization" could be wedded in distinct stages. At first contact, every Indian was understood to be an infidel and considered inferior "as children to adults, as women to men"(Hanke 1971). Therefore, a great deal of "tolerance" was to be extended toward them. It became the responsibility of the colonialists to set the example of civilized behavior. More often than not, such license cleared the way for increased exploitation and abuse.

Natives who resisted Spanish dictates or intrusion were considered something less than human. If they persisted in their pagan ways, they became subject to the full wrath of the *reducciones* (reductions) or, worse, to the *repartimiento* (slave distribution). As "infidels" who resisted all attempts to attain Spanish religion, towns, or citizenry, they could be killed or captured and exploited to the fullest extent of colonial practices (Hanke 1971). Unfortunate natives who were thus identified were forcibly removed and enslaved in accordance with provisions of the "just war." Whole native communities were so displaced, and their populations were relegated to perpetual servitude.

This abuse, which came to be known as the "Black Legacy," was the basis of the first major code regulating the manner of Spanish wardship. Called the Laws of the Burgos (Haring 1963:44), the laws were promulgated by the king of Spain in December 1512 in direct response to the widespread abuses of native labor and the unrestrained genocide of whole native populations. The various articles of these laws were intended to codify reform and to bring humane government to the natives.

The laws covered all aspects of native or "Indian" welfare. They dealt with specifics such as an Indian's proper diet, the correct deployment of punishment to be inflicted upon Indian subjects, and even the proper verbal etiquette for reproaching errant Indian wards (Sherman 1979:10). But despite their reforms, the laws also inadvertently instituted another form of repression: the formalization and regulation of the *encomienda* (estate).

The encomienda was based on a compact made between the Spanish Crown and the conquistadors (Bannon 1964:190). This compact gave license to the *encomendero* (landed commander or trustee) to appropriate profits from any important discoveries resulting from the occupation and settlement of the encomienda. Usually these profits were exacted through the toil of the natives. In exchange for such privileges, the encomendero became the guardian of the natives. As a guardian, the encomendero had an obligation to protect and "civilize" his charges. As the result of this compact, Christian conversion and civilization became synonymous (Cline 1974).

Although "civilizing" was primarily achieved through religious conversion and forced servitude, a significant amount of town infrastructure was required to support such efforts. Missions were established, and when colonial occupation was secured the Indian converts were required to erect a church and a convent for the priest and his attendants. Eventually the priest required the physical relocation of all the converted populations into centralized protovillages or *villas*. At the minimum, every converted Indian *(macehuale)* was required to become a village dweller.

As such, an often-overlooked aspect of Spanish subjugation is the planned and deliberate "urbanization" of native peoples for the purpose of securing colonial frontiers. The Spanish used Indian villas strategically for demarcating their territories, especially as borderland settlements between themselves and the colonies of the English and the French or as outposts overlooking the territories of hostile Indians. More strategically, the successful emplacement of the frontier villa became the first measure for subjugating large native territories.

The second measure was attained when the villa became established enough to become formally recognized by the Spanish Crown. The petition and transfer of authority from an encomendero to the Crown became the prelude to the recognition and establishment of a formally governed town, or *pueblo*. Once a villa was determined to meet all the necessary requirements of a township, it was elevated to a stature of a pueblo (Haring 1963:151). This was attained through a symbolic transfer of community land title *(fondo legal)*, as bounded within an open town square *(plaza mayor)*, and by the ceremonial passage of the canes of authority *(barras)* to the newly appointed town officials, who were primarily the *regidores* (councilors) and *alcaldes* (magistrates).

Such customs stemmed from Iberian political traditions that tied the legal authority of Spanish citizenship to their home towns. Like Catholicism, citizenship and civilization were nearly synonymous (Cline 1974). To be a citizen, therefore, indicated that the home community had been formally subsumed within the township hierarchy of the Spanish Crown. This practice was the outgrowth of Roman traditions that distinguished six types of municipal governments, each with varying degrees of rights and privileges (Violich 1962:172).

Citizens under Spanish rule were thus able to seek redress only through their town officials. Any further appeals were processed among higher authorities, who were located in townships that were considered more principal. The chain ended at the most senior town or *audiencia*, which for most of the early Spanish New World occupation was Mexico City. As a result of Spanish attempts to govern their own racial class of Iberians, these policies were replicated and maintained separately for the native populations through the Laws of the Indies, codified in the 1670s as the *Recopilación de leyes de los reynos de las Indias*.

The agenda pertaining to the urbanization of the New World was made explicit as early as 1523 with the issuance of instructions concerning the reconstruction of aboriginal cities such as that of the Aztec capital, Mexico City (Stanislawski 1947:97). Not until 1573, however, was an ordinance pertaining to instructions for the establishment of new towns promulgated by Spain's King Philip II (Nuttall 1921:743).

The New Town Ordinance of 1573 outlined 148 instructions concerning the "rational" procedures for evoking city planning and political organization in the New World. Among the ordinances with direct bearing upon the colonization of the Southwest were those that specified the following conditions (abridged from Mundigo and Crouch 1977:249–259):

> [that] the site and position of towns [be constructed] where it would be possible to demolish neighboring towns and properties in order to take advantage of the materials that are essential for building [Ordinance 39]; [upon] having selected the site for capital towns in each county, determine the areas that could be subjected and incorporated within the jurisdiction of the head town, without

detriment to Indians and natives [Ordinance 42]; having selected the area and having established existing opportunities for development, the governor should decide whether the site that is to be populated should be a city *[cabecera]*, town *[municipio]*, or village *[pueblo]* [Ordinance 43];

the persons who were placed in charge of populating a town with Spaniards should see to it that it should have at least thirty neighbors, each one with his own house, and it should have a clergyman who can administer sacraments [Ordinance 89];

a plan for the site is to be made, dividing it into squares, streets, and building lots, using cord and ruler, beginning with the main square and leaving sufficient open space so that even if the town grows, it can always spread in the same manner [Ordinance 110];

the main plaza *[plaza mayor]* is to be the starting point [and] should be square or rectangular, in which case it should be at least one and a half its width for inasmuch as this shape is best for fiestas [Ordinance 112];

the four corners of the plaza shall face the four principal winds [Ordinance 114];

around the plaza there shall be portals, for these are of considerable convenience to the merchants [Ordinance 115];

here and there in the town, smaller plazas of good proportion shall be laid out such that everything may be distributed in a good proportion for the instruction of religion [Ordinance 118];

a site and lot shall be assigned for the royal council and *cabildo* [Ordinance 121];

captains should persuade settlers to carry tents], and those who did not should make their huts of easily available local materials [Ordinance 128];

throughout the town arrange the structures of the houses generally in such a way that they may serve [as] a defense or barrier against those who may try to disturb or invade [Ordinance 133];

try as far as possible to have the buildings all of one type for the sake of the beauty of the town [Ordinance 134];

[natives] should be made aware of how we intend to settle, not to do damage to them nor take away their lands, but instead to gain their friendship and teach them how to live civilly [Ordinance 136];

the Spaniards, to whom Indians are entrusted, should seek with great care that these Indians be settled in towns, and that, within these, churches be built so that the Indians can be instructed into Christian doctrine and live in good order [Ordinance 148].

As seen in the above ordinances, the physical requirements of the villa were strictly regulated. Every villa and pueblo was planned around the church, the town hall *(cabildo)*, and an open town court *(plaza mayor)*. In fact, the Iberian style of architecture and town planning became the assumed standard (Mundigo and Crouch 1977:248).

The Impact of New Town Planning in the Southwest

As was the situation with the other colonial regions of the New World, the earliest Spanish explorations into the Southwest were economically motivated. The Spanish expedition of Francisco Vásquez de Coronado in 1540 was the first official expedition to explore the Southwest. Within their calling was a quest for the region's fabled "cities of gold." In the winter of 1540, they made encampments among the Southern Tiwa settlements of what was later christened as the Province of Tiguex (variant of Tiwa).

In his field report to Coronado, Captain Alvarado narrated the first foreigner's description of the province. He described the area as composed of "fields of maize and dotted with cottonwood groves" (Bolton 1949:184). He gave further indication that "there are twelve pueblos, whose houses are built of mud and are two stories high." As the Spanish continued their explorations along the network of established trails, they discovered even more settlements. They found a multitude of "cities of houses built from stone and mud" whose domesticated natives were wholly occupied with subsistence agriculture (Bolton 1949:186).

Although the region proved to be well situated and "thickly settled," it lacked the precious cache of gold and silver which the Spaniards sought. Such forays were intended to secure wealth and subjugate the natives through the establishment of the encomienda. Had these explorations uncovered riches, the region would have doubtless succumbed to invasion and pillage. Instead, ore samples from the region yielded only copper. Unable to find any wealth, the conquistadors could not command any further military expeditions, and the full subjugation of this frontier was never attained.

Coronado's expedition was regulated in large part by the Laws of the Burgos. A major revision of these laws had been instituted in 1542, barely one year after Coronado retreated from the Southwest. Called the "New Laws of Charles V," they forbade all further enslavement of the natives under any pretext and proposed, although unsuccessfully, to abolish the encomienda system (Haring 1963:51). These changes represented reforms instituted through the prompting of the Spanish priest Bartolomé de las Casas and were intended to lessen the atrocities being committed by many New World colonialists against the natives (Hanke 1971:62).

More important, this revision of the laws established the Council of the Indies, the function of which was to create and enforce the laws regulating relations between the Spaniards and the Indians. These laws were eventually codified beginning in the 1670s as the *Recoplación de leyes de los reynos de las Indias,* the Laws of the Indies. In final form, the nine volumes contained more than 6,400 laws intended to standardize and give consistency in the way native affairs were handled. Ultimately, the council lent credence to the self-regulation of domestic affairs by Indian officials over their own communities.

Coronado's troops became more beleaguered in their failure to find the *Otro México* (other Mexico). During the spring of 1541, they vented their frustrations by waging a slash-and-burn campaign against the villages in the province of Tiguex. These acts resulted in his command being one of the first expeditions to be prosecuted under the revised Laws by the Council for the "great cruelties upon the natives of the land through which they passed" (Bolton 1949:368). Although Coronado was later absolved by the Council, his prosecution coupled with the failure of the expedition to discover riches doubtless served to stave other Spanish advances into New Mexico.

The region's isolation from the *audiencia* of Mexico City, which according to accounts took a full year to traverse, served to establish New Mexico as one of the northernmost and most isolated of the borderlands of the Spanish empire. Although other legal and illegal expeditions were attempted, the various Indian tribes responded with continued hostilities. A number of Spanish priests who remained behind to establish missions were martyred but, lacking the finances for an *entrada* (military foray), the Indian communities were not punished. It became obvious that if the Spaniards were to succeed at gaining a colonial presence, they would need to enjoin them through other means.

The first permanent colonial settlement in New Mexico was attempted in 1598 by Juan de Oñate. Almost immediately, the colonial regime recognized two divisions of natives: those who were peaceable and those who were hostile. The latter consisted of the nomadic and seminomadic tribes (especially the Navajo and Apache). The former consisted of those tribes who were sedentary and whom the Spaniards christened as the *indios de pueblo* (Pueblo Indians). By then the New Town Ordinances of 1573 were fully enforced as a civilized code of settlement, and these policies regulated the manner of colonial relationships among the two.

The Spanish colonialists had made many positive comments about the communal lifestyle of the Pueblo Indians and likened them to "good people" (Bolton 1949:184). Correspondingly, nearly all the major elements of the ideal Spanish town plan were also evident in their vernacular settlements as well. Pueblo villages were geometrically organized around large open ceremonial town courts, or plazas (Ordinances 112 and 114), and the villages themselves were complex multistoried residences with extensive compartmentalized quarters and ceremonial centers (Ordinance 89), called *estufas,* or kivas. Pueblo villages were compact (Ordinance 110) and highly fortified (Ordinance 133). They used durable materials such as stone, *terrones* (sod-blocks), or compacted earth (Ordinance 128) and employed masonry and building techniques that were familiar to the Spanish (Ordinance 134). Finally, the sites of these villages were well situated with respect to water and agricultural lands.

Because these Pueblo attributes were not perceived as being the handiwork of protohumans, their communities were spared forcible relocation as specified in Ordinance 148. These parallels between the Pueblo Indians and Spanish community traditions ultimately afforded the natives the formal designation of their communities as pueblos or minor townships. This was not the case for the so-called hostile Indians, whose women and children were often targeted by the colonialists as a source of domestic servants and slave laborers. Eventually, separate villages comprising converted "hostile" Indians, or *genízaros*, were established by the Spanish for the purposes of mutual aid and protection (Espinoso and Chavez n.d.:69–73).

Otherwise, the first major test of Spanish settlement law came in the 1599 siege of Acoma Pueblo by the *entrada* of Juan de Oñate. The mesa fortress of Acoma was attacked and successfully taken by Spanish troops in retaliation for an ill-fated ambush of a Spanish envoy. Acoma men and women were forced to make retribution and were sentenced to between twenty and twenty-five years of "personal servitude." All men over the age of twenty-five had their right foot severed.

As Oñate found out, however, the designation of a pueblo was not to be taken lightly; these Indian townships were afforded superior protection under the Spanish Crown. After information reached the Council of the Indies about this incident, as well as other atrocities committed by Oñate, he was summoned to stand trial. Unlike Coronado, who was absolved by the council, Oñate was convicted on twelve counts and condemned to "perpetual banishment from New Mexico" (Hammond 1927:185).

With the banishment of Oñate, the protection of other Pueblo settlements was begrudgingly enforced by consequent Spanish colonial officials (Ordinance 136). Spanish colonizers could settle only upon vacated lands, and the main pattern of settlement became the reoccupation of abandoned Pueblo villages. In keeping with Ordinance 39, new structures recycled Pueblo Indian building materials, and colonial villas were reconstructed atop the foundations of Pueblo ruins. In 1598, for example, the first colonial capital of San Juan de los Caballeros had been located on an abandoned Tewa Pueblo Indian village, Yuqueunque. In 1609, the first royal governor, Pedro de Peralta, relocated the Spanish capital to the ruins of another Pueblo village, Analco, rechristening it Santa Fe (Crouch, Daniel, and Mundigo 1982:69).

Consequent visitations by chroniclers affirmed other aspects of the pattern of colonial settlement in the region. In particular, the Spanish colonists had cross-assimilated to a high degree. Fray Alonso de Benavides in his *Revised Memorial of 1634* described Santa Fe as a disappointing villa, which at the time of his visit even lacked a suitable church. Benavides also commented on the "houses [that] are not costly, but adequate as living quarters" (Hodge, Hammond, and Rey 1945:68). Of the 250 colonizers who had settled Santa Fe, most were described as married to other Spanish or Indian women or their descendants.

In sharp contrast, Fray Benavides's description of the Pueblo Indians was full of unending praise. For example, in the Tiwa Province, which he called the Tioas Nation, Benavides estimated that seven thousand souls were living in fifteen or sixteen pueblos with a total of four thousand houses, "all very large" (Hodge, Hammond, and Rey 1945:47). He described in some detail the "strength and beauty of its buildings" and commented about the villages being "very attractive on account of their corridors," "terraces," and buildings with "walls of stone and gypsum." Two missions and convents at the Pueblos of Isleta and Sandia he described as "spacious and very attractive."

Similar "success stories" occurred at the other Pueblo Indian provinces as well. These efforts represented the culmination of a conversion effort among Franciscan friars that had been initiated in 1598. By 1629, there were forty-six friars in New Mexico serving about thirty-five missions and ministering to thirty-five thousand Pueblo Indian converts.

Epilogue

With the completion of requisite Spanish town structures like the church, the Pueblo Indians formally became subsumed under Spanish governance sometime in the 1620s (Sando 1976:203–205). Political integration was rapid, owing in great part to the village tradition of the Pueblo people. The Pueblo Indian villages were ready-made for the New Town Ordinances of 1573, and the vernacular building traditions of the Puebloans were superior to those of the Spanish colonizers.

Nevertheless, largely because of disease, famine, and continued aggressions by nonconverted Indian tribes, the Pueblo nations gradually lost ground to the colonialists. Particularly with the advent of the Pueblo Revolt of 1680, the demographics of the region shifted so significantly that many Pueblo Indian villages were simply abandoned or reconsolidated under new colonial regimes.

An excellent case in point is the Pueblo of Isleta, which ultimately became the second capital of the colonial jurisdiction of the Rio Abajo prior to the 1680 Pueblo Revolt. After the futile attempt by the deposed New Mexico governor, Antonio de Otermín, to re-establish Spanish authority in 1682, the Pueblo of Isleta lay abandoned. Careful analysis of the testimony that related the consequent destruction of the pueblo by Otermín indicates that the original plaza was located to the west of the church, as was a newly constructed estufa (kiva), which was subsequently destroyed (Hackett 1942). From this venue, the probable village plan must have been very similar to that of the Tompiro Pueblo village of Abó, which was abandoned around 1675 and which had close relations with Isleta Pueblo (Toulouse 1949:4).

Beginning in 1710, the Pueblo of Isleta was successively repatriated by Tiwa families who had fled to both Tusayan in the Hopi dominion in Arizona and to Ysleta del Sur near El Paso, Texas. This doubtless provided an unheralded opportunity for the *custo* of New Mexico, Juan de la Peña, to give instructions concerning the repatriation of Isleta (Montoya 1978:22). In all likelihood, the newly repatriated village was deliberately planned in a manner that was more consistent with Spanish town ideals. Only the

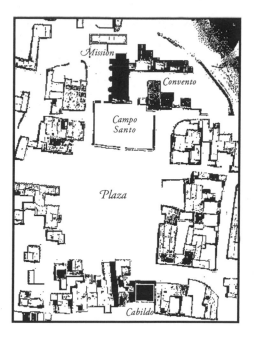

Fig. 12.1. Church of Isleta Pueblo and plaza, 1976. Source: Koogle and Pouls Engineering. Courtesy of the National Park Service

original foundation of the pre-Pueblo Revolt mission was retained, and by 1776, the transformation appeared complete, as seen in the narrative account of Fray Francisco Atanasio Domínguez:

> The pueblo consists of three beautiful blocks of dwellings, separated from one another at the corners, which are located in front of the church and convent, and form a very large plaza there to the south of them. Outside the plaza at various distances all around there are some twenty houses which would be as large as one block, or tenement, of the plaza if they were all together. Everything is of adobe, very prettily designed and much in the Spanish manner. (Adams and Chavez 1975:207)

An aerial view of the Pueblo of Isleta both confirms and dramatically indicates how the above description has persisted into contemporary time (Fig. 12.1). All the elements as contained in the New Town Ordinances of 1573 are present. The plaza, minus the *campo santo* (enclosed graveyard), maintains a ratio of approximately 1:1.5. The town hall *(cabildo)*, which

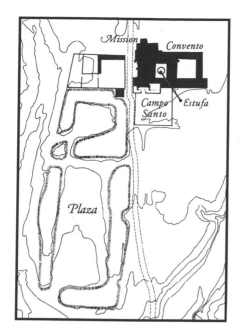

Fig. 12.2. Church of Abó Pueblo and plaza, circa 1660.
Courtesy of the National Park Service

is on the south side, fronts the plaza opposite the church. The church serves as the focus to which the rest of the village is planned. Both the plaza and church are oriented in the cardinal directions. Finally, and until quite recently, the houses and cabildo had extensive portals constructed in the manner of the New Town ordinances (Ordinance 115).

In contrast, the Pueblo of Abó typifies earlier missionary attempts (preceding the 1680 Revolt) to convert the Pueblo Indians (Ivey:37–40). The church resides on the periphery of the village (Fig. 12.2). The ruins of the village give evidence of distinct mounds and plazas that largely predated Spanish influences. The overall plan was indicative of encroachment but not native repatriation or relocation. Perhaps the most intriguing element, however, is the presence of an estufa in the center of the mission's west court patio.

This treatise necessarily concludes with this unique estufa. The juxtaposition of this estufa within the mission walls of Abó exemplifies the main premise of this essay. Pueblo and Spanish interrelations, as supported by such patterns, bespoke cross-cultural assimilation and reciprocity. Although the Spanish colonial and Pueblo Indian societies were solidly entrenched in their own civilizations, each was also aware that it could not survive in isolation. Like that estufa located in the heart of the Abó mission, both traditions intertwined to constitute the foundation of that vital archetype known as the New Mexico or Sante Fe style.

References

Adams, Eleanor B., and Fray Angelico Chavez. 1975. *The Missions of New Mexico, 1776: A Description of Fray Francisco Atanasio Domínguez with Other Contemporary Documents.* University of New Mexico Press, Albuquerque.

Bannon, John Francis. 1964. *Bolton and the Spanish Borderlands.* University of Oklahoma Press, Norman.

Bolton, Herbert E. 1949. *Coronado on the Turquoise Trail: Knight of the Pueblos and the Southwest.* University of New Mexico Press, Albuquerque.

Cline, Howard F. 1974. *The Florida Indians,* vol. 1, *Notes on Colonial Indians and Communities in Florida, 1700–1821.* Garland Publishing Inc., New York.

Crouch, Dora P., J. Daniel, and Axel I. Mundigo. 1982. *Spanish City Planning in North America,* MIT Press, Cambridge, Mass.

Espinoso, Gilberto, and Tibo Chavez. n.d. *El Rio Abajo.* Pampa Print Shop.

Hackett, Charles Wilson. 1942. *Revolt of the Pueblo Indians of New Mexico: And Otermin's Attempted Reconquest 1680–1682.* University of New Mexico Press, Albuquerque.

Hammond, George P. 1927. *Don Juan de Oñate and the Founding of New Mexico.* El Palacio Press, Santa Fe.

Hanke, Lewis. 1971. *Aristotle and the American Indians: A Study in Race Prejudice in the Modern World.* Reprint, Indiana University Press, Bloomington.

Haring, C. H. 1963. *The Spanish Empire in America.* Harcourt Brace Jovanovich, New York.

Hodge, Frederick W., George P. Hammond, and Agapito Rey. 1945. *Fray Alonso de Benavides' Revised Memorial of 1634.* University of New Mexico Press, Albuquerque.

Ivey, James E. 1988. *In the Midst of a Loneliness: The Architectural History of the Salinas Missions.* Southwest Cultural Resource Center, Professional Papers No. 15. Santa Fe.

Montoya, Joe L. 1978. *Isleta Pueblo and the Church of San Augustine.* St. Augustine Church Press, Isleta Pueblo.

Mundigo, Axel I., and Dora P. Crouch. 1977. "The City Planning Ordinances of the Laws of the Indies Revisited." *Town Planning Review* 48 (3):249–259.

Nuttall, Zelia. 1921. "Royal Ordinances Concerning the Laying Out of New Towns." *Hispanic American Historical Review* 4 (4):743.

Sando, Joe S. 1976. "The Silver Headed Canes." In *The Pueblo Indians,* pp. 203–205. The Indian Historian Press, San Francisco.

Sherman, William L. 1979. *Forced Labor in Sixteenth-Century Central America.* University of Nebraska Press, Lincoln.

Stanislawski, Dan. 1947. "Early Spanish Town Planning in the New World." *Geographic Review* 37 (1):97.

Toulouse, Joseph H., Jr. 1949. *The Mission of San Gregorio de Abó: A Report of the Excavation and Repair of a Seventeenth-Century New Mexico Mission.* Monograph of the School of American Research, No. 13. University of New Mexico Press, Albuquerque.

Violich, Francis. 1962. "Evolution of the Spanish City: Issues Basic to Planning Today." *Journal of the American Institute of Planners* 28 (3):172.

13 An Understated Sacredness

Rina Swentzell

*In an essay that will likely become a classic in the field, Santa
Clara Pueblo art historian and architectural theorist Rina Swentzell
describes the difference between European architecture as an expression
of the Western view of humankind's separation from nature and the Pue-
bloan/Anasazi view of human culture as indistinguishable from the natural
world. The created spaces formed from these worldviews are so incompatible
that a review of their differences have much to reveal to contemporary urban
designers working to retrofit parts of dysfunctional cities in the arid Southwest.*

Last summer as I stood on Tsikumu, one of Santa Clara Pueblo's sacred
mountains, I was most impressed by the wind, the beauty of the clouds,
and the flow of the hills below. There is a shrine on Tsikumu with a few
well-placed stones that define an area scattered with cornmeal and a
deeply worn path in the bedrock. No special structure celebrates the sacredness of this place. Architecturally it is understated, almost inconspicuous.

Tsikumu is typical of Pueblo shrines in that it is visually disappointing. It is, nevertheless, a special place because it is a place of access to the
underworld from which the Pueblo people emerged. It is the doorway of
communication between the many simultaneous levels of Pueblo existence. Tsikumu allows for a flow of energy between this plane of reality
and other concurrent realities. Understanding the visual understatement
of the Tsikumu shrine, and other Pueblo shrines, is important to understanding Pueblo sacred space.

Visually and physically understating shrines (or for that matter, Pueblo
community and house forms) stems from the very nature of Pueblo cosmology. At the center of the Pueblo belief system is the conviction that
people are not separate from nature and natural forces. This insoluble
connection with nature has existed from the beginning of time. The goal
of human existence is to maintain wholeness or oneness with the natural
universe. Pueblo people emerged from the underworld, from the inside

of the earth: "The Tewa were living in Sipohene beneath Sandy Place Lake far to the north. The world under the lake was like this one, but it was dark. Supernaturals, men and animals lived together and death was unknown" (Ortiz 1979:13). After emerging from the darkness of the earth, the people founded their worlds (pueblos) by first finding the centers:

> The water spider spread his legs to the north and to the south, to the west and to the east, and then he said to the priests and the chiefs, "Now indeed I have measured it. Here is the center of the earth and here you must build your city!" But they said, "We have been hunting for the center of the earth for a long time, and wish to be sure." So they asked Rainbow to measure it also. So the Rainbow stretched his bright arch to the north and to the south, to the west and to the east, measuring the distance. Then he too gave his decision: "Here at this place is the heart of the earth." (Carr 1979:17)

The "heart of the earth" or *bu-ping-geh* (heart of the pueblo) for the Tewa people is the open community space within the village where ritual dances and other community activities happen. The bu-ping-geh contains the literal center of the earth, the *nan-sipu,* which translates as "the belly-root" of the earth. Each pueblo's cosmos encircles the *nan-sipu,* and the surrounding mountains, where the sky and earth touch, are the boundaries of the well-organized spaces in which people, animals, and spirits live.

As at Tsikumu, all the boundary points, secondary-level shrines, and *nan-sipu* (center) of this well-organized cosmos are marked by an inconspicuous stone or grouping of stones. This physical understanding of sacred places is typical of Pueblo thinking because it is believed that it is better to understate than to overstate—to be one with everything rather than to be separate or conspicuous. There is, then, little need to create or cause distinctions—among people or objects or even places. Since every thing, every body, and every place is sacred and has essential worth, there is no need to individuate. The Christian myth of "fallen man," who is contaminated, has no counterpart in Pueblo mythology. Nowhere in Pueblo myths do humans experience a fall from "God's" grace. The people and their world are sacred and indivisible.

The shrines, boundary markers, and center, then, serve as constant reminders of the religious, symbolic nature of life. Because this realm of existence and other realms exist simultaneously, there is a continuous flow between levels of existence. Because the *nan-sipu* is the symbolic point from which the people emerged, the shrines (such as Tsikumu) are points where the possibility for contact with different levels of existence happen. Thus the cosmos becomes a continuous flowing whole, with visible connections between the seen and the unseen, the tangible and the intangible.

Being religiously egocentric, Pueblo people do live at the center of the universe. Their world is sacramental. It is a world thoroughly impregnated with the energy, purpose, and sense of the creative natural forces. It is all one. Sacredness, then, is recognizable in everyday life. The purpose of life for Pueblo people is to be intimately united with nature, intimately connected with everything in the natural world. Everything is included in that connectedness. Houses, for instance, are "fed" cornmeal after construction so that they may have a good life. The physical community *(O-wing-geh)*, or place where people live, is periodically healed by the Bear or medicine society. Sacralization of the entire world is easy to achieve because humans are not separate from other life-forms, not created to have dominion over other life-forms, not on a higher rung of living, not closer to God. Directional forces of the world are cyclical and move in and out of the earth rather than upward toward the heavens. Clay (dirt) is talked to because it is of the earth and shares in the flow of life. That flow described as *Po-wa-ha* ("water-wind-breath") is the essence of life. Existence is determined not by a physical body or other physical manifestation but by the breath, which is symbolized by the movement of the water and wind. It is the breath which flows without distinction through the entirety of animate and inanimate existences. The *Po-wa-ha*, then, is the creative force causing life, much as the Christian God is the originator and creator of Christian existence.

The *Po-wa-ha* is nondiscriminatory; the profane and secular overlap with the sacred and solemn. On a recent trip to Chaco Canyon a non-Indian friend expressed anger at his girlfriend for unknowingly having stepped on a part of the reconstructed walls of Pueblo Bonito. The act to him was sacrilegious. I was puzzled. I felt that nothing sacrilegious had occurred, for as a child I had climbed the Puye Cliff ruins in full view of my parents and great-grandmother, who had expressed no particular concern. I was not admonished, as a child, for enjoying sitting or standing on the *nan-sipu* in the *bu-ping-geh* of Santa Clara Pueblo. I now figure it was because I was not considered spiritually distinct from the stone or the walls of Puye Cliff. I could not cause desacralization. No one can cause desacralization, because the concept of original sin is lacking in Pueblo thought. We are not a fallen people and therefore are still blessed with being one with our natural context. We flow in the *Po-wa-ha* along with all other manifestations of life.

Further, the belief that the *Po-wa-ha* flows through inanimate as well as animate beings allows buildings, ruins, places to have life spans and to come and go as do other forms of life. Buildings and defined spaces are allowed to have birth and death. There is general acceptance that houses, human bodies, plant forms are temporary abodes through which the *Po-wa-ha* flows. They share in the essence of life, which gives them cycles of life, birth and death. Traditional Santa Clara Pueblo with its soluble mud structures is an organic unit expanding, contracting, and changing with other life-forms and forces.

For the Pueblos, then, the entire world is a special, sacred place. Tsikumu, with its few gathered and well-placed stones, is a soft-spoken reminder that all life is sacred.

Acknowledgments

This essay first appeared in *Mass: Journal of the School of Architecture and Planning, University of New Mexico,* fall 1993, pages 24-25.

References

Carr, Pat. 1979. *Mythology.* Southwestern Studies Monograph No. 56. Texas Western Press, El Paso.

14 The Anasazi Revival

V. B. Price

Although Anasazi-inspired design has had a modest role to play in the modern urban and architectural history of the Four Corners region, American designers in general have never looked to this treasury of indigenous architectural problem solving and design as a model for helping to create culturally satisfying American structures and cities. V. B. Price analyzes the influence of Anasazi architecture on American design to date and calls for a modern, ecologically oriented Anasazi revival in the Southwest, one that matches in intensity the stylistic Spanish-Pueblo Revival of the 1930s and 1940s.

Tracing the influence that Anasazi architecture and urban design has had on the American built environment leads to many puzzles and dead ends. At first glance the evidence is slight but intriguing; it seems hidden in a complicated history of terminology and aesthetic dogma, waiting to be found. But going deeper, the evidence remains elusive, suggesting little but questions and the sense that the heyday of Anasazi influence is yet to come.

Although Anasazi archaeological sites are an exotic part of our national myth, there are no great kivas in Greco-Roman Washington, D.C., no keyhole doorways in the Pueblo-Spanish Revival-style buildings at the University of New Mexico, and no clearly Chacoan urban complexes integrated into an open-space network anywhere in the suburban Southwest. Despite two world-famous national outdoor museums at Mesa Verde and Chaco Canyon, the Anasazi built environment does not seem to have played a symbolic or practical role in the American urban scene. Anasazi sites are still treated more as natural wonders than as cultural precedents. There has never been what one could call an Anasazi revival in American architecture or urban planning. If there is to be such a thing, however, it could well happen at the turn of the twenty-first century, when environmentally conscious planners and architects look past the superiority complex of first-world technology to the wisdom of traditional builders and their practices.

Perhaps it is making a false distinction to separate the Anasazi from their Pueblo descendants. Perhaps Pueblo revival styles are, indeed, really Anasazi revivals. If it can be said that Acoma, Old Oraibi, and Taos (Nabokov and Easton 1989:380) are still Anasazi cities, then perhaps it is proper to rename the Pueblo-Spanish style the Anasazi-Spanish style, owing to the immense influence those Keresan, Hopi, and Tiwa pueblos have had on southwestern architecture in the twentieth century. But I think that would be mere name changing and would cloud an essential issue—the difference between the stylistic borrowing that marks Pueblo-Spanish Santa Fe and the University of New Mexico central campus and the deeper modeling of urban and environmental forms that, as yet, remains an unexplored potential. There was no Anasazi revival at the turn of the twentieth century when Romantic and scientific interest in Pueblo ancient history first flowered, because such interest was largely artistic and commercial, dealing with surface style and design motifs rather than with more subtle matters of urban ecology and form.

Although Chaco Canyon and Mesa Verde are seen by the world as monuments to American culture, American designers and planners with deep allegiance to an American sense of place have made scarcely any direct references to these and other Anasazi sites. It has long been generally assumed that there is a direct cultural link between Pueblo and Anasazi cultures, but the founders of the Pueblo-Spanish Revival style in Santa Fe and Albuquerque made no direct references to Anasazi sites either. The founders of southwestern regionalism were mostly museum men and archaeologists, such as Edgar Lee Hewett and S. G. Morley. Though they excavated Anasazi sites, they did not work to integrate Anasazi forms into Pueblo-Spanish Revival-style buildings; nor did the chief architectural exponent of the style, John Gaw Meem. And even American organicists, such as Frank Lloyd Wright, looked south to Mayan culture and not to the Anasazi for inspiration. The great cultural parks of Chaco and Mesa Verde were treated intellectually, I think, as eccentricities, as fascinating cultural oddities, out of the mainstream of Euroamerican culture, and even out of the tributary of New Mexico regionalism.

Though they have been in the American imagination since the turn of the century, Anasazi sites were relics of what we thought of as a conquered and dependent people, of a past not our own, and consequently they were not seen as relevant to urban concerns at the turn of this century and in the heyday of Americanism at midcentury. We looked upon such sites, I think, as extraordinary but slightly minty versions of Egyptian or Mesoamerican ruins. They were even shunned stylistically, for the most part, except in Park Service buildings and some tourist architecture, most notably at Mesa Verde and the Grand Canyon. America's earliest city builders were not regarded as having anything useful to teach; their ruins were not looked upon as models for the future. Designers to this day have paid little or no attention to the utilitarian and pragmatic genius, compact forms, climatic sensitivity, and land-use conservation of major Anasazi sites.

From the preliminary perspective of this brief essay, tracing what impact the Anasazi built environment has had on American design falls into four categories of questions and potential investigations: Pueblo urban planning and residential architecture; the work of contemporary Pueblo urbanists and cultural theorists; Pueblo-Spanish Revival-style architects and Park Service architecture; and contemporary modernist and contextual architects and urban planners. Surveying these complicated subjects may start us on the path to understanding the place of Anasazi architecture in what Lewis Mumford might have called America's "usable past" (*Design Book Review* 1991:13).

Pueblo Urban Planning and Residential Architecture

The influence of Anasazi sites on historic Pueblo architecture and site planning deserves lengthy collaborative study by Pueblo scholars, archaeologists, ethnologists, architects, urban planners, and architectural historians. Writings by Santa Clara art historian Rina Swentzell (e.g., 1965, 1989, 1990) lead me to believe that Pueblo builders did not look upon Anasazi sites as architectural and urban monuments to emulate. Instead of hero-worshipping great sites such as Keet Seel, Chaco, Mesa Verde, and Puye, Pueblo builders perhaps saw the sites as simply representing patterns and possibilities available in their urban tradition. Whether the archaeological sites themselves were used as conscious models remains to be analyzed.

Following the diaspora from the Four Corners region in the thirteenth century, it seems that although prehistoric Pueblo builders did still construct huge sites, some much larger than Pueblo Bonito, they made their communities by accretion along the unit pueblo pattern rather than the great house pattern, in which a predetermined form was followed throughout many years of construction. Post-diaspora builders continued to make sacred pathways, but they did not construct networks of meticulously engineered superhighways as they did for Chaco Canyon. They seem to have built no tower kivas, no great kivas the size of Casa Rinconada, and no cliff dwellings. They did continue to build terraced house blocks at such notable sites as Taos and Old Oraibi and others, but it is unclear whether the form of these was predetermined or the product of accretion. And it is equally unclear what the distinctions in cultural, or even cosmological, meanings might be—if any—between urban complexes that added to themselves in keeping with a pattern, such as Santo Domingo, and those that grew according to a predetermined design, such as Pueblo Bonito and Chetro Ketl.

Although the great house designs were not taken up by Puebloans after the diaspora, contemporary Pueblo urban forms do follow an array of Anasazi town patterns. Peter Nabokov and Robert Easton distinguish three basic Pueblo town patterns (1989:368): the plaza type, such as San Felipe Pueblo and old Zuni; the street type, such as Acoma and Santo Domingo; and an elongated street type, such as Zia, Pecos Ruin, Old Oraibi, and Taos. The street-type contemporary pueblo was foreshadowed by such Anasazi sites as Yellow Jacket near Mesa Verde in the Montezuma Valley of southern Colorado. The plaza-type pueblos perhaps are modifications of great house plazas or, as architectural historian Vincent Scully (1989) speculates, are open-air great kivas where communal celebrations can be held. Geographer J. B. Jackson observed in 1954 that although many pueblos appear to have "no coherent plan," kivas, plazas, house clusters, and even, I suppose, street-length plazas all seem to have a common purpose, "to protect something sacred": a sipapu, a shrine, or a reverential or ceremonial space.

As to whether Pueblo builders used ancient sites as models for their post-diaspora cities, the question appears beyond answer. It seems clear, however, that Anasazi urban forms were a part of the pan-Pueblo cultural repertoire. Certain forms and materials fit specific natural environments and social needs that varied across the Puebloan world from the dry mesas of Hopi to the high mountain country of Taos. And it seems clear, as well, that some urban forms in the Anasazi pueblo repertoire, such as preplanned great houses, were not chosen for use again after the abandonment of Chaco, except possibly in transitional post-Anasazi sites such as Tyuonyi in Frijoles Canyon, south of Los Alamos. The Mesoamerican structures—the flat-topped mounds, ball courts, and porticos (except for ramadas)—also appear to have been dropped from the repertoire of built forms after the late 1200s. As far as residential architecture is concerned, Pueblo clustering, stacking, and linear addition of rooms seems to be a direct extension of Anasazi practices.

Contemporary Pueblo Urbanists and Cultural Theorists

Owing to what Edward P. Dozier (1970:24–25) describes as the compartmentalization of Pueblo "socioceremonial systems" into two separate parts—a non-Pueblo system and an indigenous system "uncontaminated" by external forces—it seems unlikely to me that the non-Pueblo world will ever gain much insight into contemporary Pueblo views of Anasazi architecture and urban planning. Nor will the non-Pueblo world have much of a chance to understand the Pueblo perspective on the relationship between ancient forms and contemporary building and planning processes, as well as their various meanings, and the role such relationships play in the protection and preservation of Pueblo culture. As Dozier points out, Pueblo peoples have survived by maintaining two cultures: one that deals publicly with the modern world, and one that is private, if not to say "wary, suspicious, and secretive" (1970:5). There is no doubt in my mind, however, that such relationships do have meaning. As Spiro Kostof (1991:25) has noted, "Physical patterns always encapsulate an extra-physical reality."

By surveying the ideas of Pueblo thinkers such as art historian Rina Swentzell, anthropologist Alfonso Ortiz, and planner Theodore Jojola, as well as recent work at Zuni and the relationship between indigenous Pueblo building patterns and HUD. housing, one can gain some glimpse into Pueblo urban and architectural philosophy and its connection to Anasazi precedents. A necessarily superficial survey discloses two broad, contemporary Pueblo schools of thought about architecture, planning, and cultural continuity as it relates to the built environment.

On one side, I would include thinkers such as Rina Swentzell and Alfonso Ortiz, as well as the leadership of architecturally traditional pueblos such as Taos, Hopi, Acoma, and Santo Domingo. In general they would hold with the idea that the built environment is an important element in keeping modern cultural contamination from polluting the essential qualities of the Pueblo way of life. They would also hold that there is an important relationship between Anasazi and Pueblo built forms, a relationship only now being analyzed.

On the other side, I would include thinkers such as Theodore Jojola of Isleta and Calbert Seciwa of Zuni. They are interested in the built environment not so much as a protector of culture, but as a pragmatic container of it. They would place a premium on adaptability rather than on design continuity. Cultural continuity, they might hold, is largely independent of the built environments in which it has existed and evolved.

As in any classification, especially one as crudely dualistic as this, there is a danger of making rigid intellectual boundaries that create differences which could easily be resolved and imply hard-line conflicts which probably do not exist in reality. My classification above should be looked upon as merely a means of organizing preliminary thoughts on a highly complicated subject.

Calbert Seciwa, writing with anthropologists T. J. Ferguson and Barbara J. Mills, holds that at Zuni "people have historically chosen function over form as they have rebuilt their village to keep pace with modern times. Innovation in Zuni architecture has been guided by a pragmatic approach that favors cost-effective solutions to basic problems of lighting and weatherproofing houses over the surface appearance of facades" (Seciwa, Ferguson, and Mills 1990:120). In such a context, continuity with Anasazi architectural forms would seem superfluous, even though traditional pan-Puebloan urban design and public-space creation still has direct ties to the past. Seciwa affirms that "though the architectural appearance of Zuni Pueblo has been dramatically transformed in the twentieth century, there are enduring features of Zuni architecture that still play an important role in Zuni society." There is, he writes, "a very strong continuity in the open-space structure of the pueblo. This continuity is due to the religious element of Zuni culture, which acts as a conservative force in architectural change" (Seciwa, Ferguson, and Mills 1990:115). One force contributing to architectural change, HUD housing, is looked upon by many at Zuni as "a Trojan horse," bringing modernizing conveniences to Zuni along with a hidden cache of extra social and financial costs (Seciwa 1989, p.c.); HUD housing has contributed to the suburbanization of the pueblo, defying conservative home clustering and open-space patterns. When Zunis make use of new building materials and housing styles, they adapt them to their social as well as pragmatic needs. By contrast, HUD housing tends to be imposed, with no concern for existing urban patterns.

Theodore Jojola, a professor of planning at the University of New Mexico School of Architecture and Planning and a member of Isleta Pueblo, interprets change pragmatically as well. Because of Isleta's early occupation by Spanish missionaries and its vulnerability to European contact, the "community settlement has not been a process of maintaining 'tradition' " (Jojola 1990:95). "What was regarded as tradition in one period would not have been considered traditional in another. The history of progress as reflected by changes in Isleta settlement and building traditions was both intense and varied. Its community remained vital because of its ability to readjust to 'new' traditions" (Jojola 1990:95). The question of Anasazi continuity at Isleta seems moot. Still, even in an adaptive pueblo, certain pan-Pueblo (and therefore Anasazi-like) characteristics remain—especially in the form of dance plazas and a kiva.

The renowned late Tewa social anthropologist Alfonso Ortiz emphasizes continuity between the Puebloans and their Anasazi forebears. Ortiz (1979:1) writes that in the Pueblo homeland "much that is vital remains as it was, timeless. Here is the oldest continuous record of human habitation on the continent outside of Mesoamerica, a habitation that has fashioned this region into a humanized landscape suffused with ancient meanings, myths, and mysteries." Although Ortiz is more interested in social organization and cosmology than in the built environment, at a symposium titled "Pueblo Style and Regional Architecture" in Albuquerque in 1989 he unraveled what he called the mystery of the keyhole-shaped kiva (so noticeable at many Chaco Canyon sites) using ethnographic material about Tewa shrines, implying a deep connection between the two. At the symposium, he explained the elusive keyhole shape of Chacoan kivas with references to a contemporary kind of shrine known as an earth navel, or a *nan-sipu,* on the top of sacred mountains, such as Sandia Crest, which are shaped like open-ended keyholes and are made of an arrangement of stones on the ground (Ortiz 1969:19, 21, 141). For Ortiz, it seems, some parts of the Anasazi built environment, along with their sacred meanings, evolved directly into the Pueblo world.

In numerous influential articles in recent years, Rina Swentzell has stressed continuity with the past as an essential element in Pueblo belief systems. While change is the essence of life, it is change in the sense of flow, or transition that the Puebloans consider important. Swentzell (1989:28) writes,

> Transition is a part of life, and is a very positive part of life, but it has to be transformation in terms of continuing. When you break the continuity, when Adam and Eve leave the garden, there's a real break. They committed original sin. We have no original sin in the Pueblo world; we are still in the garden. When you leave behind the past it is detrimental not just to yourself but to the world at large. Because you leave behind respect, connectedness—which is love.

In writing of Pueblo architecture, Swentzell connects built form with cosmological meaning, implying that there is a cosmological continuity between certain parts of the Anasazi and Pueblo built environment. Pueblo myths, she writes, "describe a world in which a house or structure is not an object—or a machine to live in—but is part of a cosmological world view that recognizes multiplicity, simultaneity, inclusiveness, and interconnectedness. . . . It is a world in which, as Castañeda recorded in 1540, 'The houses are built in common. The women mix the mortar and build the walls'" (Swentzell 1990:29). If there is to be an Anasazi revival in American urban planning, it is thinkers such as Rina Swentzell who will help lead the way from the built forms of a specific cosmology to its general, ecological applications.

Pueblo-Spanish Revival-Style Architects and Park Service Architecture

The impact of Anasazi great house architecture, Chacoan open space and road systems, and other clustering and compact forms (such as at Mesa Verde) on the Pueblo-Spanish Revival style seems to me to be almost nil. America's most distinctive regional style made almost no direct use of America's only monumental indigenous architecture. I say this without a sense of accusation or alarm; I find it curious but not somehow culturally immoral.

The Pueblo-Spanish Revival style, which dominates to this day the cityscape of Santa Fe and has contributed immeasurably to the defining spirit of America's most original and thoroughly regional campus at the University of New Mexico, is a creative synthesis of Pueblo and colonial

Hispanic residential and religious adobe architecture. That synthesis has resulted in some extraordinarily beautiful and evocative buildings. The creators of the revival style at the beginning of this century modeled their buildings on an existing Pueblo-Spanish synthesis found at numerous pueblos and in Catholic mission churches. To have used uniquely Anasazi motifs, much less great house and other urban forms, would have required perhaps too great an aesthetic and political leap of faith. The Pueblo-Spanish style was hard enough to sell: witness the firing of the University of New Mexico's president, William George Tight, in 1909 for turning the university into what writers were calling the Pueblo University.

It is also possible that early designers did not conceive of the great houses of Chaco and the cliff dwellings of Mesa Verde as being clearly distinct from modern pueblos. Archaeologist Stephen Lekson (1990:71) has written that "archaeologists at Chaco Canyon in the early 1900s . . . all saw the huge ruins as early versions of modern Pueblos." Now, of course, many scholars of various disciplines are coming to believe that the complex of great houses in and around Chaco Canyon belongs to a single urban system, designed on a cosmological model and incorporating agricultural open space, that was connected by roads not only to other outlying sites but also, and more frequently, to shrines on or around prominent landforms.

Near the turn of the century, three expositions helped set the tone for revival-style architecture in the Southwest. The Cliff Dwellers Exhibit at the World's Columbian Exposition in Chicago in 1893 was a sweetly hoked-up Anasazi dreamscape that alluded to the cliff ruins at Mesa Verde. There was a clear Anasazi connection in this exhibit, fanciful or not. That the exhibit did not lead to an Anasazi revival might be attributed to its amusement-park design. The exhibit was only incidentally architectural: a huge, pseudo canyon wall was built with little "cliff dwellings" wedged in. In 1904, the Cliff Dwellings and Dwellers Exhibit at the Louisiana Purchase Centennial Exposition in St. Louis was modeled (it appears from photographs) on Taos Pueblo, with an Anasazi connection in name only. By 1915, when Ira H. Rapp and W. M. Rapp designed the New Mexico Building at the Panama-California Exposition in San Diego, the Pueblo-Spanish style was full-born without a hint of Anasazi influence. The New Mexico Building is the model for the famous Fine Arts Museum of New Mexico in Santa Fe.

Of all the early southwestern revival-style designers, architect Mary

Colter and archaeologist Jesse Nusbaum were perhaps the most attuned to Anasazi and Pueblo forms. Nusbaum, who was superintendent at Mesa Verde from 1917 to 1931, oversaw the construction of numerous stone buildings sensitive in overall design and detail to the archaeological ambience of the area. Mary Colter, who did the interior design in such southwestern monuments as Albuquerque's (now-demolished) Alvarado Hotel, the Grand Canyon's El Tovar, and Santa Fe's La Fonda, also was the architect of numerous regional buildings at the Grand Canyon, including the often-overlooked but impressive Hopi House, which still stands today (Grattan 1980:125).

Hopi House, which opened in 1905, was designed after terraced building clusters at the Hopi pueblo of Old Oraibi, thought to have existed in the same location for nearly a thousand years. Though not a great house, Old Oraibi can be thought of as the living remnant of Anasazi urban planning, a direct descendant of larger unit pueblo sites. It is not clear whether Colter saw Hopi House as a monument to the Anasazi, but she probably did not. The distinction was yet to be drawn between Puebloans and their ancestors. Still, Hopi House is a purely Pueblo Revival-style building without any Spanish influence of which I am aware. Unlike the work of John Gaw Meem and others who solidified the Pueblo-Spanish synthesis into the revival style with which we are familiar today, Colter's early designs paid particularly close attention to Anasazi-Pueblo forms. Her interest in Puebloan architecture is only now being taken up again by young planners and designers.

Contemporary Modernist and Contextual Architects and Urban Planners

The only contemporary building I know of that is modeled after an Anasazi great house is the Indian Pueblo Cultural Center in Albuquerque. Designed in the mid 1970s by modernist architect Harvey Hoshour, the building is an abstraction of D-shaped Chacoan structures, the most famous of which is Pueblo Bonito. Not even the University of New Mexico, with its splendid blend of Pueblo-Spanish style and regional modernist buildings, has a structure that alludes so directly to the Anasazi urban heritage of the Southwest. Hoshour's building is nothing like a traditional regionalist design. Starkly modern and stripped bare of ornament, it nevertheless is unmistakably Anasazi, both in its shape and in its aristocratic bearing. The building proved a little too Miesian, however, for officials of the Nineteen Pueblos of New Mexico, which owns and operates the center: Hopi-Laguna architect David Riley was hired to give the exterior and interior a more regionalist flavor. Yet I think that Hoshour's attitude about his building was not influenced by Anasazi or Pueblo precedents in any way other than a symbolic sense.

The building, for instance, does not have a passive-solar orientation to the southeast, which is one of the hallmarks of Pueblo Bonito (the ruin is considered by some to be a model of efficient, passive solar engineering). Long-time New Mexican architect William Lumpkins of Santa Fe began building passive solar adobe houses as early as the mid 1930s. His buildings are site specific in a thoroughly Anasazi-Pueblo fashion.

Modernist architect and long-time preservation advocate George Clayton Pearl told me that there is "no point in imitating" Anazasi forms; it is the idea behind them that matters. This idea he described as "not competing with the landscape, not being divorced from the landscape, but becoming a part of the landscape." He alluded to Frank Lloyd Wright's view that a house is not on the hill, but of the hill. (Pearl 1990, p.c.)

Architect and University of New Mexico professor Robert Walters also associates Anasazi architecture with landscape. In his visionary 1984 workshop entitled "Genesis of Form," he emphasized the "variables of 'physical form,' . . . those structured by nature . . . and those structured theoretically, conceptually, and physically by the hands of women and men." The end of the workshop was spent on site near the "great wall" of the ruins of Chetro Ketl at Chaco Canyon (Walters 1985:14). Through the workshop, Walters sought to get to the essential "mood" and "visual sensuality" of ancient "sacred places," understanding form as it arises out of a spiritual and geographic context.

It is possible, I think, to discern in the work of four contemporary designers—three architects and one planner—the outlines of an evolving duality concerning the possibility of an Anasazi revival at the turn of the century. New Mexico architects Antoine Predock and Glade Sperry are contextualists interested in metaphor who have worked to liberate themselves from regionalist constraints while exploring environmental ideas latent in Anasazi-Pueblo design. Architect Anthony Anella and urban planner Paul Lusk have taken a more direct approach, conceiving projects that make use of Anasazi prototypes.

Antoine Predock is not a regionalist, but he is a New Mexican who is sensitive to the environmental and cultural context of the region. "My regionalism is portable. I can be a regionalist anywhere." Regionalism to him means "a location, a magic you draw out of a place. It's about cultural memory and overlays, stylistic overtones, responses to geography, the mystery of landscape" (Price 1987–88:72). In that spirit, he designed at the beginning of his career in 1967 the La Luz Townhouses on Albuquerque's West Mesa. Combining Puebloid masses and Spanish forms, particularly an allusion to the circular tower forms of the walled city of Avila, La Luz is a cluster development that has a decidedly Anasazi-like relationship to its surrounding landscape. Like Chacoan great houses it is self-contained, a residential island in a large body of open space which it does not invade. It does not matter whether Predock was intentionally alluding to specific Chacoan urban forms. In its entirety, La Luz is contextually Anasazi-Pueblo; it is to New Mexico what Predock's other works are to the sites they inhabit—that is, striving to be of their places, not on them.

Like Predock, Glade Sperry works to avoid the "alluring trap" of traditional Pueblo-Spanish-style materials, forms, and motifs. "To replicate the evidence of the cultures that came before dooms the culture of the present. The timeless nature of Anasazi forms signifies that there are elemental forces of spirit that pervade the architecture of this place [the Four Corners] and offer a typology in which all things are possible" (Sperry 1990:289). It is the experimentation and flexibility inherent in Anasazi-Pueblo architecture and urban forms, as well as its symbolic power, that appeals to Sperry. Rather than finding a rigid code in the past, he sees a legacy of innovation and adaptability.

Architect Anthony Anella believes that Anasazi architecture has a direct bearing on contemporary urban issues. Long interested in Mesa Verde, Anella believes that the example of Anasazi sites helps to reconcile "the dual relationship between man and nature" (see Anella essay, this volume). Anella holds that man's perception of his relationship to nature is "the central issue of our time. We live in an age," he writes, "challenged by the imperative of rebuilding a world that is in human and ecological equilibrium." He sees the architecture at Mesa Verde in particular as achieving a "compelling balance between the human program and the geological circumstances and topographical idiosyncrasies of the site" (see Anella essay, this volume). Anella is a contextualist who sees Anasazi architecture as being, to borrow a term from Edward T. Hall (1977:91), highly contexted with its surroundings. His design for a new visitors' center at Mesa Verde is deeply concerned with the symbolic, historic, archaeological, and geographic context of the site, which includes the center's orientation to nearby landforms.

The Anasazi Revival 201

The most direct, and perhaps the only, application of Anasazi architecture to contemporary urban problem solving that I know of was accomplished in 1991 by a graduate urban design and advanced planning studio at the University of New Mexico School of Architecture and Planning under the direction of Professor Paul Lusk (see Lusk essay, this volume). The studio was entitled "Learning from Ancient and Contemporary Pueblos: Application to Modern Urban Design." Graduate students visited Pueblo villages and Anasazi sites, analyzed basic concepts of their building practices, and then applied those concepts to two long-standing urban problems in Albuquerque—the design of a "Pueblo Center" on the site of the abandoned Albuquerque Indian School across from the Indian Pueblo Cultural Center, and the creation of an "Albuquerque Crossroads Center" downtown on the site of the demolished Alvarado Hotel. Some of the basic concepts they found in Anasazi-Pueblo built environments include an integrated sense of community rather than isolated individuality; coordinated rather than haphazard planning; the use of space, rather than streets and buildings, as the progenitor of form; an adaptability to natural context; compact built forms; affordable, user-made structures; sustainable materials and designs; and a sophisticated variety of transportation methods.

Efforts such as those at the University of New Mexico lead me to believe that a new era of Anasazi-Pueblo regionalism is possible at the turn of the tewnty-first century. They give strong evidence that the Anasazi are not a cultural dead end with nothing of importance to contribute to the future. In fact, quite the opposite is true. In a world of increasing resource depletion, overpopulation, and pollution, the Anasazi-Pueblo design ethos could have as much impact on the health of contemporary cities as the Pueblo-Spanish style had on the economic viability of Santa Fe and Albuquerque at the turn of the last century. Anasazi built environments are, in the words of Lewis Mumford, part of America's "usable past," still waiting to be put to use.

References

Design Book Review. 1991. "Mumford: A Usable Man of the Past." Unsigned editorial. *Design Book Review* (winter 1991):13.

Dozier, Edward P. 1970. *The Pueblo Indians of North America.* Holt, Rinehart and Winston, New York.

Grattan, Virginia L. 1980. *Mary Colter: Builder upon the Red Earth.* Northland Press, Flagstaff, Ariz.

Hall, Edward T. 1977. *Beyond Culture.* Doubleday, Garden City, N.J.

Jackson, J. B. 1954. "Pueblo Architecture and Our Own." *Landscape* (winter 1953–54):20–25.

Jojola, Theodore. "Modernization and Pueblo Lifeways: Isleta Pueblo." In *Pueblo Style and Regional Architecture,* ed. N. C. Markovich, W. F. E. Preiser, and F. G. Sturm. Van Nostrand Reinhold, New York.

Kostof, Spiro. 1991. *The City Shaped: Urban Patterns and Meanings through History.* Little, Brown and Company, Boston.

Lekson, Stephen H. 1990. "The Great Pueblo Period in Southwest Archaeology." In *Pueblo Style and Regional Architecture,* ed. N. C. Markovich, W. F. E. Preiser, and F. G. Sturm. Van Nostrand Reinhold, New York.

Nabokov, Peter, and Robert Easton. 1989. *Native American Architecture.* Oxford University Press, New York.

Ortiz, Alfonso. 1969. *The Tewa World: Space, Time, Being, and Becoming in a Pueblo Society.* University of Chicago Press.

———, ed. 1979. *Southwest,* vol. 9 of *Handbook of North American Indians.* Smithsonian Institution, Washington, D.C.

Price, V. B. 1987 1988. "Antoine Predock, FAIA." *Artspace* (winter 1987 88):72.

Scully, Vincent. 1989. *Pueblo: Mountain, Village, Dance.* University of Chicago Press.

Seciwa, Calbert, T. J. Ferguson, and Barbara J. Mills. 1990. "Contemporary Zuni Architecture and Society." In *Pueblo Style and Regional Architecture,* ed. N. C. Markovich, W. F. E. Preiser, and F. G. Sturm. Van Nostrand Reinhold, New York.

Sperry, Glade, Jr. "Pueblo Images in Contemporary Regional Architecture: Primal Needs, Transcendent Visions." In *Pueblo Style and Regional Architecture,* ed. N. C. Markovich, W. F. E. Preiser, and F. G. Sturm. Van Nostrand Reinhold, New York.

Swentzell, Rina. 1965. "An Understated Sacredness." *Mass: Journal of the School of Architecture and Planning, University of New Mexico* (fall l965):24–25

———. 1989. "The Butterfly Effect: A Conversation with Rina Swentzell." *El Palacio* (fall/winter 1989):24–29.

———. 1990. "Pueblo Space, Form, and Mythology." In *Pueblo Style and Regional Architecture,* ed. N. C. Markovich, W. F. E. Preiser, and F. G. Strum, pp. 21–29. Van Nostrand Reinhold, New York.

Walters, Robert. 1985. "Genesis of Form." *Mass: Journal of the School of Architecture and Planning, University of New Mexico* (fall 1985):14.

15 Learning from Mesa Verde

A Case Study in the Modern Interpretation of Anasazi Design

Anthony Anella

New Mexico-based architect Anthony Anella, who provided the initial impetus for the Mesa Verde symposium, contemplates contemporary design and urban problem solving through the lens of his understanding of Anasazi-Pueblo values. He illustrates his perceptions by applying them to a hypothetical new visitors' center at Mesa Verde National Park.

> Which comes first: the blessing or the prayer? It is not easy in this landscape to separate the role of man from the role of nature. The plateau country has been lived in for centuries, but the human presence is disguised even from the camera's eye. There are ruins like geological formations, disorders of tumbled stone. There are immense arrays of slowly crumbling rocks that look like ruins.
>
> —J. B. Jackson, *The Essential Landscape*

The Mesa Verde rises abruptly at the entrance to the park, revealing sedimentary strata deposited over epochs of geologic time. The Cliff House Sandstone caps the mesa; underlying it is the Menefee Formation, a layer of shale that outcrops on the steep canyon slopes (Erdman, Douglas, and Marr 1969:15–16). This geologic sequence is architecturally significant. As water seeps down through the sandstone, it meets the impervious shale, which forces it to migrate laterally to the canyon walls. There, a process of freezing and thawing undercuts the sandstone cliff where it is in contact with the impervious shale strata. This weathering process produces not only the numerous large alcoves that shelter the cliff dwellings, but also the very stones the Anasazi used to build their dwellings. At Mesa Verde, the relationship between geology and architecture is a remarkable one: the great palaces of sandstone are inconceivable without the protec-

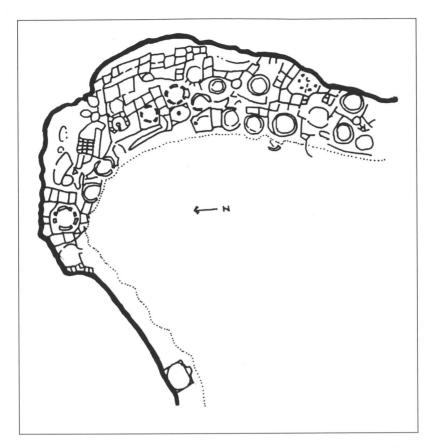

Fig. 15.1. Cliff Palace in relationship to the cliff. Drawing by Anthony Anella

tive alcoves of the surrounding rock. Here, architecture is given meaning by an order established by geology.

When we visit Cliff Palace, for example, we perceive it to be in a certain equipoise in relation to the surrounding natural setting. What makes this place so special is that the plan of the building conforms to the preexisting order of the cliff rather than to a preconceived order of human intervention (Fig. 15.1). The dry-laid masonry walls run either parallel or perpendicular to the natural slope of the alcove floor. Further, the walls are laid just inside the drip line of the protective alcove overhead. Whether this is inadvertent due to the limitations of Anasazi technology (because they had no bulldozers, they had to conform to the existing topography) or intentional is immaterial. The architecture of the Anasazi at Mesa Verde achieves a compelling balance between the human program and the geological circumstances and topographical idiosyncracies of the site. A tangible sense of place develops in their architecture because it is premised on a powerful sense of belonging to a larger natural whole.

Karsten Harries has expressed this notion well: "One task of architecture is still that of interpreting the world as a meaningful order in which the individual can find his place in the midst of nature and in the midst of community. Time and space must be revealed in such a way that human beings are given their dwelling place, their *ethos*" (1983:16). Harries links the problem of arbitrariness in modern design to our greater freedom. "To this," he writes, "one may object that freedom has here been grasped inadequately, because only negatively: true freedom is not freedom from constraint, but rather to be constrained only by what one really is, by one's essence" (1983). Modern man has emancipated himself from many of the natural constraints that confronted the Anasazi. In the process, modern man has also lost his sense of belonging to a larger natural whole.

Much of contemporary architecture is object oriented without regard for what happens around buildings. By featuring buildings as pure objects, contemporary architecture neglects the implications of what happens in between buildings.

In the Anasazi architecture at Mesa Verde, special attention is paid to the "in-between" realm: the places where the additive modules join or are purposely kept apart. For example, Spruce Tree House does not separate individual buildings from how they operate within the whole. What each part means in a qualitative sense depends on what they mean in terms of each other. Similarly, Cliff Palace is not one object but a composition of many. The object is subordinated by its repetition, which precludes hierarchy in the object-oriented sense. All modules are treated structurally and spatially the same. Only their relation to each other and the surrounding cliff gives them their quality and their meaning. The relationship between the figurative void of the surrounding cliff and the figurative volume of the architecture transcends an emphasis on either one or the other. Cliff Palace provides a counterform for the surrounding cliff: a figure to complement the void of the sandstone amphitheater. It symbolizes the other half of the dual relationship between man and nature, which an emphasis on either one or the other precludes.[1]

This is the real significance of Anasazi architecture to contemporary

American design: how the example of Anasazi architecture can help to reconcile the contemporary relationship between man and nature. It serves as a reminder of how architecture can help "the individual find his place in the midst of nature and in the midst of community." Joseph Rykwert has defined a similar idea as "the return to origins":

> The return to origins is a constant of human development, and in this matter architecture conforms to all other human activities. The primitive hut—the home of the first man—is therefore no incidental concern of theorists, no casual ingredient of myth or ritual. The return to origins always implies a rethinking of what you do customarily, an attempt to renew the validity of your everyday actions, or simply a recall of the natural (or even divine) sanction for your repeating them for a season. In the present rethinking of why we build and what we build for, the primitive hut will, I suggest, retain its validity as a reminder of the original and therefore essential meaning of all building for people: that is, of architecture. (1981:192)

The present rethinking of why we build and what we build for derives from the changing view Americans have of the land and their place within it. Informed with evidence of the greenhouse effect and the destruction of the ozone layer, we no longer abide the frontier perception of the land as a surfeit to be merely exploited. Our deteriorating environment causes us to rethink the way we customarily inhabit the earth. Must we not now develop an understanding of dwelling more appropriate to our changed environmental situation? And does not the architecture of the Anasazi at Mesa Verde suggest strategies for the design of contemporary buildings that will help man to live with the land and not merely on or in spite of it?

It is within the context of these two questions that I would like to discuss my design for a visitors' center and an archaeological research and storage facility for Mesa Verde National Park as a case study in the modern interpretation of Anasazi architecture. How we interpret the past as well as how we imagine the future are both conditioned by the concerns and preoccupations of the present.[2] The central concern of our time is man's relationship to nature. Nothing is more important to our future than rebuilding the equilibrium that sustains our life. Given this central concern, then, there are at least two possible interpretations of our Anasazi past as we try to control the development of an uncertain future. One interpretation is that the Anasazi lived in complete harmony with nature; this interpretation sees Anasazi architecture as Adam's house in paradise. The second interpretation is that the Anasazi did not live in complete harmony with nature. According to park archaeologist Jack Smith (1985, p.c.), the story of Mesa Verde is "the story of a people trying to make a living in an arid land—at first as hunter-gatherers by dealing with the circumstances of their livelihood and then as farmers by planting the circumstances of their livelihood as they simultaneously disrupted the balance of their own existence." I find this second interpretation more convincing, not only because it seems more factual, but also because it serves certain rhetorical purposes. Whether it was overpopulation, drought, a cooling trend, or a combination that caused the abandonment of Mesa Verde, the important story the proposed visitors' center and archaeological research and storage facility can help to tell is that Mesa Verde National Park preserves a prehistoric precedent for many of our contemporary environmental dilemmas.

In 1990, Mesa Verde National Park attracted more than seven hundred thousand visitors from most states of the nation and many countries of the world. They are generally unfamiliar with the area and the natural and human history that make it so distinctive. In fact, the tradition to which most park visitors belong is a tradition that tries to organize the landscape according to a preconceived grid of square-mile sections. This tradition is manifested in the way we survey the land and in the rectilinear boundaries of the states that come together at the Four Corners. It is also manifested in the string line grids that archaeologists use to orient themselves in what is perceived to be the disorder of an archaeological site before it is excavated.

The Anasazi of Mesa Verde and their descendants, the Pueblo Indians of Arizona and New Mexico, orient themselves to the environment differently. In looking at the ruins at Mesa Verde, I learned that what makes those places so special is that they conform to the pre-existing order of the cliff. In looking at the planning of the pueblos in New Mexico, I learned that the way they are organized is, again, not according to any preconceived rectilinear grid but rather according to perceivable landscape features. For example, Sandia Pueblo, just outside of Albuquerque, deflects the major axis of the central plaza away from the east-west grid to orient it toward the central horns of Sandia Mountain (Fig. 15.2).

I have adopted a similar strategy in my design. The proposed site is on the right side of the road as one enters the park just after passing through

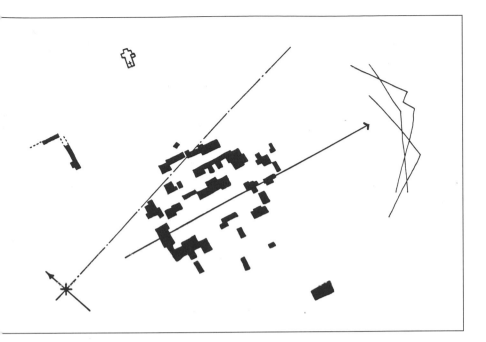

Fig. 15.2. Orientation of Sandia Pueblo. Drawing by Anthony Anella

the entry station. It is located on a ridge that affords views to Sleeping Ute Mountain to the west, Mount Hesperus of the La Plata Mountains to the east, and perhaps most dramatically, southward to Point Lookout, which is the northernmost part of the mesa which one sees upon entering the park. These three landscape features are especially important in the planning of the design. Entrance into the facility is along an axis that is anchored at one end by the landscape feature of Sleeping Ute and at the other end by Mount Hesperus. Once the visitor enters the complex of buildings, his attention is drawn to Point Lookout. From the very beginning, the visitor is made aware of these landscape features and begins relating himself to them.

I began by saying that the Anasazi architecture at Mesa Verde is given meaning by an order established by geology. This design responds to that order by including the natural landscape in a composition of built forms that narrate the story of Mesa Verde (Fig. 15.3). Upon entering the plaza, the visitor's attention is drawn to the Mesa Verde by a series of repetitive forms that make up the visitors' center. Each form corresponds to a room housing a different period of Anasazi cultural development. Each is on a

Fig. 15.3. Sketch of visitors' center. Design by Anthony Anella.
Drawing by D. E. Jamieson

different level so that the visitor's experience of walking through the period rooms, of ascending from earliest to latest, from Basketmaker to Classic Pueblo, is the reverse experience that an archaeologist would have digging down through the cultural strata of a site. The period rooms complement the existing experience available to the visitor by giving back to

Fig. 15.4. View of visitors' center model. Photo by Anthony Anella

him the excitement of seeing artifacts displayed in facsimiles of the original context.[3] They function as "life-size dioramas" and complement the miniature dioramas that are a favorite of visitors to the Chapin Mesa Museum near the center of the Park. And when viewed from the entrance plaza, the cultural strata represented by the layers of the visitors' center are juxtaposed with a view of the geologic strata of the mesa, accentuating the connection between the human story of Mesa Verde and the story of the land.

The spiral feature is an abstracted *sipapu*, or sacred spring. It consists of a sandstone masonry wall enclosing a spiraling ramp. Down the ramp, emanating from a fountain at the center, runs a stream of water that irrigates a nearby cornfield. This is a place for the visitor to get away from the crowds and have a chance to contemplate the role of water in the story of Mesa Verde.

The material to be used in the visitors' center and archaeological research and storage facility is a specially designed masonry block that matches the color of the sandstone on Point Lookout. The abstracted *sipapu* is to be made of natural sandstone and replicates the masonry techniques of the Anasazi. The juxtaposition of these two masonry techniques—the ancient and the modern—provides the visitor with a sense of the continuum between the seven-hundred-year-old masonry technology of the Anasazi and the masonry technology used today.

The profound lesson we can learn from the architecture of the Anasazi is the perception of man as a part of nature, not separate from it. My design is intended to apply this lesson by re-establishing the dialogue between the original and the contemporary, between archaeology and architecture, between the land and how we build on it. By juxtaposing the view between the cultural strata represented by the different layers of the visitors' center and the geologic strata of the Mesa Verde, this design also is intended to emphasize the connection between the story of man as told by archaeology and the story of the land as told by geology. This relationship between human time and geologic time is an important one. For when we begin to perceive ourselves as part of the larger continuum, then perhaps the choices we make will be based on less short-sighted decisions.

Seven hundred years after the Anasazi abandoned Mesa Verde, archaeologists began to excavate the ruins to deduce cultural meaning from the artifacts left behind by that ancient civilization. Seven hundred years from now, archaeologists will distinguish between the ruins left behind by the Anasazi and the ruins left behind by twentieth-century America. The cultural strata belonging to the modern era will be differentiated by the fact that

> just as modern man has fallen out of nature, so has he fallen out of history. We may know much more about history today than ever before, but precisely in making the past an object of scientific investigation, the sense of belonging to the past is lost. We have removed ourselves too effectively from the past to still belong to it. Time has been reduced to a coordinate on which we move back and forth with equal facility. With this, the past must lose much of its authority. (Harries 1983:13).

The sublime beauty of the Mesa Verde is its ultimate indifference to man's presence. It existed before the state of equilibrium that afforded the Anasazi their livelihood, and it continues to exist long after they left. And it will continue to exist despite any choices we may make to disrupt the balance of our own evolution. It is an indifference that should remind man of his place within nature and the continuum of geologic time.

Notes

1. I am indebted to Aldo Van Eyck for thoughts he expressed in his essay "Kaleidoscope of the Mind," *VIA I, Ecology in Design, 1968, The Student Publication of the Graduate School of Fine Arts,* University of Pennsylvania.
2. I am indebted to Professor J. J. Brody for the thoughts he expressed during the keynote address of the Mesa Verde Symposium on Anasazi Architecture and American Design.
3. Currently, the visitor is afforded the experience of visiting the ruins that have already been excavated, so that there are no artifacts inside, or he goes to the museum and sees the artifacts outside the context of their original setting. In between the ruins and the museum, he is not made aware of the archaeologic process. Part of the excitement of Mesa Verde, and something that is worth the visitor's contemplation, is the archaeological process.

References

Erdman, James A., Charles L. Douglas, and John W. Marr. 1969. *Wetherill Mesa Studies: Environment of Mesa Verde, Colorado.* National Park Service, Washington, D.C.

Harries, Karsten. 1983. "Thoughts on a Non-Arbitrary Architecture." In *Perspecta 20.* MIT Press, Cambridge, Mass.

Jackson, J. B. 1985. *The Essential Landscape.* Museum of Fine Arts, Santa Fe, New Mexico.

Rykwert, Joseph. 1981. *On Adam's House in Paradise.* MIT Press, Cambridge, Mass.

16 Anasazi-Pueblo Site Design

Application to Contemporary Urban Development

Paul Lusk

In this essay, University of New Mexico planning professor Paul Lusk
makes a perceptive if controversial first attempt to systematically examine
basic elements in Anasazi site development and apply them directly to solving
contemporary urban design problems in southwestern cities. Working to
understand design principles observed at Chaco Canyon and other prehistoric
Puebloan sites, Lusk pares away cultural content to reveal general concepts
that may be used as building strategies for an ecologically sensitive future.

Most of us are so familiar with contemporary patterns of urban development—urban streets, freeways, suburbs, shopping malls, and our own
lifestyle choices and habits within them—that we have difficulty imagin-
ing a different pattern. Unfortunately, though, the vast expanse of pre-
dominantly automobile-dependent urban growth that has sprawled
across America in the last fifty years (and by emulation across many other
countries) is, I believe, unsustainable. The unintended costs of these
land-use and transportation patterns have been increased travel times,
greater energy use, and expanded maintenance needs. This contemporary
urban pattern also has resulted in fewer people-friendly public spaces and
a pervasive deterioration of environmental quality. Among other aspects,
the recent war in the Middle East has shown some of the long-term costs
of our exorbitant use and consequent need to control such a large share
of the world's oil and other resources.

Ensuring continuing access to Middle Eastern oil, however, is not our
only alternative. I believe that some of the physical and cultural factors
evident in the siting, the form, and the adaptability to change of many
Anasazi-Pueblo structures contain lessons that, if applied to contemporary urban development, could provide a more livable, less expensive, and

environmentally superior model for modifying and extending our built environment.

Although many other aspects of site and building pertain, the following paragraphs describe seven of the most important: (1) site area and genesis of form; (2) location and land use; (3) orientation to the sun and seasons; (4) access systems; (5) water systems; (6) relation to surrounds; and (7) continuity and relation to time. These aspects are compared and contrasted in three settings: Anasazi, contemporary, and new urban. "New urban" in this context means new development or redevelopment of portions of existing metropolitan areas consistent with the proposed characteristics defined here: certain Anasazi land-use features—not the forms, but the apparent reasons for their location and genesis—have the potential to modify existing cities and to create new, more compact, less costly, ecologically sustainable cities.

This task of comparing Anasazi, contemporary, and "new urban" cities is inherently oversimplified, but it is intended to show that the apparent reasons for specific characteristics of many ancient pueblo developments are relevant today, particularly in the arid and semiarid regions of the Southwest. If applied within or with little modification to existing city-building processes, these characteristics would be fully compatible and could result in more efficient, less costly, and more humane urban environments.

Site Area and Genesis of Form

Anasazi

Most Anasazi and other ancient Pueblo structures in the high desert areas of the Southwest, and even many more recent Pueblo developments, are quite compact, covering a few acres of land area at most. Including water collecting, water diversion, and farming areas, the intensive land uses are all within a few minutes' walk from the primary Pueblo structure. Even remote food production, hunting, or other outposts, although varying by frequency of use, are within a defined walking distance. The operative site characteristic is *compact*. The genesis of ancient Pueblo forms involves many unknown factors. The key factors considered here, though, are the response to common needs for defense, housing, storage, meeting and ceremony, and a conscious relationship to the cosmos.

Contemporary

By contrast, contemporary urban development, including related metropolitan suburban areas, is dispersed, individualized, separated into use zones, and connected by a continually expanding network of public roads and other automobile-related spaces. Even in the relatively dense city center, many multistoried buildings stand alone, separated by acres of paved streets and parking. Increasingly, in the last fifty years, contemporary automobile-dependent urban development has been characterized by *sprawl*. In simple terms, sprawl is caused by the fact that land more distant from urban centers is cheaper to develop, especially if others pay for the access roads and subsidize the fuel costs that make it closer in time. Driven by economic and locational decisions based on and reinforced by an increasing amount and proportion of both public and private resources, the pervasiveness of the goal of uniform automobile accessibility perpetuates sprawl (Kenworthy 1990; Litman 1990).

New Urban

The premise of this essay is that a new, more life-supporting and ecologically benign urban development is needed and that careful study of ancient and more recent Pueblo structures, site development, and land use may inform and help guide a more balanced urban growth. However, because all "new" development is within the existing context, the summary characteristic of such new urban development here is defined as *compact node* or *cluster*. What this means is that rather than being built as new "improved" urban development on presently open land, new land-conserving, less automobile-dependent, multi-use development should be fitted instead into key locations and, where appropriate, over time should replace much of the existing lower-density, single-use development. The genesis of form for such new urban development should be (1) sited at a significant landform location; (2) reintegrating multiple uses; (3) reducing the need for vehicular travel; (4) accessed by diagonal pedestrian interconnections; and (5) using building form and spaces to moderate daily and seasonal sun and weather cycles.

Replacement of substantial portions of existing urban development may seem exorbitant or unlikely. However, the end-use operating energy consumption in a typical moderate density, urban/suburban area in approximately five years equals the total embodied energy investment in that area, including streets, sidewalks, utilities, houses, schools, stores, and so forth (Greenbriar Associates 1980). This means that since the 1950s, we have paid the equivalent of the total embodied energy investment for a typical development area eight times over in end-use operating costs for heating, cooling, lights, fans, water pumping, and the like. This does not include transportation energy costs, which by 1990 consumed approximately 40 percent of our total national energy use (Matloff 1990).

Location and Land Use

Anasazi

Major Anasazi-Pueblo sites are located at the edge of geographically significant places—at the edge of the valley (not in the middle), or the edge of the mesa, or sheltered in the face of a cliff. They also are located near water. The supply may be limited, from a spring or from rainfall collection areas, but access to water in a defensible location and in a manner that does not destroy potentially arable land are fundamental requirements. Land uses also are arranged conservatively, with compact, adaptable structures combining housing, storage, meeting, working, and ceremonial spaces. Water diversion, food production, and other needed activity areas are adjacent. Hunting, medicinal herb gathering, wood gathering, and other resource locations may be more remote.

Contemporary

Where we live, work, shop, and recreate tells us that land uses in contemporary urban development generally are separated by use and located according to the cost of land, the requirements of zoning, and the degree of accessibility. Excluding other unique conditions and relationships, locations usually are less expensive when less accessible or more remote. Significant geographical features may be less important than proximity to work, to services, or to other higher-density uses. Public and private use also are defined separately. The largest single-use area of any major urban area always is the public road network and related vehicular access and service areas.

New Urban

New compact node or clustered urban development should be located at regionally significant geographic locations, particularly where multiple transportation systems intersect and allow choices in access systems. Access to more than one mode of travel increases the number of people who can access a site and thereby increases economic potential. Such locations can both allow an increase in density and provide more available open space by reducing the amount of single-function, automobile-use areas. For such locations, compatible uses, including residential, service, commercial, industrial, or other economically productive work areas, should be layered over utility, parking, and waste management facilities. A proportionate volume of vegetation and a specific area of vegetated soil surface as well as a provision for photovoltaic capacity should be designed to balance human use rates and replenishment capacities at the development location.

Orientation to the Sun and Seasons

Anasazi

Detailed analyses of energy performance at Pueblo Bonito and other ancient sites by Ralph Knowles and others (Knowles 1974:esp. 20–46) have shown that these ancient stone and adobe structures not only changed and evolved over centuries, but did so in a manner that systematically improved both their daily and their annual solar-energy heat transfer and storage. Not only were new portions oriented to the cardinal directions and architecturally marked for the solstice and other celestial events, but more efficient arrangements evolved using the internal mass of the structure to store the heat of the day for the night and the cumulative heat of the summer to moderate the cold of the winter.

Contemporary

Most contemporary development is oriented to the street first and to the sun second, if at all. Although individual buildings or site designs may provide solar access to particular rooms or spaces, orientation to street frontage regardless of street direction is the rule. In many locations shadows cast by major buildings create either pleasant shaded areas or winter-long frozen islands of dirty ice in adjacent streets or properties with little evident awareness of or responsibility for the difference. Similarly, uniform facades on multistoried buildings are accommodated by additional energy expenditure to balance quite different internal building heating and cooling zones.

New Urban

New compact node and cluster development should arrange mass and void volumes to optimize (daily and seasonally) both passive solar energy and shading. The geometry of north, south, east, and west facades and spaces should provide for sun arc and seasonal differences to reduce energy use and to enhance human comfort as well as vegetative and soil surfaces (Knowles 1979). Internal mass or water thermal storage or other passive or low-energy heat transfer systems to moderate microclimate extremes should be performance requirements.

Access Systems

Anasazi

The long, straight cleared areas, or "roads" as we call them, connecting major Pueblo sites and "outliers" or other significant locations have prompted considerable interest and debate as to their nature, purpose, and method of construction. There seems be general agreement, though, that they were an extensive pedestrian network. Less attention has been paid to the ladders used in most Pueblo structures, perhaps because they are so obviously ladders. I believe, however, that they are a unique access system and are the genesis of the compactness, spatial efficiency, and environmental performance of Pueblo structures.

Ladders are a *diagonal* transportation system, primarily on the surface (although some are inside), that allow access to light and air over the surface of the tiered development that is greater than the surface area of the land covered. They create an internal volume for storage and for private rooms with each increment of rise from the base. They also create a horizontal extension of developable mass that avoids the inevitable congestion that results when floor areas are multiplied many times over in one location, such as in contemporary high-rise buildings.

Contemporary

The primary access systems in contemporary development are horizontal: sidewalks and feet, streets and vehicles, rails and trains. Such systems involve some changes in elevation, so they are partly diagonal; but at optimum they are horizontal systems. The problem is that they create extension without volume—that is, they are flat, in essence two-dimensional, and inevitably create sprawl. Our other primary access system is vertical. Its mechanized form, the elevator, evolved in the 1850s and has been applied to urban development increasingly since the 1880s. The elevator allows multiple floor areas over the same plot of land, which greatly increases the economic return from a particular land area. The problems that result are congestion at the point of access to the vertical (elevator) systems and the fact that the economic benefit is to the individual parcel while the increased cost in utility, service, and supporting transportation systems is borne by others.

Modern developments, of course, use diagonal access systems also. Stairs, escalators, and funiculars occur in varying frequency in our culture. They are *not*, however, perceived as a separate or unique transportation system with passive and mechanized components distinct from horizontal or vertical systems and with capacities that can equal or exceed more familiar road networks or elevator systems. An escalator, for example, can carry as many persons per hour as a fully loaded freeway, while using a fraction of the energy. Of course, passengers do not travel as far in an equivalent time, but each floor level is potentially a whole new development zone.

New Urban

New compact cluster developments, located where major horizontal access systems converge, should use diagonal transportation systems to interconnect the road, train, bus, light rail, jitney, interior parking, and other horizontal networks with the new three-dimensional development created by the diagonal access systems. Escalators and surface stairs should provide direct pedestrian connection to horizontal accessways and plazas created by the diagonally tiered or ziggurat skin of the new surface development. More detailed analysis and design prototypes are needed. But my estimate is that, to avoid congestion, the height of such a three-dimensional cluster development (whether in a single low-rise building or in an interconnected structure covering one or more blocks) should not exceed twice the longest horizontal dimension of the base. Similarly, to avoid sprawl, the base should not exceed four times the greatest dimension of the height.

Water Systems

Anasazi

Ancient Pueblo sites show evidence of water collection, storage, and distribution systems that changed and evolved over time to meet changing needs. Researchers differ on particulars and on interpretation of some of the evidence, but they generally agree that available rainfall, intermittent streams, and, where available, freshwater springs were used to provide for water needs. Nearby materials (such as rocks, mud, and wattle) were used, as well as the accumulated knowledge of the Pueblo inhabitants regarding flows, diversion structures, storage basins, grids of placed rocks, and other devices to provide for water where and when needed in balance with supply (Henderson 1978).

Contemporary

Albuquerque, as an example, uses pumps drawing groundwater from deep wells to store water aboveground in large steel tanks or concrete reservoirs. The tanks then deliver water by gravity to the pipe networks serving the dispersed development pattern of the city. Supply is undifferentiated, providing potable-quality water for all uses. Rainfall runoff is collected separately, generally concentrated in paved drainage structures, and accelerated out to the river.

New Urban

Water supplying most new urban cluster developments most probably would be provided by city or metropolitan systems. Providing comparable water supply from smaller-diameter deepwells within the cluster also should be evaluated. Reducing consumption, using graywater irrigation systems, recycling wastewater nutrients, and collecting all surface runoff for storage and irrigation of landscaped materials and gardens should be design criteria. Balancing water use with supply and recycling systems should be design requirements. Other elements that should be evaluated are incorporating vegetative surface and porous photovoltaic panels for evaporative cooling as well as shading, and using water reservoir tanks or ponds for thermal storage.

Relation to Surrounds

Anasazi

Land areas around ancient pueblos were used in quite different ways than in contemporary society. Evidence presented by researchers, surviving myths and stories, and the use patterns of members of contemporary pueblos indicate that land surrounding the intensive-use areas was used sparingly, differentially, and sequentially—that is, at different times of the year. The surrounding land was not divided, distributed, and used continuously by separated owners.

Contemporary

Contemporary culture also uses land as a resource, but it is viewed as separate from us—that is, as an object that can be owned, sold, used continuously, or even destroyed as a possession not involving others. Generally land is perceived as "real estate" with different economic value and, perhaps, different potentialities such as mineral, agricultural, commercial, or other uses but not intrinsically different because of its location or time of use.

New Urban

Compact, clustered development sites should have a mix of use areas such as housing, plazas, local commercial, economic production, and work areas as well as internal parking, utility, and recycling areas. External or regional use areas, of course, will be separate from compact node or cluster developments and not under their control. A boundary area of dense vegetation and living soil should be established to distinguish the outside noncontrol area from the cluster. The boundary area should be large enough to define this separation and to perform other functions such as providing a noise buffer, line-of-sight control, waste-stream nutrient recycling, seasonal color, beauty, natural aromas, and food or fiber products as the specific setting and program requires.

Continuity and Relation to Time

Anasazi

The reasons for the abandonment of many of the ancient Anasazi-Pueblo sites as well as some more recent locations are not known. Prior to these events, however, many Pueblo sites were occupied, expanded, and evolved to considerable size and complexity over many centuries. Even some currently occupied pueblos such as Acoma, Taos, and Santo Domingo have histories of continuous occupation and cultural continuity for eight hundred to a thousand years. The roles of myth, storytelling, dance, ceremony, and other ways of transferring culture and providing continuity are at least vaguely familiar to many people. One method of ensuring cultural continuity that may not be as familiar but is very effective as well as useful is the annual (or other time period) task of pueblo structure maintenance. Adobe structures—Taos Pueblo, for example—require regular repairs such as mud plastering. If repairs were not made, erosion would accelerate and even physical continuity would not remain. The mudding task not only allows for cross-generational learning, but teaches that regular upkeep is an essential part of continuity.

Contemporary

In contemporary American society, continuity in cultural norms and expected behavior may be transmitted through family, school, peers, laws, or the media. Continuity for buildings and other components of the urban environment, however, may be discouraged by our professional building process and by the choice of materials that have different life expectancies than hand-placed rocks or adobe walls. Generally, our building process does not include the concept of shared maintenance as a strategy to convey essential skills as well as responsibility. When our buildings age, the repair needs and the skill base as well as the cost may require more than is available or deemed "economic," requiring demolition rather than repair.

New Urban

In new urban cluster or node development, cultural continuity also would be transmitted through family, school, peers, laws or codes, and the media. Building integrity and renewal, though, would be enhanced with three proposed strategies: (1) the primary structure, core, utilities, plazas, and linear pedestrian ways (including platforms for houses, stores, and other changing uses) would be publicly owned, either by the overall jurisdictions or by the residents/users, while the infill housing, economic production areas, commercial areas, and so forth would be owned by the residents or entrepreneurs; (2) real economic production—that is, job and income-producing activity—would serve as an integral and continuing component of the cluster; and (3) vegetation and living soil would cover an established percentage of the total surface area. Each residential unit on each level would have a proportional open surface area with structured soil containers for water absorption, heat gain, night re-radiation, food production, or aesthetics. They also would have direct access to sun, sky, clouds, wind, and rain or snow. For each inhabitant, tending a garden would contribute to the maintenance of the building.

Summary

The following is a summary of the seven site and building development aspects described above. It lists in abbreviated form the characteristics identified as Anasazi, Comtemporary, and proposed New Urban development.

I believe that all participants in the urban building process—architects, engineers, developers, builders, and users, as well as agencies that regulate, review, or finance such development—could benefit from a careful consideration of the relevance of Anasazi site development factors and of their efficacy in enhancing contemporary urban development.

	Anasazi	Contemporary	New Urban
	Compact	Sprawl	Node-Cluster

		Anasazi (Compact)	Contemporary (Sprawl)	New Urban (Node-Cluster)
1.	SITE AREA AND GENESIS OF FORM:	- common needs - evolving structure - relation to cosmos	- individual lots - access network - distance from centers	- reintegrate uses - reduce travel need - form moderates weather
2.	LOCATION AND LAND USE:	- edges, not middle - water, arable land - multi-use structure living/storage/meeting	- economic value - accessibility - separate use zones - pubic/private separated	- geographically significant location - transportation system xing - multi-use/infill over parking, utilities
3.	ORIENTATION TO SUN AND SEASONS:	- solar mass storage day/year, improvements - season marks for planting/ceremony	- street-oriented - solar individual buildings - summer, winter shadow - building energy use zones	- sun-arc volume/void - day/year energy storage - vegetated/soil surface - water cooling/storage
4.	ACCESS SYSTEMS:	- horizontal pedestrian network - diagonal ladder system - volume/surface > base	- horizontal roads/vehicles - horizontal parking/walking - vertical elevators/floors	- horizontal systems xing - diagonal escalator system - horizontal pedways/plazas
5.	WATER SYSTEMS:	- rio/arroyo irrigation - fresh water springs - rain collection/storage	- deep well/pumps - all potable system - rain collection to sewer	- deep well/pumps - separate waste water recycle - rain collection/irrigation
6	RELATION TO SURROUNDS	- land used in common, differentially, sequentially, sparingly	- individually owned - use zoned, own well rights or use continuously	- public access/structure parking utilities interior - economic products/jobs - vegetated boundary area
7.	CONTINUITY AND RELATION TO TIME:	- myth, story, dance, through ceremony, clan - maintenance of pueblo structure/adaptation	- family, peers, law, media persuasion - building process, materials, costs deter reuse	- family, peers, law - structure publically owned, private infill development - vegetated surface, maintenance over time

References

Greenbriar Associates. 1980. *Energy Conserving Site Design, Greenbriar Case Study, Chesapeake, Virginia.* Final report, U.S. Department of Energy, Assistant Secretary for Conservation and Solar Energy, Office of Buildings and Community Systems, Washington, D.C.

Henderson, E. 1978. *Secret of the Ancient Kivas.* Mesa Publishing Group, Inc., Albuquerque.

Kenworthy, J., and P. Newman. 1990. "Reversing the Trend toward Automobile Dependency—A Rationale for Halting Freeway Expansion." Paper presented at the First International Ecological City Conference, Berkeley, California, 29 March-1 April 1990.

Knowles, Ralph. 1974. *Energy and Form: An Ecological Approach to Urban Growth.* MIT Press, Cambridge, Mass.

Villecco, Marguerite. 1979. "The Sun's Rhythms as Generators of Form." *AIA Journal* (September 1979).

Litman, T. 1990. *Transportation Efficiency: An Economic Analysis.* M. A. thesis, Department of Environmental Studies, University of Washington, Seattle.

Matloff, T., et al. 1990. "Future of Urban Transportation." Paper presented at the First International Ecological City Conference, Berkeley, California, 29 March-1 April 1990.

Epilogue

V. B. Price

Anasazi architecture has an important role to play in the future of American society. Unlike Spanish-Pueblo Revival-style architecture in modern Santa Fe, or Colonial American architecture in Williamsburg, however, Anasazi architecture has more to contribute to the health of the future than history lessons or Disneyesque "imagineering." In looking to the Anasazi past for clues about how to construct a more humane and sustainable future, we need to discard the contemporary practice of what critic Ada Louise Huxtable (1992) has called "the replacement of reality with selective fantasy," look beyond architecture as mere entertainment "packaging," and focus instead on functional and symbolic issues, on ecological utility and the social metaphors of form. As the chapters in this anthology illustrate, the ecological sensitivity and savvy of Anasazi designers is a model for restructuring fundamental Euroamerican concepts of land use and site selection as postindustrial America struggles to retrofit its dysfunctional cities and suburbs for environmental efficiency and cost-effective sustainable growth.

The basic Anasazi land-use strategy of adapting the built environment to the conditions and contours of the natural environment, working with natural forms and cycles rather than considering them obstacles to be overcome, has immense philosophical and practical values in the future. Coupled with Anasazi skill at clustering human habitations in networks of open space, the essential Anasazi strategy of designing with nature (to borrow a phrase from Ian McHarg) has the potential to transform American building practices in the twenty-first century. Imagine, if you will, a nation of ecologically sensitive, solar-oriented clustered developments, resting as human oases in agricultural or wilderness open spaces and connected by a mass-transit system that was designed not only to move people and goods, but to preserve landscape rather than obliterate it. Retrofitting inner-city neighborhoods along Anasazi principles has equal practical value.

Architecture both reflects and accommodates the cultural patterns and expectations of its builders. Anasazi clustering and designing with nature would be put to best use in a gradual accumulation of communitarian projects that reflect the values of both private and public clients. Although Anasazi city building eventually succumbed to the grandiosity that inflates and undermines most powerful societies, its basic design principles are no more prone to gigantism and ostentation than any other. If urban sprawl is the chief ill of urban America—creating traffic congestion, pollution, inefficient resource consumption, and land degradation—then the sophistication of Anasazi clustering and site sensitivity is a potential cure that must not be overlooked.

The more difficult lesson to be learned from the Anasazi is the importance of using architecture and urban design as metaphors of social values. Anasazi values and cosmology are not our own, and it is not implausible to believe that the materialism and technocracy of the postindustrial West has no cosmology beyond that supplied by transient scientific theory. But no matter how denuded of metaphor our worldview might be, the lesson that design has symbolic as well as utilitarian meaning is vital for the creation of a humane future in the postmodern world. Architecture and urban design can reinforce humane values or disrupt and disperse them. Architecture can reinforce such values by representing them symbolically in the design of buildings and in the layout of cities, and by creating structures that help to channel action in socially favorable ways. Architecture can also reinforce psychological well-being by creating environments that allude to the essential meanings and ancient values of our culture. Design can disrupt the social fabric as well by creating built environments that either neglect basic human needs or are so dehumanizing in form that they actually cause depression.

The possible symbolic meaning of Anasazi architecture, especially in and around Chaco Canyon, is a model for those designers who wish to make socially reinforcing buildings and urban patterns. It is not our way to design great houses along a cosmological scheme that creates a sacred calendar out of a built environment. But Chaco shows how useful it might be for American designers of the future to get beyond commercialism and deeply examine the metaphors and values of their own culture to see if they lend themselves to architectural representation.

Are there, for example, uniquely American design strategies that reinforce the potential for neighborliness and the practice of grassroots self-help and direct democracy? Are there American design metaphors that could embody our consistent need for privacy along with our growing need for community? What symbolic and aesthetic strategies already exist that would symbolize and help to strengthen our resolve to live in greater harmony with our natural environment?

Both pragmatically and symbolically, the urban legacy of the Anasazi is a vast resource of tough-minded problem solving and inspiring poetic comprehensions, a resource whose full potential we are only now on the brink of recognizing.

References

Huxtable, Ada Louise. 1993. "Inventing American Reality." *The New York Review of Books,* 3 December 1993, p. 24.

Contributors

ANTHONY ANELLA is an architect, author, and teacher working in Albuquerque, New Mexico.

J. J. BRODY is Professor Emeritus in the Department of Art and Art History, University of New Mexico.

BARBARA COLEMAN is a former city planner in the Albuquerque/Bernalillo County Planning Department and now teaches at the School of Architecture and Planning at the University of New Mexico.

STEPHEN D. DENT is associate dean of the School of Architecture and Planning at the University of New Mexico.

RICHARD ELLIS is the director of the Center for Southwestern Studies at Ft. Lewis College, Ft. Lewis, Colorado.

DABNEY FORD is an archaeologist with the National Park Service, Chaco Canyon.

THEODORE S. JOJOLA, of Isleta Pueblo, is a professor in the University of New Mexico School of Architecture and Planning and is the former director of the Native American Studies Program there.

SUSAN KENZLE is a master's student and teaching assistant at the University of Calgary, Alberta, and a recent research intern at the Crow Canyon Archaeological Center.

STEPHEN H. LEKSON has been an archaeologist with the Museum of New Mexico and the National Park Service.

PAUL LUSK is a professor of planning at the University of New Mexico School of Architecture and Planning.

MICHAEL P. MARSHALL is a freelance southwestern archaeologist.

BAKER H. MORROW is a landscape architect in Albuquerque, New Mexico.

V. B. PRICE is a poet and environmental critic in New Mexico.

STEPHEN D. SCHREIBER is a professor of architecture at the University of New Mexico School of Architecture and Planning.

ANNA SOFAER is an independent scholar and researcher and founder of the Solstice Project associated with Chaco Canyon.

JOHN R. STEIN is an archaeologist with the Navajo Nation Historic Preservation Department in Window Rock, Arizona.

DAVID E. STUART, a southwestern archaeologist, is an associate vice president for academic affairs at the University of New Mexico.

JUDITH E. SUITER is with Zephyr Graphics, Albuquerque, New Mexico.

RINA SWENTZELL, of Santa Clara Pueblo, is an architectural and art historian living in Santa Fe, New Mexico.

IAN THOMPSON is a writer living in Cortez, Colorado, and the former director of the Crow Canyon Archaeological Center.

MARK VARIEN is a senior research archaeologist at the Crow Canyon Archaeological Center and a doctoral student at Arizona State University.

Index